FOLLOW

FOLLOW YOUR JOY

The information given in this book is for entertainment purposes and should not be treated as a substitute for professional medical advice. Always consult a medical practitioner.

Although every effort has been made to ensure that the information in this book was correct at press time, no responsibility is assumed for any loss, damage, or disruption caused by errors or omissions and no liability is assumed for any damages that may result from the use of this information.

The views expressed in this book are those of the author alone and do not reflect those of That Guy's House Ltd.

This book is a work of creative nonfiction, however, certain elements may have been fictionalized in varying degrees, for various purposes to suit the narrative.

The book information is catalogued as follows;

Author Name(s): Jacquelyn Armour

FOLLOW YOUR JOY

Description; First Edition

1st Edition, 2021

Book Design by Lynda Mangoro

ISBN (paperback) 978-1-914447-23-5

ISBN (ebook) 978-1-914447-24-2

Prepared by That Guy's House Ltd.

www.ThatGuysHouse.com

FOLLOW YOUR JOY

JACQUELYN ARMOUR

So many people have inspired me to be who I am today.
I only hope this book inspires you.

It is dedicated to anyone taken too soon and to
the countless modern day adventurers I have been
fortunate to share a moment of my life with.

To anyone that needs to hear this: "Don't die with your
music still inside you"

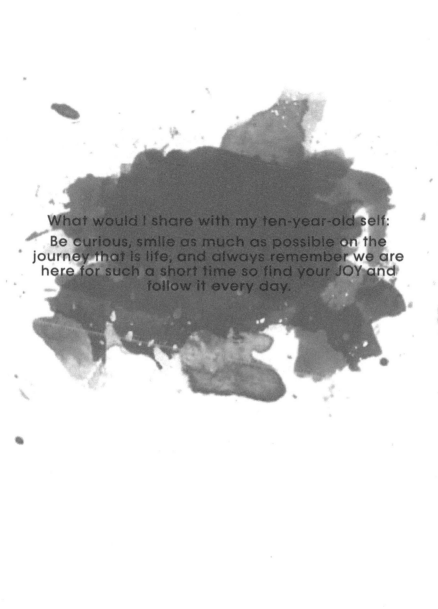

What would I share with my ten-year-old self:

Be curious, smile as much as possible on the journey that is life, and always remember we are here for such a short time so find your JOY and follow it every day.

Contents

Introduction: Welcome to my world

The thrill of glancing at your passport as you pass through customs, the sea of taxi drivers demanding your attention as you walk towards the arrival's hall. That first whiff of air, a different air. The smells of the local cuisine, and sometimes the locals. Their glances, and occasionally a shared smile. You are as exotic to them as they are to you. It feels familiar but new. To leave the daily routine and seek adventure, the thrill of the unknown. To rise each morning and follow your own carefully planned itinerary – delivering you to your wildest dreams. An indescribable need for travel, deep inside. To feel untamed and free, a desire that will never go away. Travelling is to be alive, curious and at one with the world. Travelling is to be an explorer, eager to be enlightened.

Everybody expects you to have a favourite country. Some days I do, other days I declare them all equally as wonderful as each other. How can there be just one? Italy would be high on the list if I had to pick.

As the home of pasta, we have shared many memories over the years, and it played a vital part in what would become part of my travel legacy. As travelling became my hobby, it was only a matter of time before I visited my ninetieth country. It was originally planned as North Korea to run a marathon, but with the trip cancelled, Andorra soon stepped into the frame. In the end, that didn't happen either. We can blame the covid-19 pandemic for that.

In the late summer of 2020, when the world opened up again, I found myself in Italy with one eye on the new number ninety - San Marino. It became a possibility when I flew into Bologna from Berlin and worked out you can easily enter San Marino from Rimini, a coastal town reached by train. The world of travelling back in my life - I could sense the excitement creep in.

I spent a day in Bologna wandering the historic streets, eating all the gelato and even more pizza. There were zero expectations from this Italian city, used as a base to access San Marino before heading west to Florence and Pisa - the true star attractions of this trip.

That evening I plotted out the trip to San Marino. This is when I felt that feeling, to accomplish something that seemed impossible throughout the first half of 2020 when the whole world entered lockdown due to an out of control virus. The historic tourist 'city' sits majestically perched high on top of a steep mountain - Monte Titano - looking out to the Italian coastline in one direction and the sweeping valley in the other. From the photos, it looked incredible.

The day started as expected with everything on track. I performed the 'get to the train station' walking march. Having travelled around Italy many times, I knew you could easily buy tickets from the station the day before, or even online, all to remove the travel stress. For whatever reason, I didn't bother. I considered this as I arrived at the train station and looked around. Everything seemed chaotic and everyone stressed. People milling around, wearing masks, the usual levels of life stress, now magnified with covid-19 anxiety. Here we go, I thought.

As I typed the train details into the ticket machine, my trusty and reliable credit card suddenly declined, not just once but multiple times - argh. It never gets declined, not even in the most random and remote countries – always to my surprise. After doing that annoying thing where you retry again and again as if something magical will happen, I gave up and looked around for help in the form of an actual person. From a scan of the station, I could see different systems on the go. I went to queue for the pop-up counter.

Thankfully I found myself next in line.

It became clear the person in front had one of those complex cases. The discussion seemed quite tense. "Come on," I thought while managing my stress levels with some controlled breathing. Suddenly I felt breathing down my neck. I could feel it through their mask. I turned to catch a glimpse of the culprit and came eye to eye with a nun, an actual nun, a real nun, a heavy breathing nun.

The nun took the opportunity to try queue jump right under my nose. I could see it unfold. Frustrated, the nun decided her case was way more important than mine and performed this sneaky manoeuvre, where she shuffled up and stood alongside me in the queue.

She explained she needed to sort her situation, to back this up she placed a couple of train tickets and a note with train times under my nose. After a glance, I came to my conclusion; she was a complete chancer. It seemed she missed her first train and would also miss her second. I knew if I let her jump the queue, I would miss mine. She signalled as if to say, "Can I move in front of you?". I looked her in the eye, shook my head, then edged forward to reinforce the message. "Not today lady," I thought while trying to remain calm. I needed to sort this ticket situation out or the San Marino trip wouldn't happen. A distressed nun became the least of my worries.

Eventually, it became my turn to speak at the counter, soon to be turned away as he shook his head and explained, "You can't buy tickets at the pop-up desk". WHAT, I shouted inside in my head. I didn't have time to start to understand the point of the pop-up desk. My options now dwindling. I could try the credit card again in the hope it magically worked, find an ATM to get cash to use at the ticket machine, or take a next in line ticket and wait for the ticket desk to shout my number. From glancing over at the ticket desk, I knew I didn't have time. I found myself back trying to figure this out. I couldn't see an ATM to withdraw cash from. I did what any person would do, I tried the credit card again.

I glanced up at the train station clock.

With less than ten minutes until the train departs, I'm acting as cool as a cucumber from the outside, while internally praying I don't miss the train. The ticket machine appears to be doing something more than the last time, it remains unclear though. I need some sort of validation. I look behind and ask the man standing next in line what the message in Italian on the screen says. He smiles and says, "Just wait". Arggghh, is this life teaching me a lesson? I look away, more controlled breathing underway, thinking if I don't look it will magically print, and it worked – it actually worked. I saw the ticket print like magic and appear in the collection window - thank you, trusty credit card. I grabbed it, thanked the Italian guy, who seemed unaware of his morale boosting role in this whole episode, and did a slight dash-run move where I jumped down the stairs onto the platform straight onto the train to Rimini.

What a drama over a simple train ticket purchase. Sums up life perfectly. Along the way, there will be hurdles and roadblocks. You just need to keep focussed, figure it out and go for it.

Did I get to San Marino? Of course I did!! It was super easy in the end. It always is.

I stood in the midday summer heat in Rimini, waiting alongside the other day-trippers, near the very nondescript and easily missed bus stop. I'd already purchased a ticket from the local newsagent exactly as described from a blog I read. As the bus arrived, we all popped on our Covid protective masks, handed the five euro ticket to the driver, and took a seat on the bus.

Soon heading towards the country that would become known as number ninety in my collection. NINETY. Crazy! Twenty minutes later, I crossed the imaginary border separating Italy from teeny tiny San Marino.

San Marino became probably the simplest country to tick off the European list. Leaving only four countries; Russia, Belarus, Moldova, and Andorra. Their time would come. A pretty significant milestone ticked off without even a stamp in my passport to show for such an accomplishment. No visa hassles, no security checkpoints to stress over, and no navigating customs with 100ml bottles. Thank you San Marino for making this easy. I can't say that for all the others.

I know what you are thinking. Were the people of San Marino out on the streets waiting for my arrival, and second, were you invited to join a banquet supper with the King of San Marino? Sadly, no to both. I'm not even sure San Marino has a King.

Travelling the world doesn't change your appearance. You don't earn a gold badge to wear for free hugs, but it does change you deep inside. It grants you ninety countries' worth of perspectives, at least ninety separate trips' worth of stories, and endless obstacles to tackle to reach this day. It feeds your imagination with far-flung adventure and turns your dreams into your memories. It changes how you see the world and how you live your life - if it didn't, then what has it all been for?

This was not about one day in San Marino, but much more.

This was for the eight-year-old girl who boarded her first flight on a family trip 'abroad' to Spain. Who felt that feeling of excitement when adventure awaits around the corner. When you see for the first time, the clouds drift through the sky from the aeroplane window and feel the intense heat stepping off the plane - welcoming you to a new 'exotic' destination.

This is for the 20-year-old girl who landed in New York, travelled South to Delaware to work the summer in a family-owned, beachside amusement park. Who travelled the East Coast of America with the dollar pocket money earned that summer - first South to Florida, then all the way back North beyond New York into Toronto; another country collected. Hello Canada. That trip to America provided my first taste of real freedom. Did I make the most of it? – Of course I did. Some stories will remain untold. Until that summer, I never lived away from home, not the whole time I went to university, and here I am in the United States of America. The land of Hope and Glory. 2003, what a year and what a summer.

This is for the girl in her 20s who planned all the trips in her long-term relationship. Who for years read the Saturday newspaper each week with a big cup of tea, searching for something, not sure what, to eventually apply for a job and set off to work, live, and explore the gigantic country known as 'Down Under' or simply Australia.

Eventually exploring the neighbouring continent of Asia. Can you imagine the eight-year-old Jacquelyn thinking of a future me, in Asia! Very 'abroad'. The start of the realisation that the other side of the world is not scary or unusual, but home to many awe-inspiring wonders. Maybe a little unusual, but in a mystical way.

This is for the girl in her 30s who boarded a plane to Japan, solo after that long-term relationship ended, and never quite stopped exploring after that. What would I share with anyone interested in being part of the game called Travelling the World? Keep going. Plan. Sometimes go with the flow, but always have a rough plan. Get excited. Scribble notes for future trips - it never ends. Make it happen. Lie-ins are not something to collect. Do You - Cry, Smile, but Breathe. Be Curious. Regret nothing. Embrace it all. And remember, everything is figureout-able, as coined by Maria Forleo in her best selling book.

You will eventually look back on your life and wonder how you got so far forward. Having way too much fun to realise you were creating moments of your own history, that one day may inspire someone else to leap into the unknown.

San Marino starts the collection of countries called the 90s. The collection of 80s were pretty wild. I'm not sure how I will top these but I will try hard: 89. Sri Lanka 88. Ethiopia 87. The Faroe Islands 86. Albania 85. North Macedonia 84. Georgia 83. Armenia 82. Azerbaijan 81. Kosovo 80. Slovakia.

Each country the stepping stone to the next - but in its own right, a wonder.

In the summer of 2020, I felt lucky to spend nine weeks exploring Europe, where I visited San Marino, amongst some other amazing countries. On my return to Scotland, I reflected on my life so far, that summer in Europe and all the countries I have been fortunate to explore a little.

For a couple of years now, I have asked myself that question, "What is this thing called life all about?". For me, it isn't working the 9 to 5 to pay the bills or settling in a life where society's blueprint directs you. Wishing away your week where Monday to Friday is about existing, resulting in a blur of a weekend - mainly with regrets. Repeating it all again – focussing on a break in the circuit when you embark on a summer holiday. I believe every day is a day where we make a choice to be happy, make a difference, and see the joy in the simple things. So many people around the world don't have that privilege of another day; their life is gone in the blink of an eye.

I felt guided to share with the world some of my travel tales and the experiences that have guided and influenced my life.

'Follow Your Joy' is my first travel memoir where I share stories of the world through the eyes of someone who has wandered the streets of ninety countries. It is an ode to learning about myself and discovering the joy of life along the way. I honestly believe that I found more than one person could imagine, and now want to share it with you.

Through travelling, I've learned a lot. I am fascinated by the communist regime - a time period I will never fully understand. I love the great outdoors and feel lucky to have hiked in Kosovo, the Faroe Islands and Peru, to name a few. I could lose days of my life exploring the ancient wonders in Myanmar, Thailand, Laos, and Japan. I am in complete awe of the imaginations that have brought the world the ancient cities of Petra in Jordan, Baalbek in Lebanon, and Angkor Wat in Cambodia. I adore the European 'classics', where they take your senses on an epic journey.

Each country a blank canvas to explore and learn, to which I am endlessly grateful.

Throughout each chapter, I provide a little insight into the history and culture of the country I visit, through my eyes, as I understand it. This isn't a history lesson, but I feel some countries pasts shape their present, so it is equally important I share a glimpse along the way.

I am fully aware solo female travelling can come with a level of nervousness by some. Within the book, I share tales where I date on my travels. This is my choice, and I make that choice after considering my surroundings.

As I began writing my first ever travel memoir, I wrote down all ninety countries to form a shortlist. Ninety became ten. Is this my top ten? No. But these are the ten I am starting with. Will there be more? Maybe. Colombia, Peru, India, Jordan, Philippines to name a few, have yet to be shared. Let's start here and see what happens.

I hope you read this book and see the endless possibilities in yourself and the world, so you believe you can design your own life and happiness! See each day as a gift and find joy in the simplest of things.

Remember, the secret we all seem to forget, we are only here once.

"Our happiest moments
as tourists always seem to
come when we stumble upon
one thing while in pursuit of
something else."

– Lawrence Block

Easter Island: Splash the cash - these are the once in a lifetime moments you will never forget

As I stepped onto the plane in Santiago, the capital of Chile, I knew around the corner was an experience I would remember for a lifetime. I boarded a plane to embark on a five-hour flight to Easter Island. Few people can say they have travelled to the island, even now when I look back on my photos I feel goosebumps. It's a magical place. A true wonder of nature and the product of an ancient civilisation. The definition of a hidden gem waiting to be explored.

As soon as I read about one of the remotest inhabited islands on the planet, I was intrigued. Awarded world heritage status by UNESCO, the Organization that rates sites around the world for awesomeness (my summary of their definition), I nodded to myself. I know from previous trips this is the badge of honour amongst the countless gems to explore in the world. Easter Island was instantly added as a must-see to the itinerary of my South America trip.

As I continued to work through the plans, with one eye on my budget, it was the one part of my 'big' trip that I would consider scrapping. I know, I know. One minute I am drooling at photos online, allowing my daydreamer mind to conjure up all the possibilities of being lost on this mystic island like a true intrepid explorer. Then, annoyingly, I am wondering if Easter Island is a bit too much to add onto the other eleven countries and many side trips plotted out. The flights were pricey, a lot of money for someone who quit her job to become a backpacker on a four-month trip. But we only live our lives once, right! Pretty much the most overused mantra I live my life by.

I would get overly excited gazing at the ancient and mysterious Moai statues on Google images, credited to the early settlers. The first settlers are thought to have arrived from the nearby-ish Polynesian region. It isn't until you google map Easter Island and zoom out, again, and again that you realise how far away it is from any other landmass.

So much is known and unknown about these statues and the overall history of the island, you can't help but be left fascinated. There are over one thousand monumental statues around the island - either standing solo, splattered around vast areas, or lined up like soldiers in military formation - commanding the attention they deserve.

The intrigue continued as the plane started the descent to the island. With no sign of anything other than ocean for the entire five-hour flight, I felt very far from civilisation. A bundle of nerves and excitement started to bubble away.

One week before, I found myself in a crazy scam involving a Bolivian couple posing as a traveller and a police officer. My phone and all my debit and credit cards were stolen, just like that. My instant access to money gone, and my phone – also my camera, music, internet and all forms of communication – lost forever. Three countries into an eleven-country trip and travel life got hard.

With some US dollars in my pocket and my iPad mini, which turned into my camera, awkwardly pulled out my travel bag when I fancied taking a photo - I still cringe about that now - travel life resumed. Luckily, the day before I was due to fly to the island, my wee sister, to who I owe the fact I completed my four-month trip, wired money to Western Union for collection. With this money and my iPad as a camera, I was ready to shake off the negative energy left by that scam and travel to a destination of my dreams.

With a population of less than 5000 I wasn't expecting anything crazy, or even to meet many other travellers there. It is, along with Madagascar, seen as the ultimate South America add on. I fully prepared myself for a wilderness seeking, Moai hunting, awe-inspiring experience full of happiness.

I booked to stay at the local 'hostel' on the Tipanie Moana campground, a five-minute walk into the town, and the only real budget option. Once I landed onto the stripe of an airport, I walked through the arrival lounge to spot my name scribbled on a whiteboard. Suddenly a big smile appeared on my face. I loved this. When you know for sure you will have somewhere to stay as there is someone at the airport to collect you, like a big warm welcome hug. What a treat.

There have been so many times where I have arrived in a new country and felt pretty lost, as I try to figure everything out the minute I clear customs – all under the gaze of the locals. An endless stream of thoughts to get from A to B – how to get cash, where is the nearest ATM, what happens if that doesn't work, how do I travel into the city, should I ask the information desk for directions, no I can figure this out, should I use the bus or train, or even a taxi – all while trying to work out your new playground of choice.

A local from the campground introduced himself, offered a gift and declared, "Welcome to Easter Island, the Rapa Nui people welcome you here." What a special moment, the welcome extended further with a lei, the flower garland you would instantly associate with an exotic island location, soon worn with pride.

I felt very welcome and quickly forgot the remoteness.

The island received its European name after the Dutch arrived on Easter Sunday 1722. This volcanic island was truly untouched by tourism, as untouched gets in the year 2016. The traditions I instantly encountered weren't for show, but as a gesture of their culture from their Polynesian ancestry. The island, known as Rapa Nui by the locals, emits a special energy when you walk amongst the locals who act as gatekeepers of the land.

A German traveller joined the airport transfer. As we drove along the dirt tracks to the campground, the owner seemed overly excited when I explained I was Scottish. The UK embassy has a very remote consulate on Easter Island with only one worker, the worker now part of the community and apparently Scottish. Eyebrows raised kind of moment. My intrigue continued as the owner pointed him out from the jeep window. Standing 6ft tall, bare-chested, clear signs he worked out, barefoot, a little windswept and not very Scottish looking. Who is this man!!

Eager to get out and explore the minute the jeep pulled up, I established the German traveller shared roughly the same plans - explore the full island and breathe it all in. Simple. A loop of the island involves a scenic one hour drive with some incredible Moai statues to salivate over. I researched 'Easter Island Top 10' and cherry-picked the highlights - usually those that made me stop in my Google search tracks and mumble, "wow!".

I was so ready for everything this island offered.

I am made for adventure fuelled island trips. You feel emotions you can only experience by stepping in the footsteps of those who have paved the way, who have left glimpses of a past that you will never fully understand but will keep that fire lit inside you - the fire of possibilities. Some people escape their day-to-day life to sit in a cafe or lie by a poolside and bury their nose in a book. I escape my daily routine to create memories and experiences. I will literally sit down one day in the future with a cup of tea and giggle and mutter, "remember that," as I look through the photos or replay the moments on one of my many runs when my mind wanders into my past to guide my future.

As we left the campground to explore the island, we immediately bumped into the Scottish embassy worker - still bare-chested, as I hoped! Of course, I needed to know his story. After questioning him like an amateur journalist, I uncovered he first arrived on the island as a nineteen-year-old to spend a few months. He of course, as per the Hollywood movies, fell in love with the island and continued to study the history, culture and ancient language from afar, back at university in the UK. He soon spoke the local dialect and he returned to the island after graduating. I struggle with mastering 'thank you' in most languages, so to learn an obscure language gains bonus points in my eyes.

Summer turned into a year, and he has now been living on the island for over fifteen years. Incredible. Between us, it sounded the dream, an official job where you are available to support any 'issues' that arise on the most remote and unassumingly quiet island in the world.

This is travelling. Opening your mind from the tales shared by others. Their normal is your fascination and usually nudges something inside you. These encounters grip me.

So, what made a twenty-something from Scotland call Easter Island home? Only he knows. It shows anything is possible, especially when most of the population in Scotland can't even point to Easter Island on a world globe and we have our very own Scotsman leading his life here. Some would say he is owning it.

We found a small shack type place that served fresh food, where we sat with tacos and a super chilled beer enjoying the views out to the Pacific. I felt so present and slightly delirious to be on the Island. Travelling is a funny old hobby. One minute you are getting goosebumps flicking through photos of a remote, ancient, cultural hotspot, then the next minute you are standing on the island sipping a beer. It suddenly becomes your normal, "Oh hi, I'm busy on Easter Island." I never ever forget the first feelings of a new country or place, as I know soon it will feel normal. I cannot describe Easter Island as normal - exquisite maybe, but not normal. You end up sharing these first moments with random strangers who, a few hours after first meeting, share your inner joy. Your paths collide, and you share a moment that no other person in your life will experience or even really get.

We wondered a little more in the early afternoon sunshine and bumped into a friendly local man, smelling of beer. He spoke like he knew we were new to the island - fresh off the plane. He asked about our plans. "How forward of him," I thought. I casually mentioned we would probably watch the sunset later, and he replied, "See you there."

As we walked away, I realised I was still wearing the flower lei around my neck – the symbol of fresh meat to the single men in town. How funny. Before we headed to sunset, I took off my lei. No one wants an island romance, especially one on the remotest island in the world!

As we walked into a beachside bar for a sunset drink, I got a little spooked. There sat a couple who I hung out with back in Colombia. We enjoyed a boozy rum fuelled day trip from the city Medellin to El Peñón de Guatapé, an incredible rock formation that appears from nowhere a couple of hours from the city made famous by Pablo Escobar. We spent my last night together in Medellin with some others from our hostel on a very boozy night out. I last saw them a little tipsy, code for blind drunk and high on some classic Colombian gear, a month earlier when our routes parted. It always baffles me a little how you can meet people so many footsteps, and days, in the future, when you have both been meandering through South America to arrive at the same spot, at the exact same time.

After sunset, and with bellies full of local food, we headed back to the hostel dorm for the second spooky encounter of the night. As I perched on top of the bunk bed, I glanced up as the door opened. There in front of me stood a girl who wore this shocked expression on her face at my existence. Once my brain caught up with her reaction, I said out loud, "Nooooo way."

There in front of me stood a girl I spent two days hiking with while in Peru in the Colca Canyon. I last saw her over three weeks before as we arrived back into the nearest City, Arequipa, where I said my goodbyes, not expecting to see her again, ever, and especially not on Easter Island. How magical.

Two random backpacker connections in the one day, hours apart - I felt part of the worldwide travel community. The German girl looked on like I was a bit famous, bumping into people on a remote island. Funny how small the world can feel when you are travelling around, noticing little gifts from our travel past brought back into our present. The realisation that nothing is ever final, the universe is constantly spinning us through life.

The following day, the real-life lessons of island adventure unravelled in front of me - let the travel games begin. There were three options to explore this intriguing island: 1. luxury car, 2. thrill-seeking moped, or 3. old-fashioned bicycle.

My eye was firmly on the bicycle option. I think I am a bit old school and just love a proper old-fashioned adventure where you need to use your energy and body to its max, feeling completely at one with nature and in control of the outcome. Not some backseat passenger half falling asleep in the comfy car seat.

It became apparent the German girl was after that halfway house option and a less energetic adventure. At one point, I could hear my mind explaining maybe it was best to downgrade my adventure goals and compromise - follow the German girl's lead and rent a moped. Quickly my 'I know what I want' attitude kicked in, and I booked the bicycle option. Of course, I did. This girl doesn't compromise on an adventure.

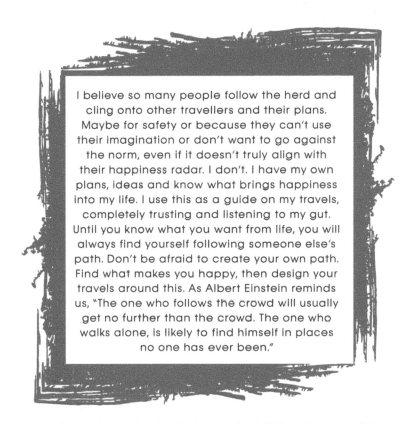

I believe so many people follow the herd and cling onto other travellers and their plans. Maybe for safety or because they can't use their imagination or don't want to go against the norm, even if it doesn't truly align with their happiness radar. I don't. I have my own plans, ideas and know what brings happiness into my life. I use this as a guide on my travels, completely trusting and listening to my gut. Until you know what you want from life, you will always find yourself following someone else's path. Don't be afraid to create your own path. Find what makes you happy, then design your travels around this. As Albert Einstein reminds us, "The one who follows the crowd will usually get no further than the crowd. The one who walks alone, is likely to find himself in places no one has ever been."

As I collected the bike, I naively enquired, "What happens if I get a puncture?"

The man shrugged, he explained how they previously provided puncture kits but hardly any came back with the bike - so stopped. Then continued to express that the island isn't that big and, somehow, I would find a way back. "Oh okay," I thought. All I could think as I jumped on the bike was, "please don't let Jacquelyn get a puncture." Not halfway round the remotest island in the world.

I cannot put into words the feeling as I cycled out into the wilderness, the glistening turquoise of the Pacific Ocean as my guide. You literally could not get lost as the road circles the island – everything was set for the best day being a curious explorer. Retracing the footsteps of the early expeditions, with a bag full of snacks and a mind ready to be enlightened. I felt free as a bird, with those happy vibes switched ON, riding solo into adventure-filled horizons. Yes to that. A proper adventure where I would decide at the last minute what sites to visit as they came into sight. Jumping off my bike when something caught my attention, trying to picture an ancient civilisation going about their olden days business - which I assume was low-key. Taking it all in. Every single second.

I would see a site in the distance and mutter, "WOW." This happened a lot.

One of the major sites is called Rano Raraku – the Moai quarry formed from a volcano that now houses a freshwater lagoon. Described as the Moai factory, home to so many statues, that sit or lie toppled around the area. Constructed in the quarry by hand, then transported around the island to honour the memory of the island ancestors. Over 300 Moai statues can still be found here, with the Largest Moai known as 'El Gigante' measuring over 21 meters. I kept pausing to take in the pretty unbelievable scenes.

After spending time exploring the site, lost in the stories I could overhear from a loudly spoken tour guide, I walked towards my chained up bike with a spring in my step. As I glanced over, I felt that feeling in my tummy - that sinking feeling when you spot your worst nightmare. I could see a flat tyre. A P.U.N.C.T.U.R.E! Surely not, not on this magical island – this wasn't part of the grand master plan. Two hours into an all-day adventure and so far from the only town. What a palaver.

All I could hear echo around in my head, the words the man expressed earlier, "somehow you will find a way back." This could only happen to me - the girl who wants to have a full-on adventure. Well, I was getting it now. With so much more still to explore, I really didn't need this - argh! After I surveyed the area to look for any sign of flat tyre help, there was only one thing to do, I jumped on the bike and cycled along listening to the crunch of the wheel at every turn of the pedal. I made that face when you know you are probably destroying the bike. After a while, I got used to it and kind of pretended the wheel wasn't flat! Full-on denial. What a tactic.

Eventually, the next site appeared into sight. I gasped in awe. There in front me stood 15 imposing statues, erected in line, their backs to the sea, used as a ceremonial site by the clans that once lived in these parts. It is thought the statues face inwards towards the villages to guard the people - representing the spirits of ancestors who held important positions. I was completely blown away. This site was the main reason I visited Easter Island.

As I researched the trip online, I saw this view countless times and felt shivers when I thought of seeing it in person. And now here I was. No flat tyre was ruining this for me. I parked up and explored the site in person, goosebumps on my skin. Taking all the photos, including some silly selfie shots attempting to eat the Moai statues. They were fascinating to witness in person, each seemed to show their personality or maybe the personality of those that designed and created them. Haunting. As I glanced out beyond the line of statues, out towards the crystal clear water glistening in the midday sunshine, I felt a sense of contentment. The flat tyre worries still there, bubbling away, but I switched off the feelings. "This is paradise," I thought, "I am experiencing paradise." Whenever and wherever, always keep bringing yourself back to the present – the thing you are worried about can always wait for a bit.

I was soon back on my bike.

Eventually, I made it to the North of the island. As I cycled along the road, trying my best to stay present and soak in the enigmatic energy emitted from the stunning landscape, I found my gaze and mind wander looking at the cars, vans, and other happy cyclists pass by trying to work out if they could help in any way. Although I felt okay to cycle on the flat tyre, I was very aware this probably wasn't quite right, and I was now even further away from the town. The show goes on and all that!

At the next site, I started chatting to the youngster guarding the area. As we chatted more, I explained the flat tyre situation. He offered to radio ahead to his friend who worked at the next site, who owned a van that could transport me back to town. 'My knight in shining armour,' I thought. As I thought of the incoming happy ending, I felt the relief slowly flood into my body, a nice warm feeling in my tummy, rather than that anxiousness you get when you know you are wrecking the bike tyre while floating about the tip of the island – still in denial mode. I thanked him so much. What a lovely human.

After more wheel crunching, I arrived at the next spot feeling happy that the situation would soon be fixed. I went on the lookout for the friend - my rescue. Well, this is where I got that sickening feeling there was no one here to help. I couldn't find anyone that looked like they worked for Easter Island, and after walking in circles, a little drained from the daytime heat and the ongoing puncture saga, I resigned myself to the fact I would continue to be a damsel. Eek.

Before trying to figure out a new rescue plan, I decided to enjoy this breathtaking sandy site – it was truly unique, my mind blown away again. Seven Moai statues faced onto the most beautiful white sand beach. No words will ever do justice for this spot. It felt like a Caribbean beach with the most special archaeological findings guarding it. Although I tried to stay present and take in my surroundings, in the back of my mind I kept thinking, "How will I make it back?". I knew the next part of the loop road involved a steep uphill - an incoming nightmare with a flat tyre. So, I went back into denial mode and I lay on the beach for a bit longer to recharge my batteries, occasionally glancing back at the protective statues. What a mesmerising site. Surely the powers of the Moai statues would deliver some help.

As I set off again and began to cycle uphill, I could feel a tantrum come on. A sign signalled 18 km back to the town, and with all the sites ticked off, I felt drained. I think I used up all my positive thoughts, and now, with no sites to use as a focus point, it became one enormous struggle. "Why could I not just be content with a moped?" I thought. I kept on the lookout for the German girl, I left her back at the bike shop hours ago, busy chatting to the guy from the shop. Secretly hoping she would glide by and sort out this situation.

After a while, I stopped cycling and walked the bike uphill. You can just imagine, slightly dragging my heels like a teenager. A lovely cyclist stopped and asked if I was okay. "Of course I'm not" I thought while pretend smiling. We tried to blow up the type with his pump, knowing fine well it wouldn't make a difference as I watched the air slowly escape. I thanked him and he cycled on. By now I was making despairing noises in my head, like a wounded animal.

The next rescue attempt rolled up - a van full of locals who seemed, well, interesting. They enquired if I was okay and if I wanted a ride. "No thank you," I assertively answered, smiling politely. They looked like they were smoking some herb life, and I did not want to be in that van. They lingered a bit, and I stood smiling. A bit of a stand off. "Look in charge of the situation", I thought. As they drove on, I felt semi relieved. We have all seen those movies where a naïve adventure-seeking traveller, with no puncture kit, is snatched in broad daylight from a seemingly quaint tropical island. I didn't plan for that to be me. Thankfully, the road was busy enough with other tourists leaving the beach in their luxury cars or mopeds, so

I never felt in any snatching danger - just pangs of jealousy at the ease they travelled up the hill. As the uphill struggle continued, I clung onto hope. Hope that a happy ending would be incoming. I kept staring ahead, expecting a miracle.

Suddenly, from nowhere, the miracle came, of course it did. We have all seen the movies. A handsome French tour guide, on his way back to the swanky eco holiday village where he worked, was my knight. Round of applause please. Of course, a handsome man was always going to save me. This was the mystical Easter Island after all – the dream. The struggle was worth it.

As the pristine van pulled up alongside me, I looked to the side and into his clear blue eyes as he peered out the passenger seat window, smiling. I instantly felt a calming feeling as he asked, "Do you need some help?" in a very sexy French accent. Soon enough, the local driving the van bundled my bike into the back of the pickup. And I found myself sitting up front, alongside the handsome guide, with the breeze on my hair and island infused tunes playing out the speaker. What a couple of legends.

This is why we travel, to experience it all. The highs and lows. The tantrums and despair. Then the euphoria of the flat tyre rescue.

And this is how quickly a moment of despair can turn into something magical. Yes, I was fully in the middle of throwing an adult tantrum, but I didn't give up. Everyone knows the moment when you want to quit is the moment when something will happen - if you only keep going. Keep focussed, determined and open to options. There are always options to any situation. Some better than others. And some more exciting, and pleasing on the eye.

He explained with an apologetic, handsome face that he could only drive as far as the eco-village. This sat at the top of the long and energy-sapping hill, leaving a final cycle back to the town - all downhill. I could have cried happy tears - this felt manageable.

We chatted on the drive that would have taken hours to walk. As he handed back my bike, he wished me well - I knew I was going to make it back to town, and I did. All downhill, wind in my hair and not a care in the world - until I cycled back into the rental place and I wondered, "How do I cover up a flat tyre?" No one wants a hefty bill for something that was technically not their doing, especially when a puncture kit would have fixed me up – not that I would have known what to do with one. The rental guy seemed distracted and signalled to place the bike against the wall. I seized the moment, placed the bike as instructed and scurried away - physically and mentally exhausted, with my mind full of the wonders of the island.

What a day. I needed a beer, or two, and a moment to acknowledge I had conquered the island, on a bike, experiencing some of the most exquisite remains in the world.

After a well-deserved shower, I sat at the top of the hill that overlooks the town. Watching the sunset out at sea with the final sunlight glistening on more Moai statues. A beer in my hand, and a smile on my face, as I reflected on the day. The German girl wasn't back yet – I considered what kind of island adventure she experienced as I recalled my energy sapping day. Later that night, I found out.

Turned out we were enjoying different island experiences – very different. She ended up on a date with the young guy from the rental bike shop - he offered her some after-hours service. They went swimming at a hidden part of the island then enjoyed a candlelit dinner, where he explained she was his first after-hours date. Yeah right! Some girls get lucky, some throw an adult tantrum over a puncture!

Well, that Easter Island adventure toughened me up a little and taught me, as much as possible, to go with the flow as you always figure stuff out and nothing is ever as bad as it seems at the time. Each trip provides a perspective, or story, to add to your resilience toolkit, ready for a future date when you need a little bit of reassurance.

During the very first Covid lockdown in 2020, I bought a new bike. After many weeks locked indoors, only allowed outside for exercise or to the supermarket for essential purchases, I needed to feel more freedom. The bike provided that. One day, while I was on the phone with my mum explaining my plans to cycle outside Glasgow, to enjoy some nature-filled freedom, she asked, "What will you do if you get a puncture?"

"I have a puncture kit," I explained.

"Do you know how to use it?" She responded. Of course, I didn't. I smiled as I thought back to Easter Island and thought "I will figure it out".

My last day crept up on me - it always does. The minute a trip starts, I instantly want to press the pause button, as before I know it, the trip is over. The adventure you have researched and obsessed over for months, the trip you have daydreamed about and imagined, soon a memory. Always be 100% present and take in every single second; as you want to collect the most vivid memories to look back on one day.

Although one of the remotest destinations in the world, the island envelops you with its incredible warmth, passed on from the people who are privileged to call this their home. Who guard the treasures left on the land.

My last experience on the island summed up my time here, magical.

With no departure lounge at the airport, you are free to wander back into town once your luggage is checked in. With my final minutes ticking away, I sat on the edge of the island overlooking the water, sipping a beer at a small outdoor bar. Allowing all the feelings to flood in, to pause and breathe in this exotic setting for one last time. You don't take any of this for granted, I knew I would never set foot on this land again – this was the end. The end of my time on Easter Island, but soon the start of the next, new, shiny awe-inspiring adventure. I looked at the wooden Moai necklace in my hand. A farewell gift from the campsite owner, who placed the necklace in my hand, and explained it would act as a reminder to never forget the time I spent on the island. Wow – another goosebump moment.

I sometimes catch a glimpse of the necklace as it sits tucked away in my jewellery box, a constant reminder of the island with the most intriguing and sacred Moai statues. A reminder to be present in the moment, as the moment doesn't last.

The island, full of warmth, tradition, connections, and adventure, will now remain part of my life forever. It taught me to be playful, embrace the culture, and wear the lei all day long – even if it attracts unwanted attention. Or just hire a bicycle, learn to go with the flow and put trust in the island. You are never really alone in life. The power and strength it stores protects you. We are all part of a bigger, more connected energy. Each of us the main characters in our own stories, but also supporting characters in others lives – some we don't even realise.

Don't be afraid to step outside your comfort zone to chase down that dream. The dream job, relationship, adventure or experience. You will be guided; you just need to be open to the adventure of life and keep your eyes and mind open. Remember, nothing in this life is really coincidence but a collection of moments shared across the universe, moving you forward in life ready for the next chapter.

It is the trips that you doubt or consider cancelling that you need to take. These are the ones that ultimately make you work for it; make you question if it's worth the cash value assigned by the airlines or tour companies. These are the ones that will blow your mind with the splendour, remoteness, or uniqueness. You know it when you arrive. That feeling of awe where you think, "This is why I came here." Splash the cash as these are the once in a lifetime moments you will never forget or regret. We are all on a journey to our end and spend such little time on this planet, so why not spend the cash you have worked for when you can? You will be rewarded - trust me. I give you permission, what are you waiting for?

Easter Island

CAMPING
TIPANIE MOAN
WIFI - ROOM
HOSTEL

JAQUELYN
ARMOUR
Roxanne Boch

"Live as if you were to die tomorrow. Learn as if you were to live forever"

– Gandhi

Albania: Where we learn that colour brings Joy

Albania sat on my travel list collecting dust for a long time. Some countries jump to the top and others need to practice patience, slowly working their way up. In 2019 I could feel the pull of Albania. I had already travelled to neighbouring Croatia, Montenegro, Bosnia, and Serbia. With Kosovo the most recent. It felt about time I finished off the Balkans. I can be a little OCD with my country collection - you can't say 'I have done the Balkans' then slip in, 'except Albania'. That just wouldn't do.

I followed a female traveller online for years, one of those full-time blogger types, she wrote a blog all about her trip to Albania. Of course, this became the base to work from – why start from scratch when the hard work has already been done. I knew across seven days you could easily experience the 'main highlights' - I just needed to work out how to get there. Countries like Croatia are 100% on the holiday map, Montenegro is a favourite with the cruise ship day-trippers into Kotor Bay, and there sits Albania 100% off the radar - very much a hidden gem. This suits me. There is so much potential in a hidden gem - your wild imagination goes into overdrive about what awaits you.

For various, mainly obscure, reasons this country excited me - a lot.

I read a book called Joyful by Ingrid Fetell Lee. In the chapter Energy, it features the Albanian capital Tirana and I became hooked. The author explains how the Mayor commissioned the introduction of street art into the grey and gritty city centre streets, previously crime and poverty ravaged. A charismatic arts graduate who knew the benefits of filling the streets with colour and energy - people felt pride again, and studies showed a crime reduction followed. I needed to see this city with my own eyes. It sounded the future.

Annoyingly for a country in Europe, it took some time to make this trip work.

Blogs spoke about vague bus times with statements describing 'lack of infrastructure makes things difficult.' I remember having this idea there would be no main roads, only pothole-filled dirt tracks. After what felt like a lifetime of plotting and planning various routes in and around the country, I remember the night the trip finally came together. I could finally see the perfect route mapped out in my notebook. I do love the research and plotting part, Albania was tricky to make work though. I hoped it would be worth it.

I flew into North Macedonia, where I spent a couple of days, before I arrived in the capital of Albania – Tirana. After a four-hour minibus journey, with no border patrol to negotiate, I cruised through from one country to the other. North Macedonia and Albania added to my travel list.

The more I discovered about the country's communist era, the more I found myself intrigued – the Albanians were locked away from the world for forty years. Forty years ruled under an ultra-communist regime led by Enver Hoxha, who rose to power in 1944 in the same era of Moa in Soviet China, Tito in the old Yugoslavia, and Stalin in the now defunct USSR.

Albania eventually dissolved ties with their communist allies. First, they broke away from the treaty of friendship they held with neighbouring Yugoslavia then left the Warsaw pact, truly isolating themselves from the rest of Europe. After the death of Mao, the unique trade and military relationship between China dissolved, leaving the Albanians in dire need of aid. Even their ties with the Soviets crumbled.

To put it in perspective, Albania – a European country – found itself completely shut off from the outside world. TV and all media were state-controlled. No one could leave or enter the country. Regardless of your education or potential, the communist regime treated everyone the same. As explained by a tour guide on an evening walking tour in Tirana, there was no point in having an imagination as it would never flourish. People learn to dampen their fire and stay quiet. Turning into ghosts. Anyone who questioned the regime would disappear. Paranoia was rife in the country. Families would turn against each other. This was not living, but survival.

Their crazy egocentric dictator convinced himself and the country there would be an imminent attack – I'm not sure why. As Western Europe continued to flourish, where the old Yugoslavia radically changed following the second world war, just next door, Albania found itself stuck in the 70s. The dictatorship finally crumbled when Enver Hoxha died in 1985, along with his ego.

He may be dead, but his legacy is everlasting. There are over

175,000 bunkers left dotted around the country, built to protect the country from the attack Hoxha was convinced would come. None ever used! Most now remain as lasting memories of those crazy times. There are two famous sites - Bunk'Art 1 & 2.

I visited Bunk'Art 2, the underground bunker in the centre of Tirana. Located on the main block of ministerial buildings in the city's centre, this underground shelter was hidden from the public eye until its unveiling in 2015. Secretly built from 1981-86, each of its 24 rooms now recounts stories of the political persecutions during this dark period of history. The exhibition sends chills down your spine with stories and photos across the 40 years – some of what you see and read doesn't feel real. The Primo Levi quote grabs your attention above the entrance - 'All Those Who Forget Their Past Are Condemned to Relive it'.

I remember pretty quickly saying to myself, "You will return one day." Albania, as I found as I travelled through it, gets under your skin. So rich in culture, with a few surprises up its sleeve. Home to a fjord. Yes, a fjord. A fjord in Albania. I need to return for this alone. Fjords are up there in the 'must see' category In any country lucky to have them. A gift from mother nature. When I lived in Melbourne, I visited the world-famous fjord and wonder that is Milford Sound in New Zealand. When I finally made a trip to Norway happen I became obsessed with the Flam Railway, a train journey that ascends through the most stunning scenery to Bergan where you can take a boat trip to witness the UNESCO rubber-stamped fjords. That train ride, Bergan and the Norwegian fjords need to be seen – trust me. Did I know fjords can be found in Albania? Absolutely not and I call myself a fjord fan. Fjords are the travel gems people visit countries for, but in Albania, they keep it on the down-low until you arrive – like you earned this information. I am now passing it on for free.

This is Albania, a country that will constantly shake up every perspective you have of it.

So back to my first day in Tirana. I dumped my bags at the hostel, grabbed a map of the city from the ultra-friendly reception staff and went off to explore. This is Europe with an Eastern twist. The main religion in Albania is Islam, leftover from the Ottoman Empire. All around, you see the distinguished mosque minarets. I love Islamic architecture and find mosques mesmerizing.

As I approached a site I spotted from afar, I could see the partially complete grand mosque fenced off from the city by a corrugated iron wall. I noticed a slightly open door in the wall and peeked through. From what I could see of the architecture style, it looked elegant and magical. As my face sneaked a glance of the under-construction wonder, I caught eyes with a slightly stern-looking guard. I smiled as I pointed up to the mosque and explained via my body language, "beautiful." His stern look melted into a proud grin, and he seemed so happy. I thought, let's chance our luck here and asked, again through body language, "Can I come in through the corrugated iron wall door and have a wee nosey, maybe take some photos." He looked around sheepish and ushered me in - I strolled in. Result!

The next thing I know, I am in a photoshoot with the, now, over-friendly security guard, who is directing the photoshoot. Sadly, he lacked the most basic camera skills and went full portrait mode on me with the tiniest sight of the mosque in the shot - I wanted it as a backdrop. I smiled as he handed back my phone to check his work, I gave him a thumbs up. I sensed his playfulness as he dropped the 'I am a security guard' persona and things soon escalated further. We performed that universal activity, which solidifies a new random friendship, where we took a selfie together. Now left as a memory of our five minutes of mischief together. We giggled as we viewed the photo – the cheesiest of grins on display. I thanked him, before expressing my happiness for the sneaky peek of the mosque. Thank goodness for the use of body language as a form of communication. It has proved to be a life saver on many trips when no one speaks English. A true-life skill to develop. Take note.

I stepped back through the door and waved goodbye while giggling to myself – these interactions make my trips and lift my energy. For the rest of the day, I kept giggling at the most awkward selfie and his big cheesy grin. As I walked away from the mosque, I watched as two serious-looking French tourists asked if they could enter the construction site to take photos. From across the road, I watched as the lovely jovial security guard turned stern again. He gave them the universal sign that signalled, "No chance, this mosque is off-limit." He shook his head and shut the fence door. How funny.

Serious and straight-faced gets you nowhere – as I saw. I think there is something in being a bit playful, with an inquisitive and child-like nature.

Tirana keeps you wanting more. Grand Neo-Renaissance style

buildings found in Skanderbeg Square, the vast plaza connecting the outer regions of the city into the heart of the capital, with street art murals and graffiti dotted around most corners grabbing your attention and bringing a smile to your face. This is so typical of a country reborn. The people find their imaginations are now free. Free to explode all their creativity, previously stifled, onto the streets. They do not hold back. Nothing left untouched - Batman, Salvador Dali and even Jesus were all spotted painted onto pavement utility boxes.

The city, at times, still felt grey and sad, stuck with the bland brutal concrete communist-style architecture. Then you were reminded this is a country taking the visitor on a journey of growth and rebirth. I stood on the edge of a roundabout and looked ahead where a rainbow inspired mural was splashed across a nondescript white building, jumping out at you grabbing your attention. All around the city little pockets of quirky and thought-provoking artwork popped out. Sometimes when you least expected. Alongside some bleak buildings were entire districts that would fit in with chic New York, foody Athens, or trendy Tel Aviv. I was surrounded by hipster bars, independent boutiques, and the coolest coffee spots – even some arty pop ups. All splashed with colour, sparkling in the blue skies of the Albanian summer. The city felt alive and so did I.

The main attraction in Tirana is a little hard to explain and grasp. A structure described as a glass framed pyramid. Opened in late 1988 as a museum to the late communist leader, showcasing his legacy. Soon repurposed as the country quickly looked to remove all traces of their dictator following the breakdown of the party. Now it sits truly abandoned, having experienced dilapidation and vandalism. It felt poignant for what it once represented. The brutal architecture now left to the city – perhaps as a reminder of the past or a gift to the future.

Tirana felt like organised chaos – a little unruly. This is Europe but more. A melting pot of the empires that influenced Albania over the years – Ottoman, Roman, and Byzantine, to name a few.

So now to introduce two main characters into the Albania travel story. First up, I met Teacher Tony on the Tirana evening walking tour on my first night in the city. I spotted him while keeping myself to myself, as you do, wandering the streets, following the tour guide and listening to all the facts. I spotted Tony as he asked a question and could distinctly hear a London accent. Maybe in his 50s with this eccentric vibe about him. At first, I thought he seemed annoying - like a know it all. What is that saying, 'Don't judge a book by its cover'. By the end of the three-hour walking tour, it became clear we were pretty much on the same fast-paced route. We first connected over some chit chat, and once we both sussed each other's travelling credentials, we developed mutual travel respect for each other. Tony, like me, doesn't mess about and knows what he likes. What a legend. We need more Tony's in the world.

As the tour ended, I jokingly said, "Probably see you on the minibus tomorrow to Berat" - the next town on my itinerary. I felt this warm feeling inside, Albania oozed this small-town community vibe. I felt like I belonged here. I could sense true travellers and, maybe, eccentrics visit countries like Albania. These are my people! In small doses, though.

I arrived back at my hostel tired but excited. The city had been my playground all day and I knew more waited in the morning on my planned run. I felt tired and wanted a quiet night. That was what I thought before the second main character arrived onto the scene.

As I walked through the hostel, I slowly felt my gaze stumble onto this untamed character, sitting in the chillout area, looking deep in some travel planning. "How handsome and interesting looking," I thought. I could feel my mischievous side come out.

"Let's Play," I thought.

I did what any red-blooded single girl would do when presented with this opportunity, I sat at the comfy chair next to him. We caught each other's eyes and acknowledged each other with a smile – how polite.

We soon went from politely acknowledging each other to arranging a breakfast 'date', he was also travelling to Berat the next morning. The new guy in my travel life seemed very eccentric. Of a similar age, Israeli born but now based in Melbourne before he set off travelling - three years ago. Three years of travelling. How wild. My mind in overdrive.

I could feel myself get overly excited. He explained he worked as a social worker. My heart melted. As we got to know each other, he started to get very animated when he received an email confirming his visa for Russia, all so he could take an epic train journey into Mongolia to experience a lake – standard. I felt a pang of jealousy. Russia sits high on my travel list. The Saint Basil's

Cathedral in Moscow gives me goosebumps every time I google it – which is a lot. I felt a travel crush bubble away. He seemed to be playing in the advanced level of the travel game. The one I look on and admire.

He continued to surprise me as he explained he recently visited Scotland and guess his favourite city - Glasgow. He sat listing all his favourite spots in the city. I felt my heart grow with love. "This is the one," I thought. I knew it, I was pretty sure we were going to have a travel romance, then I would convince him to return to Glasgow where we would sit trading travel stories like a couple of legends. I went to bed with that feeling, knowing the next day some fun things would happen. This is travelling - each day is a whirlwind of emotions and adventure, where you decide the outcome. Earlier, when I stepped through the hostel door, I planned a quiet night, there was nothing quiet about that night.

After a sweaty early morning run, I got chatting to another traveller at the communal breakfast table while waiting for my date. She casually explained she planned to travel north to the Albanian Alps. The Albanian Alps. They sounded the hiker's dream. Albania again handing out more hidden gems – the Alps like the type in France and Switzerland. More surprises from this country and noted on my future travel list. First fjords, now the Alps. Who would have known!

My future boyfriend soon joined us. I played it cool, he didn't. I could sense he was looking for a holiday romance too. He soon earned extra brownie points when he couldn't finish his breakfast, and I enjoyed two servings of yummy pancakes – what a breakfast date. With a full tummy, we needed to get moving.

We made our way to the edge of the city, where I felt flashbacks to Asia. As we jumped out of the taxi to cross the highway into the bus station forecourt, the whole place emitted this crazy vibe. Each minibus stood with an attendant shouting the name of the destination, everyone trying to get your attention. As we continued to walk through the mayhem, I could hear our destination, Berat, and we were soon bundled into a moving minibus.

It felt frantic and organised at the same time. The minibus was practically full, and luckily I spotted two seats together. I could feel a set of eyes on me from a seat near the front. They belonged to Teacher Tony. Tony seemed distracted with something, but I sense Tony is constantly distracted. After a lowkey journey on the highway south – remember the blogs that made travelling in

Albania sound perilous – we soon reached Berat, the town with a thousand windows.

Mr Boyfriend and I, yes he got upgraded on the bus journey, went our separate ways after we arrived into town after sharing a taxi with Tony. Don't worry, only for a 'to freshen up' break! From now on I stayed upmarket - Albania upmarket - whoop. I picked this rustic, authentic hotel that sat perched on one of the cobbled streets leading to the clifftop fortress. As I entered, they treated me like a special guest and instructed I look at two rooms to pick my favourite. The room I picked was stunning, all wood-panelled walls, original wood beams on the ceiling with all these little quirky touches. A wooden balcony facing out to the internal courtyard, with the peacefulness oozing back into the room. It felt like luxury - £30 a night luxury.

After a coffee, I met up with Mr Boyfriend to explore Berat. I knew the town itself would be the main attraction. The scenery and views all around were stunning, like walking through a scene from when the Ottoman Empire reigned. The town, built into a cliff, looked like an oil painting. A painting with a fortress perched on the top of the cliff, rows of windows from the Ottoman styled houses staring back, the cobbled streets winding along the cliff face. Definitely a reflection of the town nicknamed 'thousand windows'.

We wandered the streets ticking off some sites and found ourselves on a windy, cobbly back street with an arty hand-painted sign 'I LOVE BERAT' on one of the giant steps leading to locals' houses. A photoshoot got underway – I sat for mine, while Mr Boyfriend lay across the step modelling an overly dramatic pose. Very much an eccentric.

As we walked along the river, we caught a glimpse of a building ahead that looked like the White House. It stood mesmerising, completely out of place in Berat, or anywhere else in Albania. Before we reached the White House building, I spotted the state library. As a book geek, I adore libraries. I grabbed Mr Boyfriend's hand and dragged him into the library. He seemed to go along with my tour, as he half clawed at me affectionately. I know it sounds strange that on my day date we visited a library - correct. I can see the line of future boyfriends waiting for their chance of an afternoon date with me - in a library!

The scene inside filled me with despair. The library shelves were sparse, and the books that were on display seemed from the olden days. I even found a book about the United Kingdom.

The front cover displayed a deary grey Birmingham from some time warp known as the 70s. We left and headed towards the White House building, recently a privately funded university now converted into a 5-star hotel. Again confused. "Where were all the five-star tourists coming from?" I thought.

As we peeked around the hotel reception and got the attention of some workmen, we asked in basic English about the building. They pointed to an older man who seemed in charge of the site and thankfully spoke a little English. He seemed very excited to show us around the under-construction 5-star hotel.

What waited inside was truly spectacular, marble imported from Italy and Roman-inspired columns dotted about the spacious reception area. Following a tour of the hotel interior, we were ushered to a hidden stairwell. As we walked up, I glanced back at Mr Boyfriend as if to say, whatever next and he shrugged his shoulders. "Maybe we were being led to a rooftop," I thought.

When the door opened, I nearly fainted. We were walking into the massive White House dome - home to a private library. Honestly, I could have cried. Think of the inside of a majestic marble dome, with the bottom half clad in wood panels with each panel arch acting as a bookshelf filled to the brim with books. There were thousands and thousands of them. Such a bright and airy room where the books seemed to sparkle. "Whose collection even is this?" I thought.

I paused as I took it in. We were standing in the centre of one of the most extraordinary book collections I have ever seen. It's likely no one will ever have the privilege to witness this, and all I could think about was the state-run library with the most uninspiring collection ever. You could see that building from the hotel. There is no justice or equality in the world. It makes me feel sad at times, but I know I can't change it - only observe it. And hopefully, lead my life in a way where I keep my mind open, so I never take for granted the opportunities and privileges I have. We thanked the man for the most wonderful and random tour ever. What a hidden gem, only discovered as we were being curious souls.

We stepped out into the most intense heat; it must have been 36 degrees, and the streets were deserted. It felt like we had the entire town to ourselves. Slowly I could feel the late-night, and early morning run, along with the intense heat, catch up on me and declared I needed a nap. After a nap-a-thon and change of outfit, we were ready to enter the last stage of the date that started 12 hours ago at breakfast - we were heading to experience the sunset from the clifftop fortress.

But first, let's talk about Mr Boyfriend. We shared breakfast at the hostel, the bus ride to Berat, enjoyed our day date exploring the riverside views. Now as we strolled up to the fortress, still in the intense heat, I heard this thought bubble up - I don't think I want him to be my forever boyfriend and move to Glasgow.

He was fun to be around and a total diva character at times – have I mentioned he wore a Spice Girls tee-shirt from their concert in Manchester and odd socks. But for most of the day, he moaned. Mainly about the heat and the fact I made him be a tourist during the peak hours.

After three years of travelling, he seemed pretty ungrateful and no longer saw the beauty or cherished the mystic of a new town with all the charm of the Ottoman Empire. He shrugged it off like he'd seen ten Berat's in his lifetime. There is only one Berat. With this is in mind, I sensed the end was near for the short-lived Albania romance.

We shuffled up the cliff, still sleepy from the nap. We seemed to save the best to last. We reached the edge of the castle walls, which sit perched on the cliff, as the sun set with the most spectacular views all around. What a way to end our day in Berat together, and what a time to pause and enjoy a moment with another traveller. It felt poignant. A symbol that nothing is final, people will come into your life, and leave again – let them go and enjoy the moments you shared. It became time to say goodbye. As we reached the foot of the steepest hill, Mr Boyfriend looked me in the eye and said he needed sleep.

Secretly relieved, I formed my own plan on the stroll down the cliff. As we hugged and wished each other well, I soon found myself on the same street that was deserted at 3 pm, now alive. I choose a restaurant with a live band playing outside, ordered a Quattro Fromage pizza and checked in with friends back home. Back to being a solo traveller, and pretty happy with that.

What a whirlwind romance. I wasn't sure what was around the corner, but I knew it wouldn't involve my boyfriend - soon downgraded to someone I shared 24 hours with. It's always nice sharing a part of my trip with someone, but no one likes someone who moans all day!

Now that we know what happened to My Boyfriend, what about

Teacher Tony?

Well, I never bumped into him during my Berat stay – too busy entertaining My Boyfriend. But he soon reappeared. The next day when I arrived at the bus station, I heard the shout of Gjirokaster, and I nodded to the driver who grabbed my backpack and ushered me into the minibus. As I looked up I recognised the next face I saw. Teacher Tony. And wait for it, I claimed the seat next to him – separated by the minibus aisle.

Usually, the thought of spending over three hours sitting near someone I vaguely know would make me feel uncomfortable. That feeling of awkwardness if the chat dries up and you are stuck with them, nowhere to hide. In the end, we chatted the whole journey, non-stop, constantly - I laughed a lot. Especially during a moment, maybe two hours into the journey where the driver turned around and gave the universal sign for 'shut up tourist people', and did that Albanian 'shush' noise. Well, Tony looked shocked and mouthed, "is that to us?" I shrugged and giggled. Of course it was to us. It didn't stop us chatting though, and we hushed our voices and spoke quieter. When you sit two kindred spirits together in a new country, who are massively vibing off each other, the chatting does not stop for a grumpy Albanian man. We have obscure stories to share – come on!

Tony was great, completely unfiltered. He, like me, likes to max out his trips and would be known to fly back to the UK on the last possible flight to then stroll into the school classroom after a few hours' sleep. Yes, Tony! He seemed spontaneous, a true explorer - planning on the go.

As we arrived in the UNESCO listed Gjirokaster, we were practically flung out the bus onto the side of the road. The next thing we are in the back of a jeep of a handsome local man, the owner of the local hostel. Neither of us were staying there, we befriended a girl during a break in the bus journey who was. We talked her into asking the local to drop us into the old town – her booking included a pickup and we extended it a little further. Tony and I wanted to arrive in comfort. As I mentioned my hotel, Tony raised his eyebrows. My hotel was number one in town. Another steal at £30.

After a quick outfit change, I was soon ready and exhilarated to explore. This town was awarded its heritage symbol for the rare example of a well-preserved Ottoman town that sits in the valley between the mountains and the river. All the attractions stacked on top of each other, layered to provide the most authentic experience of Albanian life. The Gjirokaster fortress is perched on the top of the hill, commanding views of the valley below, leading towards the cobble-lined old town - which feels like an open-air Ottoman Museum.

Rather than be sensible and hide in the shade from the 40 degrees heat, I became an explorer and walked up the slippery cobbles to the Castle with the most stunning views. After some time exploring, I heard a familiar accent asking if I wanted my photo taken. Yes, it was Tony. Tony is an actual photographer – well, he took the photos at a family wedding and allocated himself that title. It turned into an elaborate photo shoot with sweat dripping down my back as Tony shouted, "work it!" Let's just say we were causing a scene as I returned the favour. I waved him off as I went to explore further.

Later in the day, I sat enjoying the stillness from my huge hotel room balcony, reading my book and appreciating my surroundings. I napped as the day caught up with me, I suddenly felt exhausted. Dressed for the evening, I wandered the cobbled streets looking for food options. The old town was made up of maybe four streets that ran off a crossroads. As I turned the corner of the first street, I could see Tony. Yes, Tony was deep in chat with another English gentleman enjoying a cold beer. Turns out he'd been on the go all day. That is Tony. When I asked if he'd seen the Ali Pasha's bridge, part of a 19th century commissioned aqueduct complex, he looked at me from over his glasses. Tony seemed torn – now that he knew about it, he must see it, but the sun was setting. He asked if I was joining him, I smiled and shook my head. I didn't need to see the bridge right that second. Sometimes we need to pause for a bit.

I recognised myself in Tony. I remember my solo trip to Japan. On my last day in Kyoto, I thought I completed all the attractions. As I glanced on Trip Advisor, I noticed an attraction not yet ticked off. I knew I would need to visit. Even though I saw every other attraction, walked for hours and ran in the morning to see all the sights, my brain was always hungry for more. I went to visit the Temple. Did I need to see it? Or could I have instead appreciated what I had seen and spend the leftover time to rest and be grateful? It's always a fine balancing act - something I am still working on.

That night I started to feel unwell, the urge to be sick swept over me. After I fell asleep, I soon woke to be sick, this continued for most of the night. When I woke in the morning I felt drained. But like Tony, I wanted to hike to the bridge - it was how I planned to finish my time in Gjirokaster.

If only I could learn when to listen to my body, I would have stayed in bed for a bit. Instead, I went to find the bridge. My tunes playing for the easy hike, the outskirts of town felt very rustic. Cattle roaming free and the occasional local popping into view, I even saw a real-life shepherd herding his goats along the valley. I could hear their bells in the distance. Reassuring at first, then at times spooky. I thought, "Is this a potential kidnap scenario?".

Most of the time as a female traveller I feel safe, but your mind is constantly assessing every scenario for potential kidnap opportunities. I completed my assessment and determined the shepherd would not turn into a kidnapper. Phew.

I carried on the hike thinking of how Tony must have been scrambling his way along the route in the dark. After finding the bridge and taking some photos, I walked back to my hotel. I felt so lethargic from the lack of sleep, and my tummy still felt yucky. Lost in my head, worried about my next minibus journey, I heard this loud clatter noise disturbing my thoughts. Still on the outskirts of the village, deep in the rustic way of life, feeling startled, I looked up to see an old Albanian lady dressed all in black at the window of her cottage, knocking on the window shutters to grab my attention. She definitely caught my attention. As we caught each other's eyes, I saw the biggest and warmest smile appear and soon forgot all about my yucky tummy. She shouted, "Italiano?" I shook my head, and she looked confused as if to say, "yeah you are" I smiled back and replied English. Her eyes widened and she repeated the word, "English." I smiled and waved as I walked on. I smile as I remember her wide eyes and inquisitive face at my existence.

These are the moments that take you out of your head and make you feel the most present and connected. If I didn't think my tummy was going to explode, I would have stayed around to chat a bit as from her expression it seemed she didn't see many foreign visitors.

After checking out, I soon found myself back at the side of the road where Tony and I arrived the day before, ready for my next minibus trip to the beachside resort of Sarande. Only a one-hour journey, surely I would be there in the blink of an eye. Between us, I didn't think I would get on the minibus or survive that one hour journey as my yucky tummy was back. After waiting around for all the traveller types to arrive, the minibus was ready to depart. I asked two English girls if I could sit at the edge of the front row as I needed to feel free. Does anyone get like this when feeling ill? You can't feel boxed in. I needed to be near the minibus door. I mentioned to the girls I felt poorly and hoped they would take this as a hint to stop chatting to me. Well, they didn't.

Normally I would be so up for some chat, but honestly, I thought I was going to pass out. The minute the minibus started, I just felt the weirdest I have felt in my life. Less than one minute into a one-hour journey, I could have cried. My tummy rumbling, sweat dripping down my back with sweaty palms – I tried to feel calm and decided to focus on my breathing. One girl continued to chat, constantly, while I politely nodded. I felt a little guilty as I don't like to be rude, but my insides were exploding and I thought I was about to spew at any minute. Whatever next.

Well, then the strangest experience happened - I started to lose my vision. Subtle at first, then quickly down to a blur, then into blackness. There I am with sweaty palms, no vision, and the strongest urge to be sick. I felt petrified. I have never experienced a migraine before, so assume it must be similar. I didn't have a clue what to do. As I couldn't see, I didn't want to turn and tell the English girl as I didn't know what I wanted her to do. Then I thought about putting my head between my legs, but clearly, that would have attracted all the unwanted attention. I could have cried. It would pass I reasoned. I wanted to cry again and started to feel sorry for myself. I thought that if I was travelling with someone they would look after me, or at least say those words you want to hear, 'it will be alright'. I felt all pathetic.

Slowly my vision returned, the darkness eased and I felt such relief until I realised the bus journey continued along the windiest road. I couldn't deal with this. The entire time up to now I kept thinking "where can I be sick?". I knew it was only a matter of time as the rumbling from my insides continued to intensify. The next thing I know I am being sick into the sick bag I managed to grab from a local, with the two English girls sat next to me and two German girls squashed to the other side. I felt the shame surge up within, and a tear come to my eye. Please let this journey stop.

The English girl shouted at the driver to stop. He looked back confused until he saw my pathetic situation, next I am outside the minibus being sick at the side of the road. The English girls were so sweet, handing over a fresh sick bag and some tissues as I rejoined the minibus. The Germans meanwhile looked disgusted. I shrugged.

The bus finally left the windy road and I arrived at the seaside town, the last destination of the trip and home to the Albanian Riviera. I thought I would be high on life at this point in the trip - especially when I first saw a glimpse of the sea. Instead, I still felt in survival mode. I wished for this day for most of the trip as the Albanian heatwave sucked the life out of me. The minute we stepped outside the cramped minibus, I could have dropped to the pavement and lay there in the foetal position. Instead, I thanked the English girls and scurried away to find my hotel. Mentally drained. That one-hour minibus journey was an emotional rollercoaster – I still remember the 'I have lost my vision' fear and those sweaty palms like it happened yesterday.

I adore travelling. I love the solo adventure. I enjoy being in control of my journey. But travelling the world solo makes you the most vulnerable version of yourself, and you need to put trust in the amazing humans that walk this journey with you. I experienced the worst feelings on that bus journey and had to soothe myself.

When I think back to that minibus trip, I can feel all the emotions like I am back there squashed in that front row. I can even feel the sweat drip down my back trying to keep the panic at bay. You always survive these moments, and although I travel alone, I know there are lovely strangers, like the two English girls, to remind me I am never truly alone. We need to be comfortable asking for help. I toasted my minibus survival by popping into the nearest supermarket to buy two Ice poles. My previous hangover soother of choice and now used to soothe my dehydration, providing a much-needed sugar hit and a short burst of energy for the walk to the hotel.

When I arrived at my seafront, family-run hotel, I wanted to crawl into a ball and cry. I must have looked like I'd been dragged through the Sahara Desert.

The next two days unfolded as expected. That minibus nightmare soon a distant memory as I jumped straight back into doing what I do – maxing out every single minute, knowing it will all end soon. I felt I was on the mend, though still not 100% as my morning runs would remind me. "Slow down," my body shouted but I knew there was one last gem to experience.

The reason for the whole trip to Albania finally arrived - a day trip south to the ancient city of Butrint. Seven days crisscrossing through Albania all to arrive at this ancient city once the home of the Greek and Roman Empire. Here I am about to step foot into a world, a world that pulls me in like a magnetic force. A world where my imagination, and some research, fills in the blanks. I imagine emperors, wives and mistresses, open-air theatres showing performances based on Greek mythology - like an olden days Netflix. Where naked outdoor bathing is casually accepted and ceremonies are held in grand forums, for whatever reason a ceremony is needed by the Roman Empire.

An archaeological site that dates back almost 2,500 years, Butrint has the imprint of Greek and Roman civilisations. The Romans took over from the Greeks and adapted and extended it to their philosophy and way of doing things. The city is considered one of the most important archaeological sites in Albania. The site of a Greek colony and a Roman city, eventually abandoned in the late Middle Ages, sat on a hill overlooking the enchanting estuary, providing the most amazing setting for all those tranquil moments where I pondered the ancient site's grandness. The ruins represent each period in the city's growth where it also fell into occupation by the Byzantine, then briefly by the Venetians. My geek alert was switched on.

After a couple of hours exploring this majestic ancient city, in complete awe of what I experienced with my own eyes, I headed back towards the Riviera. What a day, all designed by me - a sunrise run along the promenade, before a morning exploring the ancient wonders left to fill our minds with all the possibilities in the world, followed by an afternoon at the beach to reflect on everything I experienced during this trip. I jumped off the local bus at Ksamil. As I strolled through the village streets just off the beach, I smiled as I knew a slice of paradise waited around the corner. I read blogs about this sun-drenched beach haven. As I strolled over the dune, I glanced wanderlust at the cobalt coloured sea – I could feel the tranquillity that comes from nature envelop me. The coastline in front of me, blessed with dozens of pretty cove beaches and a small collection of dreamy islands within swimming distance of the shore. There were taxi designed paddle boats bobbing out at sea, used by the locals to navigate the wavy waters, much to the entertainment of the sandy sunbathers and myself. Whenever I looked up from my sunbathe spot I would giggle at how ridiculous the water taxis were.

I spent the rest of the afternoon chilling on the white sand listening to music, swimming in the turquoise waters, avoiding the taxi paddle boats, and enjoying the yummiest bowl of pasta ever. What girl cannot be happy with a big bowl of pasta overlooking a dreamy cove?

This to me is travelling on my terms - a full day researched, planned and experienced by me. Full of all the treats, the things I love from life. Experiencing the hidden gems that Albania had to offer, but also pausing – providing an opportunity to feel wholly present and grateful. Grateful to the girl that is curious and who doesn't settle.

I reflected on Albania. A country that sat on my travel list for over two years but always seemed too much effort to reach. Not quite ready to negotiate some vague bus route or deal with unwanted attention in a predominantly Muslim country. Instead, I found the most unbelievably effortless trip with the warmest of people. There is no online bus timetable or booking system, but who cares when local knowledge is worth ten times that.

A 'developing' European country heavily influenced by the cultures of the empires that conquered and invaded it. It felt familiar but unique. Heavily impacted by the communist era which we struggle to fully understand in the west, a country on a path to freedom, demonstrated by an abundance of free art on the streets. The capital engulfed in the most colourful, striking and thought-provoking art. Thank you to the old Mayor of Tirana, Edi Rama, an artist before he moved into politics. He encouraged the city to let go of its grey, cold past and walk into a bright, colourful and vibrant future it had a right to be part of.

On my last day, I arrived at the port greeted by a sea of colourful rainbow inspired umbrellas floating in the sky, bobbing along bringing a splash of colour to the early morning stillness. This art display, a true reflection of my trip. Little pockets of colour splashed in your face to bring you back into the present and, well, make you feel something. I boarded a fast boat sailing to the port of Corfu Town. As I glanced back over my shoulder, I felt a gratefulness that I followed my instinct to explore this country, when I could have easily overlooked it for something 'easier' and a nagging feeling that one day I would return to Albania.

In a world where we want everything to be perfect and glossy, Albania felt real. It's imperfect, complex, intriguing, friendly, and refreshingly unique but also familiar! Probably forever shadowed by its past - remember those 175,000 bunkers spread across the country, to prepare for the attack the paranoid communist dictator thought was imminent. It is so much and more. The more is the stuff I've not seen but is the reason I will come back to Albania. I would love to experience the breathtaking fjords, Albanian Alps, and all the stunning white sand beaches I never managed to enjoy. And there is an abundance of street art that needs to be seen.

Every one of my trips starts as an idea, like a seed, that grows into an epic adventure. This is why we travel. There is still so much wonder out there that isn't even on my radar. This excites me. As long as you remain curious and grateful for the natural and man-made wonders in this world, you will always have something to aim for, to strive to see or simply check in on from afar. My travel list constantly grows as I read books, stumble upon blogs or hear whispers of places like Lake Koman, home to the Albanian Alps. Will I ever get bored of travelling – of course not. The minute you tire of this is when you know you have dampened your own spirit. Find your fire, be a geek, read books, watch documentaries – explore and find that one thing that makes you excited and go find it. What is stopping you – plant a seed today and watch it grow. If nothing else – be curious.

Will everyone race to visit Albania after reading my tales - probably not. But can we learn from Albania - 100%. If we learn nothing else, we learn that colour brings us Joy. Albania is alive and so are we, so let's enjoy life! Not everyone survived the communist regime - we owe it to them!

Albania

"Live the full life of the mind,
exhilarated by new ideas,
intoxicated by the romance of
the unusual."

- Ernest Hemingway

Cuba: Don't ever lose what makes you unique!

Cuba became the last country on my four-month trip around South and Central America in 2016. The minute I extended my trip into Central America, I knew there was no way I was stopping there and not visiting Cuba. It is the dream destination – Spanish colonial and baroque architecture, communist history influencing everyday life, off the beaten track towns and the Cuban Culture: music, rum, and we cannot forget Cadillacs. There was no question really to answer. I was travelling to this enigma. Mexico, Belize, and Guatemala - welcome Cuba to the Central America mix.

Cuba is difficult to explain.

Even now, I find it hard to understand. It's tricky - tricky to manoeuvre, tricky to understand how they live under a communist regime, tricky to fully relate to their life as you stroll through a country stuck in a time warp. For so long, they have lived under international sanctions and restrictions. You feel it the minute you arrive, a strong desire to be set free but I'm not sure they are ready for what this country could become if allowed to flourish on their terms.

To fully appreciate Cuba, you need to understand its world. It is delicate - there feels an underlying tension. On the surface, everyone seems to follow the rules and keep in line. But under the covers is a country operating outside its own rules.

The trickiness of Cuba started when I considered how to get money. US dollars are not accepted due to the turbulent relationship with America, ATMs are notoriously unreliable, most American Credit Cards are blocked and there are no Western Union branches. After travelling seven weeks with no access to ATMs - thanks to that scam in Bolivia - my only option involved bringing in Mexican Pesos to exchange. Travel blogs gave an idea of the cost of things and I figured out a rough budget for my eight-day stay. My little sister transferred the money and after a visit to the Cancun branch, where they spoke no English and I spoke no Spanish, I held onto my stash of cash like the precious cargo it was. My only thought, please no one steal my money. There was no plan B when in Cuba. My travel money anxiety bubbled away.

Finding suitable accommodation became tricky, more vague than tricky. Backpacker hostels didn't seem to exist. Eventually, I found some options through reading blogs and some time-consuming research. They have hotels in the capital Havana and there is an area of Cuba most people visit for an All-Inclusive holiday, but outside this, most options are homestays. It seemed vague if locals were allowed to rent their rooms under the Cuban rules. I never knew 100% what waited on the other side of the booking.

Every traveller seemed booked in with some random family, stated as 'for cultural purposes' on the immigration form. For my first two nights in Havana, I made a booking with Enzo. He sent over some helpful instructions in the booking email, and my eyebrows raised at the text in bold – I sensed Cuba was going to be crazy. Not even on the plane yet and the anxious feelings were there. Look at that last statement, "Is not very simple but it's possible." Thanks Enzo!

FROM THE AIRPORT (2016)

The prices of the taxis from the airport is 20-25 CUC, **fight for that price**.

In taxi never is less than 25 CUC, but you have other two options:

a) Share a taxi with **another people that you "meet" inside the plane or airport**. If you share a cab, always is around $10.

b) If you arrive at terminal 3, and you can go to the terminal 2 you save a lot of money. **You can walk (is 1.5Km away)** or take Connexion Bus until Terminal 2.Connexion Bus is like **a ghost bus**, is every 1 hour.

Terminal 2 is 200m away from Boyeros Ave, there you can take P12 or P16 bus until National Bus Station, after Revolution Square. From there you can walk until my building 600m away. Always the reference is the Latinoamericano Stadium.

Is not very simple but it's possible.

With no time to talk myself out of tackling Cuba, I soon arrived at Cancun airport to check in. On the other side of a one hour flight, costing the grand total of $90, awaited one of the last few remaining communist countries in the world. I was about to fly into a real-life museum - a country stuck in the 50s, when Castro gained power.

Cuba's history is remarkably interesting and complicated. Back in 1492, Christopher Columbus arrives as the first European and claims Cuba for Spain. Cuba first fought for its independence in 1868. In 1898 the US gained control of Cuba and, in 1902, gave Cuba independence. In 1952, president Fulgencio Batista took control of the country and made himself the leader - a dictator was born. Up steps rebel leader Fidel Castro who organised a revolution to overthrow Batista, and grant freedom back to the Cubans. In 1959, Castro overthrew Batista's government to gain control of the country. Cuba became an ally of the Soviet Union, and was a major player in the Cold War between the United States and the Soviet Union.

The United States unsuccessfully tried to overthrow Castro – with that infamous Bay of Pigs invasion. Then, the Soviet Union tried to establish a nuclear missile base in Cuba, causing the Cuban Missile Crisis. This led to the enforced trade Sanctions and travel restrictions in 1962 by the US, and the decline of Cuba became real. Fidel Castro remained in power for 50 years before handing the government to his younger brother Raul. On 25 November 2016, Fidel died leaving the majority of locals distraught. The country respected a nine-day mourning period – with everywhere closed, and no music allowed. Life stopped; People wept on the streets. I flew into Cuba on 11th December that same year – over a week after the mourning ended. Thankful Cuba, the vibrant country we all imagine, was back and in full swing. The music was ON and the streets were alive again.

At the Cancun check-in queue, I observed the backpacker next in line chatting to the Mexican man standing in front. The Mexican seemed to casually befriend him. Feeling a little on edge with Cuba, knowing there were rules and restrictions to the tourist entry, I felt hypersensitive to my surroundings. Alert mode switched ON. I noticed the Mexican slide a duffle bag towards the backpacker right in front of the check-in area. "What is happening?" I thought.

The queue was long and slow, allowing me to make friends - as encouraged by Enzo in the airport instructions. The backpacker in front turned out to be German, well half German and half Egyptian. He shrugged when I enquired about the duffle bag. I remember at the time thinking how wild - everyone knows the rules. Whatever happens on your travels, you don't bring anything into a country for anyone. Especially not in the check-in queue and into a country known for strict sanctions and restrictions.

After completing the check-in stress-free, I bumped into the German backpacker again in the departure lounge. With two hours to kill, we sat with a coffee sharing travel stories before we both looked up to see the Mexican standing over us. I felt a little apprehensive around him. He explained it would be useful if the German could carry an extra bag onto the flight as the Mexicans' friends also had too much to carry - the friends were nowhere in sight. The German again saw nothing suspicious with this and took full ownership of another bag. Meanwhile, I'm sitting open-mouthed, trying to manage my uneasy feeling. He seemed cool as a cucumber. All I could hear was my mother's words before every trip "Don't talk to strangers".

When we boarded the plane, I took my seat relieved to be sitting far away from the German and Mexican. This suited me perfectly - I wanted to use the quiet time to reset my busy mind. On the flight I got chatting to an American – I am pretty sure at one point I got up and sat next to him instead of shouting over the aisle. How bold. I acquired another friend – Enzo's advice now seemed to make sense. The airport and plane were backpacker magnets.

All the backpackers stuck together as we walked off the plane and entered Cuba – well the airport. As each of us successfully made our way through customs, we met again at the baggage area, giving each other a silent nod as if to say, "we are nearly in, we are nearly in." To describe the scene that waited as chaotic is an understatement. All sorts of boxes and luggage came flying off the conveyor belt, practically flung into the air. It became a case of stepping over boxes to claim your backpack - I felt relief to see mine. Everything seemed tense, but also going to plan.

The Mexican popped up again, of course he did, to ask if the German could carry the checked-in bag through the final customs check. I knew nothing about the final checkpoint. I thought we passed all the checkpoints when we were interrogated about our whereabouts in Cuba. I can hear myself now, "I am staying with Enzo." Turns out we had to complete a form declaring we knew the contents of our luggage - it would help if all the luggage was ours. As I grabbed the form from the custom lady nearby, she explained to complete it for the entire group I was travelling with – she must have spotted I was part of a larger group. I kind of wanted to complete it only for myself.

By now the Mexican and his mysterious friends were through customs – I could feel their curious eyes on us from the other side of the terminal exit. "Aww man," I thought, this is feeling very dodgy. All the guys who I acquired along the way from Cancun airport, the flight and at the baggage area were ridiculously overexcited and distracted after successfully conquering the first security checkpoint with no challenges – back then there were still strict restrictions on tourist entry, in particular for Americans. No one else seemed worried about the Mexican – still watching us from the exit. He made me feel uncomfortable. Maybe it is a female thing, where we trust our intuition. He did seem the nicest and friendliest man on the surface, but aren't those the ones we should be wary of?

I walked in front of the guys, smiling like an angel at the female custom officer, my tummy performing cartwheels as I handed over the group custom form. She looked each of us up and down, glanced at the bags and handed back the form, then nodded through to the exit gate. Gulp, we were finally stepping foot into Cuba. I felt the tummy cartwheels again – a mix of travel anxiety and 'I am in Cuba' excitement.

The Mexican stood waiting for us as we strolled through the airport exit. As we approached, he whispered to keep the bags for now. Whaaaat. By now my attention shifted from the Mexican as I tried to work out how to exchange money and grab a taxi based on the advice from Enzo. As I observed the chaos all around, the humidity hit, I noticed every single person from the plane seemed in one of two lines - either waiting for the ATM or the money exchange desk. Neither seemed to move. This was going to be a long day hanging around the airport.

As everyone stood discussing options to arrive into Havana, the Mexican reappeared to explain he could help us, as a thank you for carrying the extra luggage. At first I felt wary, then my narrative caught up with the situation and this invite became music to my ears - the queue for cash still hadn't moved and there didn't seem to be any taxis. Cuba began to hurt my head.

Alongside the German and the American from the flight, my two amigos, we were soon in the pick-up truck of a local who seemed to be friends with the Mexican. Vague – like Cuba. By now I eased up a little as we drove out of the airport into the quiet highway, the wind in my hair sitting squashed in between the two guys - of course I took a selfie as a memory. I look back on that photo now and all I can see is a girl in love with life, who probably deep down couldn't believe she was in Cuba. Very abroad. Travelling truly is wonderful. Whenever possible take the photo. Yes, be in the present but capture the moment. I love my memories, but sometimes a photo triggers so much that I have forgotten.

Now, viewing my Cuba trip with a fresh perspective, I can see how awkward I was around the Mexican. On the surface, and in that photo, I looked relaxed and in love with Cuba, excited at spotting my first Cadillac, a glimpse of the massive Fidel Castro and Che Guevara portraits on the side of the Republic Square buildings, a nod to their Cuba. But secretly, I kept one eye on the Mexican.

The German had no accommodation plans for Havana – who are these wild travellers? Meanwhile, the American had plans with some others at a local homestay in the centre. We formed a plan, the Mexican would make sure we made it to our homestays, and the German would come to my homestay to see if they had space, but first we were going on a detour. "What?" I thought.

As we turned off the highway towards the 'detour', I could feel unease creep back in. I had let my guard down for 5 minutes and start to get excited. Trust me, it was back up. The Mexican constantly chatted during the car journey, explaining life in Cuba. I smiled along. When he wasn't chatting, I kept my eye on him. The other two were too busy having the best time squashed up in the back seat, pointing at everything that signified Cuba like the most eager versions of themselves. Men!

The car pulled up into a residential street. Is this the rendezvous spot?

We all jumped out, and the next thing I know we are in this Cuban house where two men appear from a small kitchen. I remember taking in my surroundings, making mental notes of everything and also realising the exits were blocked. I'm giggling writing this now as I remember at the time thinking to myself, "these are the kingpins," convinced I was part of some sort of dodginess. I kept smiling and, importantly, breathing while trying to figure out what I had walked into. The Mexican looking at me, as I nervously looked around and at him. No idea what the other two were up to, they were still buzzing to have made it to Cuba.

I giggle now as I unravel the real story from that day - the two men were a couple. The Mexican showing us off to his friends as examples of tourists. Of course, he was. The two men seemed in awe of us as the Mexican described our nationality. "This is Jacquelyn, from Scotland." Me, standing with my humid hair, becoming more confused as to what was going on here. "Is this a cultural exchange?" I thought. You can not make this up.

As we all headed outside into the street, the trunk slowly opened and they carefully opened the various bags - in broad daylight. Surely this couldn't be the 'drop off' point! Only then did I glimpse what they smuggled in. It confused me even more. The bags crammed full of various supplies, at first hard to work out - then it became very obvious, so obvious. First out came a car radio, handed to the driver - he looked like he would cry. I felt overwhelmed at the situation unfolding. More bags filled with dancing costumes, ballet shoes, and lycra outfits handed to the two men. As they opened each bag, I realised nothing dodgy was going on. The story would melt your heart.

It turns out the Mexican, Carlos, is a dance teacher at a local school on the island. With the sanctions in place the Cubans have nothing, they can't freely buy what they need, except from the black market, where the price is inflated because of the lack of supply. Carlos' friends and dance school rely on his 'visits' back to Mexico to return with much-anticipated essentials for their life to have meaning and purpose. To bring joy that you and I take for granted.

As Cubans have little money, he gifted them all the supplies. The driver without music for months, now the proud owner of a new car radio. Now the upcoming dance show with much needed new outfits. I smiled - it all made complete sense. I felt silly for thinking anything else. He thanked the German again and said those extra bags contained all the dance school supplies. Carlos, a real-life angel, giving back to the community he now proudly called home.

He continued as our angel. We grabbed our backpacks from the truck, ready to walk into the city to flag down a taxi to our accommodations. Carlos took my backpack off me, and insisted he wanted to help. What a true gentleman – he carried it on his back. He looked me in the eye and said, "Do you trust me now?" I was a little taken aback. We giggled as I explained what I thought was going on – or what my wild imagination conjured up – an elaborate tale of modern day smuggling. But not cute dance outfits for the local dance school. He softly explained, "You will soon realise these people have nothing, and by offering some items that we take for granted you are changing their lives." Carlos reminds us all there is so much good in the world, and sometimes one small act amplifies into massive change.

There is a worldwide movement which encourages you to show a random act of kindness to a stranger or even someone you know to brighten their day. It can simply be a smile to a local shopkeeper, asking someone how their day is, or surprising someone by doing something that brings them joy. If we all make small changes in our day and life, we would become a more connected, joyful community. When every person becomes aware one small act can cause that ripple effect and spread it naturally amongst their community, then big change can happen. Carlos created a massive ripple in Cuba and my trip! I pass on the challenge to you. Act today.

As we walked to the local currency exchange, it felt like Wall Street. People milling about the actual building doing deals and exchanges outside on the street. Now with some local cash in my hands, it was time to sample the Cuban cuisine for the first time. The hunger levels were sky-high. After spending the last part of my trip in Mexico, where I was in daily foodie heaven, I was super keen to discover what spice Cuba had to offer. We were starving by now. Soon the four of us were sitting ready for our first meal experience.

As the waitress handed us the menu, Carlos started to speak a little angrily in Spanish to the waitress. Soon new menus arrived. They have government-issued menus, where all money is received by the state. They handed us the pretend tourist menu first, so they could charge more for the same food and, well, pocket the difference. Carlos explained to be patient with the locals, which I think translated into, "they don't mean to scam you."

As I glanced at the menu, there looked to be two options: meat, rice, beans, chips and salad. Or the same without meat. I ordered the meatless meal with a beer. When it arrived, I looked at my first Cuban meal – my heart sank a little. My plate looked empty with five chips, one scoop of rice with about two kidney beans, and a sprinkle of thinly sliced cucumber as a side salad. Carlos smiled and shrugged.

"Welcome to Cuba," I thought. Time to adjust my expectations to manage my happiness.

The time came for the gang of four to split up, we had spent less than a day together, but I felt like we formed our own bubble. I didn't want the bubble to pop. The American easily found himself a taxi into Havana – we waved him adios, not sure if our paths would cross again! If only it was that easy for us. All the local buses drove past full to the brim, argh! After lots of time standing on the corner of roads waving down taxis, only to be waved away each time, we continued to stroll the streets looking for a way - there is always a way. We finally persuaded a driver to fit the three of us, and our bags, into his rickshaw. Carlos insistent he would accompany us to our hostel building, so we stayed as a gang of three.

Now approaching 5 pm, as I arrived at the hostel, Enzo, the owner, appeared glad I finally made it as I'm sure I told I would be there safely by midday. He explained he started to get worried – as he eyed up the Mexican and German standing next to me.

Carlos made himself comfortable and enjoyed some chat with Enzo – learning more about the 'hostel' and what types of travellers he hosts. He was so lovely with a really curious, thoughtful, manner about him. I think in the end he just loved being around the international backpack vibe, enjoying our new to Cuba curiosity and energy. Carlos made my first day in Cuba, he treated us like guests to his country, when in fact, we were all guests to Cuba.

These moments stay with you. If one man can take you under his wing and ensure you arrive safely at your accommodation, with food in your belly and money in your pocket, then we can all take time out of our day to smile and connect with the community we live in. We need more Carlos' dotted around the world.

The hostel wasn't a real hostel. I'm not even sure how to describe it. Housed in a huge apartment block with maybe twenty floors.

The neighbourhood was located pretty far away from the tourist trap of downtown Havana. It was really a local guys apartment, turned into a hostel – four bunks with eight beds crammed into the self-labelled dorm. We shared the lift with the curious locals who looked baffled at our existence. The lift felt like it would break down at any minute, probably not serviced for decades. This is one of my fears, like a scene from a scary movie. Prone to electricity cuts, every time I stepped foot in that lift I would risk my life. The dorm crew shared a story where a group before them got stuck in the lift with the locals shouting down the shaft - the actual fear. Makes me shudder thinking about it now.

I finally said goodbye to the Mexican, Carlos. I thanked him for being the most selfless and hospitable person ever. It was also time to say goodbye to the German. My pretend hostel was full, so a neighbour took in the backpacker overflow. We exchanged details so we could connect once I found Wi-Fi. I never saw him again, well not in person. We still follow each other online.

To access the internet in 2016, there was a system where you would buy an internet card from a stall, stand in a designated zone, then wait to connect to the mega sllooooow internet. The day I finally decided to buy some internet I was told it was sold out. "How can the internet sell out," I thought. This is Cuba.

In front of the apartment building stood a Wi-Fi zone next to a massive baseball stadium – you couldn't miss it as everyone stood around gaining those slow internet vibes.

Enzo used the same Wi-Fi to reply to online bookings. He worked out if he stood at the communal stairwell window, the faint Wi-Fi signal from the baseball park would still work ten floors up – I will never complain about slow internet access again in my life. By day Enzo worked in a bank in the back office, until he discovered a gap in the backpacker market. He continued to work in the bank but also opened up his pretend hostel.

That night I went for dinner at the neighbourhood restaurant with a young scouser staying at the hostel. Only 18 and studying history back in Liverpool. With news of the death of Castro, he emptied his savings to arrive in Cuba for Castro's funeral. He didn't make it to the funeral - of course he didn't, it was impossible. Every bus heading South to the funeral was full. During the nine-day mourning period, the whole of the country effectively shut down. With two weeks in Havana during this period, he had nothing to do but walk the streets in a Cuba none of us would recognise –

empty and closed. They took the mourning very seriously.

With no money left. He hadn't managed to explore Cuba choosing to stay in Havana the whole time. He may as well have stayed in Liverpool if you ask me. To say he was stir crazy was an understatement. Bless the 18-year-old for his bold attempt to be part of history. As we walked to the local restaurant, the streets were pitch black. With limited street lighting, I sensed an edgy atmosphere. Enzo explained the men are passionate here. They notice outsiders and make it known - but also reassured me that they will do nothing untoward as the punishment is too much to risk. "Oh Okay," I thought.

I soon found the men made it very vocal when they saw you. I remember at one point a local man kicking a bin after he catcalled me. What an experience, living on that solo girl tightrope - rather the bin than him taking out his fire on me! I scurried out of sight.

On that first night, all I could see were people hanging around the streets, with no street lighting, their eyes peeking out from the pitch-black streets. As we entered the local 'restaurant', a garden furniture vibe greeted us. I glanced at the menu. I recognised it from earlier today - serving up the same meal options. 'Welcome to Cuba', I thought again.

That night I sat up with the bunkbed crew like a sponge, taking in all the information and lessons learned from their travel stories. Number one – sort out bus travel ASAP. The transport system sounded like a drama waiting to happen - limited and restrictive. The cross-country buses sell out days in advance. That feeling in my tummy signalled tomorrow I would be getting my Cuba plans together. I didn't have time for any sold out buses or any mishaps. Leaving Havana and exploring Cuba was the dream. No one wants to be stuck like the 18-year-old. I wanted the full immersive experience this country had waiting for me.

I woke on day two excited and eager to experience my first full day, now ready to be let loose in Havana with two goals – buy bus tickets to travel around this vibrant country, then walk, wander, stroll, and completely lose myself in the city of Havana. I set off on foot navigating an offline map since remember - no internet access.

In some countries, I choose to keep the flight mode on as I want to be so present and enjoy my time in the country, rather than distracted by the notifications of the mobile world. This 100%

works, but it is always good to know you have that internet safety net if you get lost. In Cuba, my safety net came in the form of the Lonely Planet book picked up from a hostel in Guatemala. And asking locals if I got stuck. Never be afraid to go old school and ask the local community. They live here and, as I found out from a day with Carlos, can help. But remember to remain alert for any scams! Travelling – a constant tight rope of being alert, present and also lost in the moment.

As I arrived at the bus station on the outskirts of the city, it seemed chaotic. This brightly, stylish, and very glam lady seemed annoyed when I presented a list of destinations and dates to buy tickets. I wanted it all – give me the bus tickets lady! In between shouting in Spanish at anyone not following the bus station rules, she would type all my requests aggressively into her archaic computer while looking angry. As she printed the tickets, she explained, "The buses are full." Gulp. Mission one ticked off successfully.

As I walked into Havana through less touristy streets, my eyes were as wide as space hoppers. So many buildings with the most exquisite architecture. The streets of Havana transported you to a time in Cuban history when they were free and independent with the grandeur to show for it. The buildings once so grand and ahead of their times were now a shell of their former glory, left with character but no soul. Dilapidated is the only way to describe them. On some pavements stood columns, a nod to the colonial era but now out of place. That is probably a symbol of Cuban life. A mismatch of styles.

Washing would hang from neo-classical building balconies with all the features hidden behind everyday dust and dirt, now looking like residential squats. Everything band-aided together, clear signs of decades of abandonment. It would leave you feeling in dismay at how this happened, then suddenly in front of you would be the most beautiful colourful restored building. Teasing you and taking you on a journey showcasing how stunning Havana once stood and again could become. Some architecture styles were simply out of this world.

Havana is complex. I looked for a supermarket but found none. There were what looked like shops, but when you glanced in, they had limited stock - sometimes one type of something. Like the end of a clearance sale, but this was their normal. Because of the sanctions they never knew what items they could get their hands on, so everything seemed unplanned, chaotic and like what you would imagine during the times of war – rationed food and queues. If you wanted to find a shop with something to buy, you would look for people queuing, then you knew they had something worth buying.

The Old Havana district of Cuba's capital is a time-warp. A journey into a postcard full of classic cars, dilapidated colonial buildings, and music. I stood open-mouthed as I felt I walked into a movie set - a place unlike any other. I walked through the maze of art-filled streets manoeuvring around men cycling ice cream carts or bicycles darting around the dusty back roads, my eyes drawn to the socialist propaganda – endless portraits of Castro on every street. Leafy courtyards would appear hosting pop up musicians, market stalls selling books and endless memorabilia - Cuban flags flying in the dense, narrow streets that would open into huge vast plaza squares. Havana – simply a walking museum. I would do anything to transport myself back there now.

Havana's old town square is a colonial masterpiece dating back to 1559. The square is Havana's most architecturally eclectic square, where Cuban baroque nestles next to Gaudi-inspired art nouveau – my inner architecture geek alert switched ON. I am a Gaudi fanatic. Sprinkled with bars, restaurants and cafes, Plaza Vieja even has its own microbrewery – how very trendy of Cuba. It is the tourist hub after all.

I sat with my nose in the lonely planet - without WI-FI it felt like the olden days using an actual physical book as a guide while sipping a couple of beers listening to live music. What a feeling – now this is the Cuba I came to experience.

An eccentric Norwegian lady invited herself to join my table of one as there were no other free tables – she plonked herself down with her mojitos like we were long lost friends. How forward of her. She was the chatty type, maybe in her 50s, with a son in his 20s. She last visited Cuba six months before, for a month, now back again for another month. When I tried to understand her intention with Cuba, she insisted she's not here for the sex. "Oh Okay," I thought. She ended up giving me a headache with her constant chit chat.

Done with the Norwegian chat, I switched bars to sample my first 'Papa Hemingway'. A cocktail created in the bar he called his local. I sipped the drink while enjoying the live music, impromptu tourist dancing and a photo with a life-sized bronze statue of Ernest Hemingway. Cuban tourist activity 101 ticked off the Lonely

Planet list.

From the extreme Papa Hemingway experience – the tourist crowd seemed very American and very energetic, I was ready to explore the Malecón. Havana's evocative 7km-long Oceanside boulevard with a mishmash of architecture that mixed sturdy neoclassicism with whimsical art nouveau. Now a busy six-lane highway that carried Chevrolets through the blue sky of Havana.

After strolling the Malecón I found another bar and another cocktail, this time a mojito – we are in the country of rum after all. Sitting in a trendy bar I reflected on some of the most exquisite architecture I have seen, probably ever.

The Bacardi Building, one of Havana's main landmarks - an extravaganza of Art Deco. The façade, floors, and interior covered in marble and granite, according to construction records imported from at least seven European countries, including Germany, Sweden, Norway, Italy, France, Belgium, and Hungary. Followed by the building where U.S. President Barack Obama addressed the Cuban people during his historic visit, the Grand Theatre of Havana. This Neo-Baroque building has an elegant façade featuring four sculptures that symbolise charity, education, music, and drama - it is a standout. Ahh, Cuba was ticking all my boxes.

After dinner, it felt time to head back to my hostel. I'd been gone for hours. Leaving bright and early to march to the bus station, and now my watch showed 8 pm. Enzo would be worried again! I wasn't sure how to get back. I considered the options – a one-hour walk to the hostel in the pitch black, no thank you, or a taxi ride but the drivers didn't seem interested, too busy deep in chat. Thankfully, I spotted a young boy hovering around, trying to grab my attention. In the end, I agreed to his service to cycle back to my hostel in a makeshift rickshaw with his tunes blaring. He kept shouting "lento" back at me while energetically turning the peddles, heavy breathing along. At the time I thought he meant far, when in fact he kept repeating "slow". I loved our slow journey back, but I am not sure he would agree. It felt the best way to finish my electric day in Havana!! What a day. I waved him off as the sweat dripped from him, as I started to think ahead. In the morning I would leave Havana for the start of the true Cuban adventure.

The next day started pretty hectically. I am not a fan of hectic. Booked on the 7 am bus south to Cienfuegos, I set off to arrive in plenty of time – famous last words. By 6.45 am, I was nowhere near the bus station and my stress levels were sky high. With no taxis to be seen in the blackness of the morning and every public bus whizzing past overcrowded, I felt those stress vibes and beads of sweat appear as I pondered a solution. The clock was ticking and I could hear the words of the bus station lady, "the buses are full" rattling around in my head. I was going to end up like the 18 year old Scouse - stuck. Surely this wasn't how my Cuban adventure was going to end. Stuck in Havana. After pacing about like a madwoman, with my backpack rattling about my back, I spotted a taxi parked down a side street – it seemed he appeared from nowhere. I glanced at my watch - it showed 6.50 am.

I tapped on the window and pointed inside towards the back seat; I didn't wait for an answer. I flung myself into the back seat awkwardly, still strapped to my backpack and agreed to pay him double before shouting, "Rapido" and "Bus Station". The stress levels didn't ease up as he drove casually along, not a care in the world. Everyone knows "rapido" translates to "foot on the pedal, we have a bus to catch."

With two minutes to spare, I flung the money at him and jumped out of the car into the station shuffling with my backpack. As I glanced at the ticket I collected yesterday, it stated, "Arrive by 6.30 am." I asked the lady at the counter for the bus stand, and she pointed over. Scared to look, I felt that feeling of relief rush through my body when I spotted it - my bus. As I dashed over, the bus driver stood chatting to the ticket attendant like they had all the time in the world. It felt like they were waiting for me. When I checked the bus destination – they proclaimed "just in time". I am one lucky girl, I thought, as I took my seat on the bus, sweaty and out of breath, feeling very smug and a little exuberant ready to start exploring this exotic island. Just when the universe is presenting hurdles, stretch and jump over them - never quit this game called life. Obstacles are to be tackled because on the other side is an awesome adventure waiting for you. I still have no idea how I made that bus, but I did.

Four hours later, I arrived in Cienfuegos. Perched on the coast, a world away from the hustle of Havana, ten times quieter and nowhere near as dilapidated as the capital. A colonial town mixed with the elegance of the French, their European style passed on from the founders, melted together with the feisty Caribbean spirit of the locals to provide an intriguing vibe to this new location.

Another UNESCO delight, recognised for the classical architecture in the town centre, centred on the Plaza with archways and columns straight out of the colonial era. I strolled around, taking it all in. Enjoying ridiculously cheap and yummy ice cream from the diner-style café, before walking open-mouthed along the bay, home to outrageously grand palaces built by the money from the 1920s, with tennis courts, lavish grounds, and ocean views. Cuba, a country of contradictions.

I soon arrived sweaty at the grounds of the majestic Palacio de Valle, this architectural gem featuring Moorish Hispanic art with Gothic, Romanesque, Baroque and Mudejar influences – what a combination. This as described by the travel books – I don't speak that elegantly. To me, it was grand, exquisite, and very European with a Caribbean twist in the form of an outdoor bar perched in the gardens. Naturally, I enjoyed a tropical Pina Colada chatting to the barmen while gazing at the panoramic views out to the bay. The way of life here seemed a lot slower than in Havana. This was a chance to unwind after nearly four months of navigating 11 countries, and all the fun and games travelling brings to the party. I felt mega relaxed.

On the walk back to my homestay casa, I spotted a supermarket. This surprised me. An actual supermarket. I never found one the whole time I explored Havana. Intrigued, I popped in for a look around and soon remembered this was a supermarket, in Cuba – expect the unexpected.

Let's just say the supplies on offer were limited. An entire aisle displaying only one type of food - crisps. One flavour. Filling an entire aisle. One tub deep. Then another aisle with only pasta – one type. An eye-opener. In the west, we are so consumed with a disposable society, driven by next day delivery and instant fast food dropped to our doorsteps, all one click away. These moments force you to confront everything you realise we take for granted with our lives and even complain about.

Just like that, it was time to move on again. On my fourth day, I travelled an hour south to Trinidad. A one of a kind, perfectly preserved Spanish colonial settlement stuck in the 1850s. Donkey drawn carts transporting locals around quaint rustic cobblestone streets, lined with single-story colonial buildings plastered with enchanting pastel colours. Cuba's oldest and most enchanting 'outdoor museum' - a true gem. This is why I travel – to experience this first hand. Even now, when I look back at my own photos, I take a deep breath as I remember wandering those streets in complete awe of their way of life. Life seemed slow and simple, but vibrant and explosive. I felt like a fly on the wall, experiencing their daily lives, tiptoeing around trying to understand it, all of my senses switched ON!

Strolling into the backstreets where men played dominos on the street, Soviet cars worked on in makeshift garages and kids roaming free as school finished. Locals buying fruit and veg from carts, even a pig head hanging from a hole in a wall signalling 'The Butchers', and pop up bars found around most corners. This town, as raw and real as it gets.

I meandered through the streets, following the route from my guidebook. Finding myself lost, lost in a way where you would stumble upon hidden gems, tempting you away from the main route. The more I strolled off the tourist trail, the more I felt myself warm to Cuban life. Each colonial building a piece of art. With a mismatch of coloured wooden slant doors, colonial style shutters, crumbling walls with blocks of colour - a colour palette lovers paradise.

From sunset, sleepy Trinidad comes alive with live music on all corners of the town. As I sat enjoying dinner in the place to be seen, the waiter brought a female traveller to my table and sat her down. "What is actually going on," I thought. There I am, having my dinner, and now I have a girl sitting with me - like a travel blind date. He explained as we are both solo tourists this should be ok. "Oh, Okay," I thought while making awkward eye contact with her and smiling. How very bizarre. You can't make some of this up.

Of course, it eventually became ok after the initial awkwardness of it all. Turns out my dinner date lived in Northern Ireland, and we immediately hit it off. I think we were both secretly glad for a friend to enjoy this lively town with all the electric street music.

After an intimate dinner – squashed together around a tiny table – we went to explore the streets heading to the famous stairs. This is the spot; everyone sits enjoying the live music from the main square bandstand. It felt alive. This is what I love. Sitting amongst other like-minded souls enjoying the sound of music and tourist chat filling the air, you can't help but feel that vibe. The vibe of freedom and possibility. We were chatting like long lost friends.

We moved onto a bar we both heard about from the backpacker blogs. As we stood at the door, we were told 'not tonight' by the doorman as all the tables were full. As I peeked my head in to check, I caught a guy's eye and we both shouted, "No Way!" There sat the American I met on the plane over who became part of the day one gang with Carlos. I last saw him when we parted ways in Havana, not sure if our paths would cross again. Now here we are having big hugs in this mega lively bar – the place to be with the backpacker crew.

With my connections, the doorman let us in as we squeezed into the table already full of backpackers. Just a minute before this exchange, I expected one last drink with the Irish girl before figuring my way back to my casa by midnight. The universe had other plans. We were part of a melting pot of different backpacker nationalities, all high on the fact we were in Cuba. We drank, laughed, and laughed some more into the small hours. I sneaked back into my casa as the morning sunlight came up, with a plan to repeat it all again the next night. With no internet access, we agreed on a time and a place for round two – talk about the olden days. I hadn't accessed any Wi-Fi since I landed, fully enjoying that feeling of being off-grid.

I woke the next day, and as I opened my eyes, the first thought that appeared in my sleepy mind, "How best to sleep off a hangover in Cuba?". "Head to the beach," the response. Bikini on, and very much beach ready, I queued for the bus with the other beach seeking backpackers ready to spend the day at Playa Ancón, a long stretch of soft white sand with pop up Caribbean style wooden bars selling cool cerveza. I, of course, treated myself to one. It was just what I needed to prepare for round two. After an afternoon of all the sun, sea and snoozing a girl needed to recharge, I arrived back at Trinidad.

That night we arranged to meet at 8.30 pm for round two. I woke at 8 pm after a siesta. Now, even more rested and ready for more Cuban surprises. I found myself in the plaza knowing where I would bump into everyone - at the cocktail place. The cocktail place sold takeaway mojitos, full to the brim with local rum to fuel the party vibe. The cocktails soon woke me up. Now reunited with the gang from last night, we seemed to attract more backpackers, all sharing cocktail fuelled travel stories. We were a massive group now. The Irish girl had left that morning for Havana, so I replaced her with some overconfident American girls hungry for some Cuban fun. The new gang were keen to experience a full Cuban night, so off we went to find Disco Ayala, a natural cave disco. Of course the local disco had to be in a cave. How very Cuban – surprise after surprise.

The cave full of locals, and the odd group of tourists all buzzing off this fiery passion-filled sweaty cave. The music, blasted from the frenzied DJ booth, seemed to bounce off the high cave ceilings and echo all around us. The crowd would go crazy every time the DJ played a new tune. The females in the group were receiving lots of attention from the locals, who were clearly keen to experience the backpacker thirst for fun.

In the end, the attention got a bit much, it started with subtle eye contact, then escalated to a more intense level as the locals moved forward into our circle - to grind. I am not a grinder; the Hispanic intensity slightly too much. I hid amongst the American boys who were drunk dancing – 100% no grinding. Ahh the perfect combination. To dance, with no hidden sexual agenda. I danced into the wee hours, and once again sneaked into my casa. Trinidad was a blast. A little relieved that I survived that cave experience in one piece.

My last day in the deep south arrived, I intended another chilled day at the beach, to sleep off another mojito hangover. Yes to that!

As I waited for the local bus, a guy approached shouting, "I remember you," while smiling with the confidence of a male traveller who has no worries in the world. "How forward," I thought, while attempting to place him, "Was he at the cave disco?". Turned out he saw me on the bus to the beach yesterday, where I caught his attention.

After chatting on the bus journey, we agreed to be beach buddies. I could tell I wouldn't be able to say, "Hi, I would quite like to be at the beach alone to snooze off my hangover," so went along with it. Sometimes you need to slow down, let go and trust the universe to decide the day's plans for you, as this is when the best experiences happen on my trips. There are times when my plans are non-negotiable, where I charge about soaking in all the sites knowing my time is limited, but not always. That day I enjoyed someone hijacking my plans. The snoozing on the beach could wait as fun was around the corner.

While strolling the beach, we bumped into a lively group he randomly knew from the day before – I think he is a serial beach befriender. People like him are naturals at making travel friends. We joined the mix of backpackers who were vivacious and untamed, drinking all the local beers while serenading each other with a guitar, encouraging nearby locals to join the sing-a-long. This day made me smile a lot. We all lazed about chatting and enjoying the sea - a cool relief from the humidity of the town. Sipping on cold beers also kept last night's hangover at bay. This felt special, especially as we sat watching the sunset. I asked my beach buddy to take some photos, my last Cuban sunset by the beach. Forever a reminder to keep that fire burning deep inside, slow down – sometimes – and go with the flow.

The people of Cuba keep their passion alive in a society full of complex rules. They make the most of what they have. I found it a truly inspiring country and thought of it a lot in 2020 when life got hard. We are all living in cages with the door wide open. Sometimes when the rules of life are trying to keep us caged in, we need to adjust our expectations and continue enjoying life.

I opted for a quiet last night after two rum fuelled sweaty nights drinking and dancing Cuban style. In the morning I would head to Havana for my last day in Cuba. Not only my last day in Cuba, but the last day on a four-month trip. A trip that changed so much in me. A trip that began in Colombia, where four months later I acquired a deeper understanding and perspective on making the most of life - making choices on what brings joy to your day to day and ultimately being grateful for the simple things.

After a relatively smooth return journey back to Havana, I found myself back at that bus station where I was last seen 'racing' for my bus and soon back at Enzo's. Talk about full circle.

With mixed feelings, I strolled through old town Havana, knowing there were two attractions left to experience kept for my last day. Some would say I left the best for last. First up, Hamel Street splattered full of the most amazing art. Colourful paintings splashed on building walls, sculptures popping up and out of buildings, and other forms of creative art by different artists grabbing your attention all through the street. All this on show while locals spread the good vibes with live music. I wandered open-mouthed at the large scale mosaic creations, the constant surprises on offer, in this little pocket of arty dreamland, q complete joy. My creative imagination on overdrive.

Last on the list, the Museum of the Revolution, housed in one of Havana's architectural gems – Cuba's 1920s Presidential Palace. I love the idea of museums, but if I am honest, I usually get pretty bored, much preferring to enjoy the open-air museums of real city life infused with the locals. This museum felt different – I was engrossed. I spent hours learning about the revolution, the communist regime, Bay of Pigs, and of course the Cuban Missile crisis. Peering at photos, memorabilia, and transcripts. It felt like research for a movie, the movie of Cuba.

I decided to stroll back to the pretend hostel, now feeling a whole lot more comfortable in this fiery passion-filled country – the sexual tension still existed, but behind a pair of sunglasses, I felt invisible to it.

Cuba – I never quite worked you out and maybe that is your charm. The elusiveness and mystic will live on forever. You taught me to take a leap of faith, to then be rewarded with an abundance of surprises. You showed how important it is to put trust in others. Each time I walked up to the homestay casa, I was welcomed in like I was family. I brought to you my travel tales and you shared with me hope that one day Cuba will be free.

Through the random acts of kindness and warmth constantly shown on this trip, I have realised we are all equal. Simply humans trying our best. All on a journey with the same ending, how we get there is partly choice, and partly circumstances, but we can make it more joyful for each other and ourselves. You showed life doesn't need to be filled with expensive, grand items to be happy. The sound of live music, a takeaway cocktail shared with some like-minded backpackers, sweaty dancing in a cave or the sight of a bus you were sure you had missed are all little treasures. You are proud and rich, rich in history and culture. You are passionate and fiery - the music may pause for the passing of Castro but will soon restart as the spirit of life drifts on by.

Back then, you were on the cusp of moving forward into a modern world as some sanctions eased. I would love to revisit and only hope I can still party in that Cuban cave. No one is too old for a sweaty dance. That is when you feel the most alive.

Don't ever lose what makes you unique!

What are you passionate about? Find that fire deep inside, and ignite it. That is where your joy compass can be found. That is what Cuba taught me, get passionate about life - then live it. Don't hold back waiting for the right time. The right time is now.

Cuba

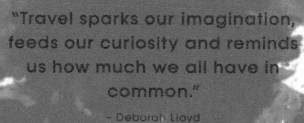

"Travel sparks our imagination, feeds our curiosity and reminds us how much we all have in common."

– Deborah Lloyd

Myanmar: Open your heart a little and let the pure joy of life flow in

In between a pre-festive trip to the Philippines – land of picture-perfect white sandy beaches with the dreamiest of sunsets - and a New Year trip to mysterious Myanmar, Christmas 2018 happened.

After a 48-hour family Christmas, I departed Scotland on a voyage to Myanmar.

"This is Burma," wrote Rudyard Kipling. "It will be quite unlike any land you know about." Almost a hundred years after these words were written, it was time to discover all that there Is to experience from a country with over four thousand sacred Stupas scattered across the plains of Bagan – famous for the breathtaking sunrise hot-air balloon rides. Bagan, the reason Myanmar kept my attention when it seemed a little tricky to explore.

But first, a stopover in Beijing.

From Glasgow, I flew into London Heathrow to start my journey out towards Myanmar involving an eleven-hour stopover at Beijing airport. After a bit of online research, I worked out you could easily sort a visa on arrival at the airport, manoeuvre the airport train into the city, to then tick off some of Chinas most iconic attractions. All before arriving back at the airport in plenty of time for the overnight flight Into Myanmar. Talk about being an opportunist. I wholeheartedly welcomed in the idea of sneaking in some Beijing delights.

On arrival, I walked straight into the airport chaos. Bleary-eyed and half asleep, I tried to work out the queue system while on the lookout for a 'get your tourist visa over here' sign. In the end, I hunted it down by following a handful of hardened travellers who looked as time-challenged as me. After a pretty confusing time securing a visa, I left the airport and jumped onto the next train into Beijing. The eleven hours now down to about eight. I soon found I can accomplish a lot in eight hours.

First stop, Tiananmen square - which stands in the heart of the city. Still a symbol of the fight for freedom by the student protestors involved in the 1989 massacre by the military. Weirdly you do feel you are being watched. Maybe paranoia kicking in, maybe not.

From the square, you can see the enchanted Forbidden Valley

tempting you over into the Palace complex from the early Ming Dynasty. Constructed in 1420, it is China's best-preserved imperial palace and the largest ancient palace structure in the world. The grand halls and walls of the imperial living quarters and traditional gardens take your mind to a period in time you can't even imagine, once home to the 24 emperors who controlled these lands during the Ming and Qing dynasty. It is a sight to behold, even for a weary traveller.

I continued the Beijing walking tour into Jingshan Park, perched on a hill with stunning views back towards the Forbidden Palace. Even though I just walked from there, seeing the majestic palace perched as a symbol of the dynasties it represents still took my breath away. I find this happens a lot. I try to see things through the eyes of a child - unfiltered. The local vibes were echoing through the park - teenagers enjoying makeshift photoshoots, energetic Ti Chi displays in full flow, and families enjoying the crisp winter day. Soon I found myself exploring Gulou, a hip neighbourhood with original Beijing charm where the streets are mainly narrow alleyways lined with fluffy pancake shops. This side of Beijing filled me with Joy, a complete hidden gem.

I felt part of the local young crowd enjoying their weekend of freedom. It felt very surreal.

One day you are sitting eating Christmas dinner with your family in Scotland, then you are standing in zero degrees in the vast and eerie Tiananmen square, likely being watched by this communist giant. The Beijing alarm buzzed on my phone, signalling I had to return to the airport. This girl had another new country to tick off, I was leaving nothing to chance. Soon back at the airport and boarding another plane, I arrived in Yangon - the largest city in Myanmar - five hours later. Scotland – Beijing – Yangon. Just like that.

Talk about cramming in all the travel experiences.

When I arrived in Yangon, a blast of humidity greeted me – from zero to thirty degrees in an instant. This country, once locked away from outsiders, instantly warm and welcoming. Running on empty, I felt energised to explore. A mixture of jetlag, overnight flying and the usual travel tiredness couldn't dampen that feeling I get on arriving in a new destination. The feeling of endless possibilities and adventure, knowing every footstep is leading you through a country you once didn't know existed. Now your playground. My senses were ready for a journey into this southeast jewel.

Any other time the tiredness would envelop you. Instead, Yangon's old colonial charm, dazzling Buddhist temples, and fascinating day-to-day street life tempted me out of the hostel bright and early, on little sleep. Everywhere you wandered, you were greeted with genuine curiosity from the locals.

Myanmar has a history - its past is clear from wandering the streets. A melting pot of the countries it borders and its colonial past. Bangladesh and India in the northwest, China to its northeast, Laos and Thailand to its east, and the colonial architecture - a nod to the British Empire. With a delicate history, still divided by the ethnic groups that make up this complex country.

The British East India Company seized control of Myanmar in the 19th century, and the country became a British colony. Myanmar finally gained independence in 1948. Following a coup d'état in 1962, it became under a military dictatorship controlled by the Burma Socialist Party. For most of its independent years, the country has been engrossed in intense ethnic strife, and its ethnic groups have been involved in one of the world's longest-running ongoing civil wars.

In 1989, the military government officially changed the English translations of many names dating back to Burma's colonial period or earlier, including the country itself. Burma became Myanmar - in the country they use both names interchangeably – and tourism developed. After almost half a century of military rule, the National League for Democracy won a landslide election in late 2015. The first democratic election since 1990, but the military overturned the result.

It is continually tainted by the systematic human rights violations which hang over the country. In the summer of 2017, a deadly crackdown by Myanmar's army on the Rohingya Muslims sent hundreds of thousands fleeing across the border into Bangladesh. The country's leader Aung San Suu Kyi, once a human rights icon, repeatedly denied allegations of genocide. The Rohingya Muslims are one of Myanmar's many ethnic minorities. They have their own language and culture, descendants of Arab traders and other groups who have been in the region for generations. But the government of Myanmar, a predominantly Buddhist country, denies the Rohingya citizenship and refused to recognise them as people. It sees them as illegal immigrants from Bangladesh. Complex. The year I visited, Myanmar again made headlines for the continued, and disputed, ethnic cleansing of the Rohingya.

Talk about complex.

This country first popped onto my horizon when travelling through Vietnam in 2015. It sounded way off the beaten track. Back then I had no idea of its complex history or even where it was on the world map.

Ten minutes after I left the hostel, a sarong wearing elder suddenly approached me. "American?" he asked. I already worked out the Burmese weren't big fans of their British Colonial past, so wisely choose "Scottish" as my response. We were soon in a deep one-sided chat and he was very quick to educate me on the crisis. He explained the West - the Americans, French and British - should stay out of the issues in Myanmar as it is a situation they don't understand. He believed the country could sort out their own troubles.

All. Very. Delicate. I wasn't here to judge but listen and experience. Keeping a perspective on everything I saw and heard. I'm sure no one deserves the treatment described as genocide. He expressed I enjoy his wonderful country, and we parted ways.

"Welcome to Myanmar," I thought.

Yangon's main attraction is the Buddhist way of life. The streets were full of energy, the mix of traditional and modern customs all around you. The traffic seemed intense with an expressway cutting through the city only broken up by a massive roundabout, home to a majestic golden stupa - Sule Pagoda. Right around this large Buddhist place of worship sits a Muslim mosque, a Hindu temple and a large Catholic church. Your senses heightened at this cultural diversity. A reflection of Myanmar.

This the first of hundreds of Stupas I would visit or glance at on this trip – they were everywhere. This one glistening in the daytime sunlight. As I wandered around the site, I shared my next local encounter of the day. An educated man stood in front of me, reciting all the facts you would ever want to know about the stupa and the Buddhist religion. Insistent he didn't want money for any of these facts - always nice to know as I had no plans to hand over any cash. He wore a leather jacket in 30 degrees heat - if that doesn't make you suspicious, then what does. I smiled politely as I explained I would not require his free service of fact telling.

As my protective mother reminds me before every trip, "keep your wits about you and don't talk to strangers." On every trip I talk to strangers, of course I do, but there is one rule I do follow as I hear her whisper in my ear if I look to embark on anything dodgy, "keep your wits about you." An expression most of us will be familiar with, loosely translating to 'be constantly alert and vigilant.' It doesn't mean you are not warm, friendly and curious. You are all of that. Those who remain open and alert can play the travel game and wriggle out of most situations that turn a bit weird. I am the product of that mindset, and sometimes the wriggling is intense!

For all the recent changes, Myanmar remains at heart a rural nation of traditional values slowly transitioning into the modern age. Men wear the sarong-like longyi, while also using the latest mobile phones. Women with faces smothered in thanaka, a natural sunblock, showcasing the most beautiful jewellery.

A Myanmar tradition close to home is drinking tea. A British colonial custom enthusiastically embraced in thousands of teahouses around the country. And that leads to my next stop, the Rangoon Tea House. The owner returned to Burma looking for inspiration to open his first restaurant, having left the country aged four. His favourite memories from the trips back to his home country were the noises, smells, conversations and most of all, the food that brought together the community in the local tea shops. As you walked into the air-conditioned colonial dream, you felt that vision, a social club vibe with a mix of affluent locals and eager tourists all ready to be taken on a journey back to the colonial days. I sat with some exotic tea and cheesecake. It felt like a slice of luxury in the middle of a very dusty, humid city.

Sometimes I question whether these types of places are authentic when you know right outside your door is real poverty, and here I am sitting amongst wood-panelled luxury. And that is life and travelling. There is privilege within every country I visit - it can't be ignored.

I feel very privileged to travel. I suppose to experience it all, you need to witness all facades of a country – privilege and lack. This type of establishment is for a certain type of local, not everyone can experience this colonial grandness. As I sat taking in the social club's chitter-chatter, I spotted a girl from my hostel with a couple of other travellers. I ended up in their booth and we all went off exploring together. They all seemed fun and keen to eat from the local food markets with all the wonderful eye-opening dishes. We explored the side streets, sharing travel stories and our plans for Myanmar. Countries like Myanmar belong to a certain type of traveller, those not jaded with complex human rights issues, limited infrastructure and a dusty low-key vibe. This country is for those who are curious and willing to be taken on a journey – eyes wide open.

After a few hours, we parted ways. I like this style of travelling where you can dip in and out of groups but don't feel obliged to follow their plans. I meandered to the main square. As I stood open mouth at the renovated colonial architecture mixed against modern high-rises and Buddhist temples all around me, I spotted a local approach me.

In front of me stood a young monk wearing his traditional orange robes, holding out an alms bowl signalling for donations to the Buddhist cause and to put food in his belly. I smiled politely and walked away. I'm not sure how comfortable I am with this and the protocol. He seemed undeterred and wandered over to the next tourist. These monks are resilient.

After walking through the city streets experiencing more Buddhist temples along the way, I arrived at my next destination during the golden hour, the hour before sunset, when the light is super soft. What stood in front of me took my breath away, the out of this world Golden Pagoda, Shwedagon Paya. This is the one you see on Google images, read about in blogs and one day imagine walking around with Buddhist monks in view and the murmur of chanting - all as the sun sets around you. Honestly, I could have cried with joy. Sometimes travelling the world can lead to great disappointment as something that looks so delicate and atmospheric in a photo turns out to be overrun with tourists or completely lost to the world of commercialised doom. Not in Myanmar. The sounds, smells and sights take you to a place of serenity and wonder. It forces you to stop and ponder on life a little, as you stroll around barefoot, at one with the Buddhist religion.

Described as the most sacred temple in all of Myanmar, a popular pilgrimage for Buddhists, legend has it that this golden pagoda and complex was built more than 2,500 years ago - theoretically the oldest Buddhist temple in the world.

What a perfect end to my first day in Myanmar. Watching the groups of locals who sat and read from passages as the sun glistened off the stupa, monks capturing selfies with the Stupa backdrop – loved that - and young couples walking hand in hand smiling at each other. That night I arrived back at my hostel one tired girl, in need of sleep but with a sense of excitement for the next day, full of curiosity and appreciation. This is how you should fall asleep - tired and exhilarated. In the morning, I had a flight to Bagan – potentially the trip highlight.

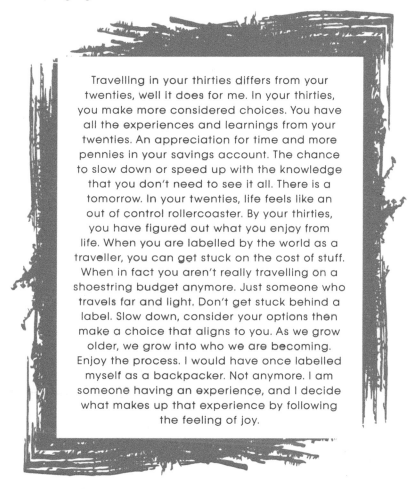

Travelling in your thirties differs from your twenties, well it does for me. In your thirties, you make more considered choices. You have all the experiences and learnings from your twenties. An appreciation for time and more pennies in your savings account. The chance to slow down or speed up with the knowledge that you don't need to see it all. There is a tomorrow. In your twenties, life feels like an out of control rollercoaster. By your thirties, you have figured out what you enjoy from life. When you are labelled by the world as a traveller, you can get stuck on the cost of stuff. When in fact you aren't really travelling on a shoestring budget anymore. Just someone who travels far and light. Don't get stuck behind a label. Slow down, consider your options then make a choice that aligns to you. As we grow older, we grow into who we are becoming. Enjoy the process. I would have once labelled myself as a backpacker. Not anymore. I am someone having an experience, and I decide what makes up that experience by following the feeling of joy.

To travel to Bagan, there were options and choices to be made:

» Fourteen-hour train ride – no thank you,

» Ten-hour bus ride over bumpy roads – again no thank you,

» One-hour plane ride – yes, please. Choice made!

The flight departed at 6.30 am. An hour later, I stood in the valley home to over 2,000 ancient temples built between the 9th and 13th centuries - rightly a UNESCO World Heritage Site. At one point, during the height of the Kingdom, there were over 10,000. Can you imagine. After paying the site entrance fee, I arrived at my hotel - I knew instantly I would like it here. Hut style apartments with balconies faced out into lush nature filled gardens. Greeted by the female receptionist, dressed in the local traditional clothing, with a welcome drink and all the knowledge of the area to share. After a quick change, I rented an e-bike for two days and soon got stuck into exploring this rust-coloured red sand town where Pagodas, Stupas, and Buddhist temples would appear – first on the horizon, then quickly in front of your eyes. To describe it as breathtaking doesn't do it any justice. Some of what I saw and experienced felt straight out of a movie.

Looking back over photos, I felt those feelings of that first day. They describe the vast site as the Myanmar Angkor Wat – a nod to the famous site in Cambodia. I love Angkor Wat. This felt more spectacular. Your mind can't truly believe what it sees, I said wow a lot as I cruised around the Buddhist equivalent of a theme park – full of manmade wonders.

Driving the e-bike is similar to a moped. I started feeling overconfident, until I tried to reverse, mistook the reverse for 'drive forward' and nearly drove into an elder from the village. The more the locals shouted stop, the more I drove forward. It makes me feel sick thinking about it now – can you imagine if I drove over a village elder. After that stomach-churning experience, I became the most cautious version of myself and would smile whenever I saw others making the same mistake. I have never allowed myself to be in control of a moped, now I know why. Reckless springs to mind.

You don't just turn up and decide at random what you plan to visit for a destination like Bagan, you research and plan like your life depended on it – that is my strength. This is a once in a lifetime location and it deserves all your attention. After a morning of exploring all the sites on my day one list, I found myself at this amazing vegetarian restaurant sitting on the floor of the garden eating the most amazing fresh curry. As the bill arrived, the host handed this little bowl full of wrapped sweets. They were the sweetest thing ever. I opened them one after the other, soon hooked. I will forever remember Myanmar for my first Tamarind

Flake experience – if only I could go back and enjoy those wee sweets. I ate them all. I needed the energy for an afternoon of more e-bike action, hopefully not involving any mistaken reverse manoeuvres. Wind in my hair, sunglasses on, gazing up at the passing clouds – if only you could bottle this feeling. I felt so happy, very much alone but full of everything that brings joy into my life. All those small moments, which together fill your soul.

The sheer scale and beauty of Bagan blows your mind. It is an open-air museum to the Pagan Kingdom, the first Burmese kingdom from 1044 until 1297. Today the area is home to the largest and densest concentration of Buddhist monuments in the world - at the kingdom's height, there were over 10,000. Each site is different. Different in material, texture, colour, shape, condition, size, decoration and location. Some sit solo, others in a cluster, some stretched out across the plains, some have grand archway entrances, while others are due to collapse, some you can walk into to witness the grand statues and frescos representing the Buddhist religion. No two are the same, as unique as you and I. Then there are the ones where you can climb up to the top and sit perched on the edge looking out in complete awe and disbelief.

As I sat observing an entire complex of pagodas stretched out as far as the eye could see, I felt a couple of people watch me. Two local teenage boys. They seemed curious, watching as I took photos, I kept catching their eye. Then one asked if he could have his photo taken, then the other; they both wanted a selfie. This moment, the start of feeling like a celebrity in Myanmar. They were genuinely in awe of western people, and it surprised me a little as Bagan is a complete tourist haven. I still have their photos. Me and the lads.

After our impromptu photo shoot, I left the last pagoda smiling. Smiling that a country and UNESCO site can be your dream, and for the locals they just want a selfie. Life is funny. For their entire life, they have seen these temples every day, so to them, it is normal. But to me, I am wandering around the travel mecca.

As the sun set, I headed to the chosen spot for my first Bagan sunset experience. This is the moment, your whole day wrapped up by one event – the sun setting over the plains as you sit on the edge of the pagoda listed as one of the top ten sunset spots in Bagan. After driving down the dusty red sandy road, I walked through a pitch-black temple, clambered up some crumbling steps for that view. The view that waited - simply breathtaking. The night light changing across the horizon, dancing in front of your eyes as you feel the day disappear in front of you. I felt grateful to be the girl who sees the world as one giant playground. All this is waiting if we dare to turn our dreams into reality. To be the creators of our own lives.

Safely back at the super relaxed garden villa, with my e-bike locked up for the night, I sat on the balcony with a cold Myanmar beer, reflecting on a magical first day. This to me is what travelling is about - feeling so free, energised, and full of joy. Maybe even feeling a little like a celebrity with the local photoshoots.

The next day I woke early, still not fully caught up on my sleep, but who cares when you have a sunrise to invigorate you. Half asleep and feeling the cold air, I layered up for the e-bike ride towards the sunrise spot – full of tourists. On most trips I like to wander off myself, but in cities like Bagan the tourist community felt welcoming to be around. They appreciated it all and I love being in that environment. Plus I took it as a sign that I was at the correct sunrise spot. No one wants to make that mistake.

As I walked through the pitch-black temple and clambered up to the roof of the temple, I heard myself mumble, "Wow." The sunrise hot air balloons started their ascent. Even though I've experienced quite a few breathtaking sunrises in my lifetime, this perhaps was one of the most enchanting in the world. Like a performance, balloons floating through the air, all for our entertainment.

There are two places in the world known for the sunrise hot air balloon experience – Cappadocia in Turkey and Bagan in Myanmar. I've visited both and both times haven't experienced this joyful activity – I know, I need to revisit. For Bagan, there is so much demand and my dates were sold out way before I even considered a trip here. First world problems.

Viewing the balloons rise from the horizon is something I will never forget. As the sun rises, the shadows of the pagodas appeared on the plains, all effortlessly shifting as the sun floats higher. The dark sky starts to project colours from the sun – purples become blues, then pinks and oranges. As I looked to the horizon, I caught my first glimpse of the hot air balloons dotted against the calm morning sky, slowly floating along, completely mesmerizing as they glide past like clouds. You stand staring into a beauty you can barely comprehend, as the hot air balloons dance around the sky above all the temples and pagodas left by the ancient Pagan Kingdom from the 9th century, full of mystery waiting for you to explore. What a scene.

Although no photo does any of this any justice, in a second I can take myself back there and feel all those feelings. Trips may fade into your memory bank, but they leave an imprint in your soul. Something to cherish when life feels tough.

After a couple of hours sleep, still wearing my sunrise chasing outfit, I needed some energy for round two of temple chasing. I walked into the breakfast room greeted like a princess from my waiter. We met the day before over some scrambled eggs, where we shared a few stories. The Burmese are the kindest and most curious. They want to know your plans so they can make sure you are having the best time. I sat feeling that jet-lagged fogginess. I knew a plate (or three) of the breakfast buffet and the strongest coffee would set me right.

Soon filled with energy, I was back on that e-bike ticking off the temples. At one point, I glanced down from the roof of a temple to see a monk, on the ledge below, set up a tripod, with a professional-looking camera taking photos of all the wonders in front of him.

We see monks as all-knowing, but deep down they are like us – curious and enjoying the wonders in front of them. I try to never take anything in life for granted, and even though I saw every type of temple possible on this trip, each one was unique and deserved my time and attention. Always remember you will soon be back in your Monday to Friday, 9 to 5 life.

There is one temple that sits perched on the edge of the Irrawaddy River. From afar, a striking and sacred bulb-shaped golden stupa, originally built by the 3rd King of Pagan. It catches your attention as you approach. As I parked up, I felt like I was entering a pilgrimage site, with more locals than tourists heading towards the river. I felt that feeling again.

The eyes of the locals, watching and following my every movement as I walked barefoot around the site taking photos and enjoying the cooler river backdrop. I caught their eyes. A group of four teenage girls, at first acting shyly. Then, once we smiled, one - pushed over by her friends - asked for a photo. I stood with each girl separately while another took our photo, then we shared a group photo, then a selfie. One would get pushed out and another pushed in. As they looked back on the photos they would giggle. It was hilarious to be part of and exhausting at the same time.

This tall, white, western girl from Scotland seen as an icon by the Burmese. As it played out I asked the main girl to take some photos on my camera. There is one I love where she captures us as a group while the girls are taking a selfie with me. What a memory of this playful moment. As I walked away, I could still feel their eyes. I knew it was time to get food and head to the last sunset spot. Bagan, what did you have left to show off? Turns out something special waited.

Bagan produced one last stunning sunset, way more stunning than the first, which at the time I thought to be the best I'd ever seen. This time I sat perched on top of a temple at a different spot. This spot quieter, so I used the time to embrace it all, including the stillness of this vast Kingdom as the sun set. This trip to Bagan is not normal. The sunset allowed me to recognise a truly special moment in my life. I would love to return to Myanmar, it felt on the cusp of something, and we know once countries fully open to tourism, their culture is changed forever as the influences from the outside world stream in. I only hope Bagan will remain unique and wholly enchanting. Goodbye Bagan – you were truly the highlight, just don't tell the others.

I arrived in Mandalay on 31st December. I booked into the top backpacker hostel in the hope there would be some New Year's Eve plans - though I wasn't expecting much as Myanmar is the most chilled country ever. I spotted a poster announcing a rooftop party. Count me in!

I travelled to Mandalay as a stopover on the way to the lake. I didn't have many plans for a city most people miss off their travel itinerary, and mainly used it to chill. First up, I treated myself to a little bit of relax and recovery with a full body oil-tastic massage followed by some reflexology. This turned into my dream day. They provided endless ginger tea, and my eyes lit up when out came a little bowl filled with my favourite treat – tamarind flake sweets. This became my absolute happy place. I felt mega chilled and ready for NYE – Mandalay style.

After a power nap, I started NYE 2018 with cocktails at the reception bar, chatting to the barman, before I moved onto the local beers at the rooftop 'party'. The rooftop hosted a mixture of locals who worked at the hostel, their friends, and a collection of hardened travellers with some random people I couldn't quite place. I hate this part of travelling, especially solo, where you are trying to play it cool while scouring the room to make eye contact with someone that looks half normal and not a maniac. To then strike up some 'what are you doing in Myanmar' conversation. In the end, I felt relieved with who I made eye contact with - a couple of guys, both very different and 100% not maniacs.

In the end, I enjoyed a fun night filled with random firework displays, local beers and the company of some super chilled travellers with the odd drunken silliness, relieved the night wasn't massively awkward or dull.

I woke up the next day and glanced at my watch as it displayed 1st January 2019 - my last day in Mandalay. An overnight bus would deliver me south to Inle Lake for my final destination in this fascinating country. But first, with a bit of a hangover headache, I struggled along the bumpy tuk-tuk ride to the main attraction - the Myanmar famous 'U Bein Bridge'. On the journey, we practically drove into a New Year's Day parade. They go all-in with their parades here - horses dressed in what looked like woollen pom-pom decorations, people dancing inside an elephant acting out a show, and everyone parading the streets wearing their Sunday best.

I felt grateful to see the bridge appear in sight as I knew I could escape the bumpy tuk-tuk. My driver instructed, "One hour," as I walked towards the bridge crammed full of locals enjoying a New Year's Day stroll. This is not just a bridge, but a focal point of local life. Local men fishing in the moody waters, farmers transporting their produce across the bridge, a meeting spot for teenagers and where couples in young love come to hangout.

As I walked the bridge taking it all in, I felt that feeling again and looked around. Every single person seemed to be staring at me and whispering. Some followed me, stopping when I stopped. I soon stopped in the middle of the bridge where a group of lively, and very drunk, teenage boys were playing their guitar and singing along erratically, using a gathering area as a live music venue. I didn't know the tune, but I signalled if I could take some photos and videos. They, of course, loved this and started to play up for the camera. They offered some whisky - yes, they were drunk on whiskey at midday. It sounds like Scotland. What a bunch of rebels. In the end, I danced along to their enthusiastic music giggling at how ridiculous the scene must have looked to passers-by. It was so much fun and distracted me from my hangover headache. I wasn't sure if I needed a nap or a sugar hit.

As I turned to walk on, a small group of locals were waiting patiently for my attention. Eventually, someone brave enough asked for a photo. A photoshoot of selfies, group photos, and those intimate one-on-one shots followed. It felt like the strangest thing ever, the most ridiculous experience. I wanted to ask what they did with the photos. Am I being tagged on Facebook as the tall, western girl?

I eventually excused myself to keep walking along the bridge. Anytime I stopped to take photos of the scenes around me, more locals surrounded me. They are the friendliest people ever, but not what you need with a hangover. I needed space and to be left alone. I scurried back to the tuk-tuk driver, and, after another bumpy ride, he returned my delicate body to the hostel ready for part two of Mandalay sightseeing. This time on foot.

The Sandamuni Pagoda is a Buddhist pagoda south of Mandalay Hill, commissioned by the King in 1874 as a memorial to his younger brother, and the hallmark is a central golden Stupa, with hundreds of mini white versions used as a site border. As I approached the entrance, I took my shoes off and looked up to notice a monk. I quickly looked away.

I had seen monks before on this trip - it is a Buddhist country and they are everywhere - and read in a travel book that you should respect their culture and not make eye contact. I took this very seriously. As I walked around taking photos of the lines of white stupas, with locals milling around, I felt that feeling. As I looked around, the monk and his friend were following me. Surely not.

Yes, the next thing I am in a photoshoot with a young monk. A monk with who I avoided all eye contact, while he tried to make eye contact as his friend took control of the photoshoot. I eventually eased into it once I realised the guidebook was being a bit strict. I have a photo of the monk and I - and a sleepy dog looking very candid! These Burmese people just love a photoshoot.

After enjoying all the views from Mandalay hill, I scurried back down to the base of the hill. I was about done for the day. Hangovers when travelling are not advised. Having negotiated a moped taxi back to the hostel, I could think of only one way to kill some time before my night bus – I popped next door for a leg massage with ginger tea and my favourite tamarind sweets. Yes to that. The massage boy recognised me from the day before – I'm not sure if he has encountered someone that gets so excited over a tiny bowl of tasty sweets. Always remember to appreciate the simple things, and the big things will take care of themselves.

As I sat with the overnight bus backpackers waiting for the pickup to the bus station, I got chatting to an Aussie girl called Alice. She still cradled a major hangover from the NYE bash – we worked out we were near each other on the night but hadn't chatted. That feeling of happiness appeared when I found out she was also travelling to the lake, and we were both staying at the same hostel. She seemed fun. We arrived at the bus station to the standard chaos, but kind of organised operation where you were never quite sure what bus was yours. The locals signalling to sit down on the plastic chairs, stop asking questions and chill out. They knew the bus would arrive, and it did. It always does.

When it arrived, I got a surprise. I didn't expect a proper full-size bus and felt relieved not to be cramming in a minibus where it would be impossible to sleep, just a squashed body and sore bum. Hello luxury. Alice and I sat on the same row on either side of the aisle, where I sat next to a local lady. As I settled into my seat, my eye mask perched, ready to start the bumpy bus sleeping challenge, I felt that feeling. I caught the local lady attempting to take a selfie - of us. What is going on? When I caught her, she displayed no shame. Once satisfied, she sent the photo to her friend. I watched as she sat typing something and smiling back at me. What is it with these people? I shook my head and popped on my eye mask. Mandalay was done. Let's see what is next.

Eight hours later, we were flung out at the crossroads towards the lake - my watch displayed 5.30 am, and we spotted one taxi waiting. Half asleep, we jumped in the taxi with a French guy towards the last new destination of this trip. We paid the fee into the lake, thankful for a bed in the early arrivals dorm when we arrived at the hostel – what a treat. We were snug, like little caterpillars, tucked in the cocoon beds, grabbing a few more hours shut-eye to re-energise us for our first day at the lake.

We met the hostel gang over breakfast. After hearing everyone's travel stories, we were soon all renting local bikes for a day out as a big backpacker gang. I loved this. A kiwi guy took charge of the route – the self-appointed designated leader of the group. All we needed to do was follow his lead cycling along in single file or chatting away in mini-groups. Up to now, Myanmar felt like a big bubble of humidity. Inle Lake seemed a different country – misty and chilly, experiencing the coldest weather in years. Not what I expected, but we all know travel life goes on whatever the weather.

As we meandered along the road that runs alongside the lake, we stopped off for some amazing, fresh curries with yummy tea to keep us warm. Along the way, we incorporated another traveller, the kiwi group leader like the pied piper encouraging anyone who looked like a backpacker to join the bicycle gang.

With full tummies, we were soon at the foot of the massive lake walking along the jetty, looking around in awe of the floating villages bobbing in front of us. These villages are neighbourhoods on stilts, where locals live in huts built above a maze of marsh and grass waterways. We arrived at the end of the school day, surrounded by the kids walking along the jetty towards where the boat taxied them to their village home on stilts. An energy buzzed about this community. I found it a peculiar and a restrictive lifestyle, but they seemed free, even walking with a skip and a jump. When we reached the end of the jetty, we met a group of young boys playing the flute. They seemed shy and a little suspicious of us. I popped on some music from my phone and signalled for them to play along. They seemed puzzled and very unimpressed. Noted.

Five hours later we were back at the hostel, preparing for quite possibly the highlight of my trip. Alice and I bonded over this possibility back on that night bus. We were booked into the number one restaurant at the lake, Innlay Hut India Food House, run by a die-hard Eminem fan. It sat perched at the end of a dusty road in a bamboo hut. His 'joint' popped up in every travel blog I read and the trip advisor reviews described it as the most intense experience. The bamboo hut is a homage to the rapper and the city that spawned him – the memorabilia covering every inch of the hut walls a clue if you happened to stumble upon it.

The hut is booked out every night, so we were lucky to get in as a big group. The excitement levels were high - mine were sky-high. We were expecting a performance from the eccentric owner, and he greeted us all like long lost friends. Instantly talking in Eminem song lyrics - this is how he learned his English as the character Stan. He would start swearing and shouting "damn fool" like the chorus of an Eminem song, stressing as they were busy and the kitchen were a little behind. He explained, he felt the pressure of remaining as the number one restaurant on trip advisor and took this very seriously. Recently, a Scandinavian family gave him a bad review for poor service - you could tell this haunted him.

I felt exhausted in his presence, and we hadn't even sat down yet.

He hailed from the gemstone-rich region of Myanmar, where the government forbade foreign visitors for fear they may steal the precious stones. At times his Stan character would slip and he seemed like a normal guy in his 20s trying to capitalise on the backpacker fascination to his story. It felt like a spoof restaurant. We were here for Stan, but also the dishes rated highly. After ordering the group banquet, Stan promised the best home-cooked food from his mum's family recipes. Sipping on some local beers, we waited a little on edge as Stan stormed about. Finally - the poor service reviews accurate - the food arrived served by Stan. He swaggered over, still acting up, to make sure we were having the best time - the dishes explained to us in between rapper quotes and hip-hop slang. It took all my willpower not to burst out laughing. He asked if we wanted anything else – I chanced my luck and asked for a group photo. Alice and I had dreamed of this moment since we both met and giggled at how much we wanted to meet the Myanmar Stan. We posed beside him at the top of the table next to a quote on the wall that states, "I am Stan, Eminem biggest fan." Everyone got into full rapper gangster mode for the photo. What a treasure - I laugh out loud every time I look at that photo. If you ever need an energised, surreal night in a bamboo hut - head to Inle Lake and ask for Stan. Recalling this memory has made my day. Inle Lake, full of all the random, fun, hidden treasures we seek out but in the form of a real human. We need more Stans in the world. Eccentric behaviour is a gift to the world.

The giant freshwater lake is tucked into a valley surrounded by lush green hills, where everyday life focuses on the network of canals connecting the floating villages. In the travel blogs, it sounded a nature-fuelled dream. On my second day, the weather was still less than dreamy. I headed off with the kiwi to find a boat to take us out on the lake in the moody weather. My last chance to experience the floating villages up close. Alice stayed in bed. With travelling, and in life, you need to make the most of your situation. Full Stop. Sometimes there is no next time. I don't want to look back on my life and regret anything.

With my waterproof jacket on, I felt lake ready. Soon we were zooming past the traditional fishermen who stand one-legged on the edge of their small boats while pretending to fish. It is a real traditional fishing method, but most of these men now charge tourists for a photo – cue eye roll. With this first site ticked off, we shared a fun day exploring, experiencing, and enjoying local village life. After taking part in a cigar rolling 'factory' experience, we eventually found ourselves warmly welcomed into a local's stilt house. They prepared the most amazing banquet lunch laid out on a low table in the centre of what seemed to be their living and sleeping space. This lunch blew me away. The local people put so much love into their lunch offering. I have never seen so much food in my life. In the end, no matter what I ate, which trust me was a lot, they kept bringing more food. Eventually, I had to explain I couldn't possibly eat one more mouthful or I would explode. They didn't seem convinced. With very full tummies and after lots of warmth from the local family, including a group photo of them with us looking like we had met our long-lost Burmese relatives, we headed on the journey back across the lake.

To experience life living on the water - relying on food farmed in the grassland or fished - completely puts our western life in perspective. These locals work every day to survive. The surrounding scenery was breathtaking with low hanging clouds and vibrant green hills - it reminded me of that saying, 'to be at one with nature.'

With blue sky weather, I am sure the return trip would have been dreamy, sitting in the canoe cruising through the maze of stilt houses watching daily life unfold. Instead, with the moody weather, my waterproof hood firmly tied tight around my face, the waves lashing into the boat. It felt like survival. I could hardly see with the water splashing in my face. As we made it to land, I laughed out loud. We were cold and wet – some would say soaked through to the bone. But with a greater understanding of the Burmese way of life, I felt a deeper perspective on the privileged life I live. Who cares about the weather or the fact I was soaked. I can't moan or complain about a bit of wet and wild weather. That night I said goodbye to Inle Lake with a local massage - sadly, no ginger tea or tamarind sweets were included - and goodbye to Alice and the Kiwi. I was back being solo.

The next day I flew back to Yangon, where the trip started six days earlier. A local tuk-tuk driver dropped me off at the makeshift airport, near the lake, first thing in the morning. Another eye-opening experience waited and, if you feared flying, would have led you to the calm pills. Heavy fog drifted in overnight, so much so I couldn't even see the airport terminal when the driver told me we arrived. After a fog delay, we were soon on the small scary plane flying high over the plains of Myanmar. I gulped as we took off. With no time to pause on the short flight, I found myself back in Yangon, walking into a five-star hotel greeted with an outdoor pool, fluffy towels, chandeliers in the grand reception, a bowl of fresh fruit in my hotel room and some fresh flowers. What a nice surprise!

Now 100% ready for some chill time with the hard part of travelling a new country done – I felt a little smug knowing I travelled this country with no dramas or incidents. The highlights tour pretty much complete. Along the way I heard about Goteik Viaduct – when I googled it, I gasped. It seemed next level. I just couldn't make it happen though. I learned a long time ago you can't see it all, and sometimes need to let go of having it all. What I experienced from this country is more than enough and you never know, I might return, or I might not. Don't get fixated on what could have been – as it never was. Enjoy what you did experience and allow yourself some time to soak it all in.

Like most trips, there is a massive change in the girl who arrived six days before jet-lagged, curious, but also a little wary of a country known for such internal conflict. Six days later, I felt so content. The people are genuinely incredibly warm. For those I met, we enjoyed some fun experiences, I sensed they would not know how to harm you if they were given the chance, and that is the side of Myanmar I remember. Not the continued conflict through the country where some states remain closed and the plight of the Rohingya population is very real.

I always get this weird anxious feeling on my last day anywhere, like part of a dream is coming to an end, and soon I will wake up back in the daily routine of normal life. I know it and when I feel it, I just breathe it out. I can't live in a travel bubble my whole life, now that would be the dream. I use it as a reminder that I need to make the most of every day on a trip, as when that feeling comes, the end is around the corner.

And just like that I find myself travelling to the airport waiting for my overnight flight to depart back to the UK.

Myanmar felt special. The locals I encountered throughout this trip were gentle, humorous, engaging, considerate, curious and passionate. They leave you with a connection to their mysterious country, making this trip unique. It isn't a Southeast Asian country that is often on travellers 'must see' lists. Maybe that is why I felt a connection.

This country makes you work a little for the travel highs it offers. It is one of the most culturally preserved and exciting destinations in Asia. It will change for sure - that is life. Evolve or be left behind stuck in the past - this country forces your mind wide open. Should we shy away from complicated, delicate countries with a dark past? I don't think so. But instead, we should experience what we can first-hand and make our own judgment of an area of the world jam-packed with gems - some natural, some man-made.

Myanmar will never be 100% free of its past. It is definitely in the process of learning how to live alongside it. It taught me you shouldn't be scared to let go to move forward or you will forever be chasing the shadow you are hiding behind. I learned a lot from watching the monk take photos of the temples in Bagan. Sometimes the beauty is in something you see every day, but until you pause and really look at it, you are forever chasing something else. Bagan and Myanmar, you will forever hold a piece of my heart! You taught me to open it a little and let the pure joy of life flow in. What joyful practices can you bring into your life?

Mynamar

"With the new day
comes new strength and
new thoughts."

– Eleanor Roosevelt

Lebanon: Learn, experience and grow from travelling

On a fresh September Sunday morning, I ran my seventh half marathon - you could call it Super Sunday. My parents were even waiting to greet me. The minute I crossed the finish line, I wanted to be sick. I just ran a personal best and my body likes to remind me of this. My dad demanding a post-run photo, my mum trying to feed me a pastry she had brought along. I glanced at them both - sensing they were eager to parent me - and asked for five minutes.

Why were they even here, you ask. Well, that night I had a flight to catch into a new exotic country and would be in Lebanon for my birthday. The finish line reunion, more a 'we might not see you again' goodbye as they both gave the usual pre-trip advice – "don't speak to strangers!". To which I eye rolled.

Back in 2018, life was hectic. I wanted it all, the runner's high and the escapism travelling brings. Run your heart out to claim your fastest half marathon, followed by a celebration lunch with the parents, then a quick bath to soothe those tired legs before the next adventure started. Twelve hours after I stood on the start line of the Great Scottish Run in Glasgow's George Square, I boarded a flight from London to Beirut – tired, but quietly excited. The perfect combination for an overnight flight.

Lebanon, I wasn't exactly fresh and springy to see you but trust me, I was 100% ready.

After two years of research and online stalking, here I am flying to a country with the most impressive ancient ruins from the Roman Empire. More 'famous' for the civil war that engulfed and destroyed much of the country, including the capital Beirut, I sensed there was more to this country waiting to be found.

The temple complex of Baalbek grabbed my curiosity and popped Lebanon firmly onto my radar. Comprising two of the largest and grandest Roman temple ruins: The Temple of Bacchus and Jupiter. A world heritage site, obviously. Its colossal constructions built over two centuries; Pilgrims thronged to the sanctuary. I had screenshots of all the ancient sites stored on my phone – flicking through them anytime I needed a reminder that the travel game is never done. I knew it was only a matter of time before my own modern-day pilgrimage began.

From a small town on the west coast of Scotland to the war ravished Lebanon. The curiosity of the world that developed as a teenager never quite left me as I grew into an adult. There was only one thing for it, to finally board a plane to Lebanon and explore. Literally that easy.

Not everyone shares that same curiosity. There are a handful of countries that receive a blank expression when I explain proudly I am visiting. Lebanon is on that list. When I reply to the blank look with "Lebanon, the Middle Eastern country where the capital is Beirut," they look back astonished. The expression 'it's like Beirut' is a much-referenced metaphor still used today to describe everything from violent riots to a teenager's messy bedroom. I no longer defend the 'unusual' countries I plan to visit and only hope by sharing my stories and photos that people realise how wonderful the world is – if we free our minds.

My flight arrived at 5 am. With a hotel room reservation booked for the night before, I knew after hopping into a taxi I would soon be tucked up in bed for a few hours sleep before a full day exploring. But first, I needed to tackle a taxi driver. I read the airport taxi drivers could be tricky. As I jumped into the first taxi in line, I naively assumed it would be as easy as the airport immigration checkpoint - I sailed through that. I forgot to agree on the price upfront or at least state 'meter', an indication we agreed on the fare structure. As we drove through the streets of Beirut, the meter ticking along, with no worries, I eagerly peered through the window into the early morning darkness trying to catch my first glimpse of Beirut. This was too good to be true, I thought, as we safely arrived at the hotel.

It was too good to be true as he suddenly demanded some made-up price.

I quickly worked out he was charging at least double. "No way," I thought. I sat upright, explaining I wasn't paying. He started the usual sob story about having a family to feed. So, I explained I would happily go into the hotel reception for them to help us agree on the price. I was all words. I didn't intend to leave the taxi, worried if I left, he would drive off with my backpack.

We sat in silence for a bit, surrounded by the usual awkwardness, him staring me out through the rear-view mirror. In the end, he caved in, and we compromised. Effectively I was still overcharged but not as much. I went from sleepy to assertive – ready to rumble. Luckily, I don't allow taxi dramas to ruin my mood or expectation of a country. Life is way too short to hold any anger or frustration with the taxi driver. He is an opportunist. Full stop. Plus, I wanted to sleep. My hotel check-in went smoothly – restoring all faith in the Lebanese. Ten minutes later, tucked up in the comfy hotel bed, I drifted off to sleep.

A few hours later I woke a little confused. Looking around my unfamiliar surroundings, I soon remembered I was in a hotel room in Beirut. Beirut. Still sounds crazy today saying out loud, "I have visited Beirut".

With a full day to experience the Middle Eastern city where East and West intertwine, creating a Mediterranean hub, I could feel the excitement bubble away. A hotspot for food and wine, nightlife and art, design and fashion, and anything else you could ever want from a city. Following the first World War, when Lebanon was handed over to the French, Beirut rose to become the playground of the rich and famous. In the 60s it was nicknamed 'the Paris of the Middle East' thanks to its French influences and vibrant cultural and intellectual life, before falling from grace during the bloody civil war.

From all the blogs I read, you could tell this was a modern cosmopolitan city alive and kicking with the Middle East's most vibrant nightlife. From the West, we see it as a conservative Muslim country, but within the Middle East, it is seen as a liberal country, with wine freely produced and drunk.

Hello Beirut, I am ready to explore. I think.

Before I arrived, I googled "what to wear / how to dress in Lebanon." This kind of travel prep stresses me out. The response was relatively mixed. Some sites require you to cover your ankles, shoulders and your hair. While outside on the streets, it seemed standard casual wear. Some blogs explained you may receive curious glances. One even explained if you use public transport, sit up front and preferably not next to a male - to ensure you were not offending anyone or at risk of encouraging unwanted attention. "What!". I always feel a bit jaded after reading these blogs and found my travel suitcase a mismatch of clothes. This was the trickiest part of the trip.

I glanced out the hotel window, trying to gauge the situation. What were the locals wearing? How were the men acting? I was looking for some sign I would not step outside wearing a knee-length dress, showing a bit of upper arm, and get dragged off the street by over-eager Lebanese men or arrested by the police. Welcome to my life when travelling. All the crazy thoughts, worryingly they are real.

That day I moved hotel to a slightly more upmarket version with an indoor pool. As I took the short taxi ride, my confidence grew as I stared out the window. The Lebanese walking the streets looked exactly the same as those that walk around London, New York or Athens. The elderly dressed more traditional, whereas the young crowd were very mainstream. Sometimes you shouldn't read travel blogs.

As I explored that day, and for the rest of my time in Lebanon, not one male gave me any attention or a second look - well not in a sleazy untoward way. They were far too busy getting on with life. Every time I turned onto a street to find myself alone with a local man, I would immediately think, "be alert, be vigilant, and keep your wits about you." They would look at me, look away, and walk past without a second glance. Not a care in the world. Like most Muslim countries, the men seem to hang out together a lot. In coffee houses, on street corners, in the local kebab shop, or playing a game of chess outside. Not one man in these groups gave me any attention. They didn't care. Forever thankful to the girl that doesn't put off travelling as a solo female traveller by hiding behind what we expect to happen.

After my first few hours of exploring and once I concluded the streets were safe, I knew Lebanon and I were going to be friends. Once you realise the locals will not bundle you into a waiting car, your shoulders drop, you look people in the eye more and you no longer feel self-conscious. We need to constantly update our negative bias to some cultures and situations.

The plan for my first day was simple - visit the Grand Mosque.

I walked along Zaitunay Bay with a spring in my step, home to Beirut's finest and trendiest open-air bars and restaurants overlooking the yacht-filled marina where the locals strolled along the promenade enjoying the warmth of the Autumn day. This felt a million miles away from the image people have in their heads of this city. Even I felt surprised. As I continued towards my next attraction, my eyes were drawn to the modern high rise apartment blocks, plush hotel chain rooftop bars and modern sky rises - home to the top tier corporate firms. All mixed together to give that Manhattan city skyline vibe.

As I approached the next location on my map, expecting to find the traditional buzz, chaos and noise from the Middle Eastern market stalls of the Beirut Souks, I became pleasantly surprised. Surprised by the silence and design of the market. There stood the modern Beirut Souks, a massive entertainment district with over 200 shops, restaurants and cafes, including a cinema complex. Not a place to haggle but instead pop into a coffee shop to use their Wi-Fi and grab a coffee. A maze of well recognised 'high street' shops and some of the most expensive designer boutiques in the world. The older locals wearing traditional throbs blending in with the high maintenance and designer style of the Lebanese youth.   Meanwhile, I looked 100% like a western tourist trying to blend in with the Muslim culture and failing. I felt very drab in comparison to the glam crowd. The Lebanese females are super stylish and very beautiful.

After a coffee break to recharge my jetlag batteries, I switched into a mosque geek. I love mosques. I remember my first experience when I visited the Masjid Jamek Mosque, recognised as the oldest Islamic place of worship, in Kuala Lumpur. It is breathtaking, the combination of Moorish, Islam and Mughal architectural styles and distant views of KL's other iconic landmarks make it a stand out. Wearing a borrowed purple robe, I collected a leaflet on the five pillars of Islam from the Visitor Centre and strolled about open mouthed. I remember my partner eye-rolling as he knew I had lit a new fire inside, that fire still burns today. That day my intrigue with the Islam faith and architecture style started.

As I turned the corner, I stopped and felt a lump in my throat, as a rush of raw emotion flooded my body. I think life caught up with me - the rollercoaster of the half marathon, only the day before, the overnight flight and the realisation I was standing in Beirut. I can share photos and try to explain what a country means to me, but no one feels this. This raw emotion when you are glancing at one of the most stunning mosques, in the most intense setting. This is why I travel, to feel alive. Standing in complete awe. Shaken to your core.

The Mohammad Al-Amin Mosque sits at the rear of an excavated area showcasing Roman ruins, with the blue minaret of the mosque demanding your attention. A symbol of Beirut, and Islam— the most practised religion of this country. Once dressed in the loaned black robe, I entered and immediately felt at peace. There is something about Islamic architecture and witnessing people deep in prayer. You instantly feel at ease with the feeling of calmness flooding your body as if time slows down. Your thoughts are brought back to the present. For every mosque that takes your breath away from the outside, there is even more waiting inside. They are welcome to us all, regardless of your faith.

Downtown Beirut centres on Martyrs Square, named for those executed under Ottoman rule. Today the vast mosque, a modern reincarnation of a 19th-century original, sits next to the 19th century Saint George Cathedral. Another symbol of how the Lebanese religious sites now stand side by side. As I continued to explore the city, you were constantly reminded of the past with bullet-scarred buildings in full display. Buildings completely left to decay, and the presence of checkpoints still with soldiers on patrol - more as a symbol of peace than to control any expected aggression.

I eventually found myself at Pigeon Rock, perfectly timed for sunset. A natural stone arch, perched out at sea, one of the city's most famous landmarks after the mosque. As I arrived, I gazed out at the Mediterranean Sea smiling as I appreciated this natural wonder, and excited to experience the rest of my planned week. I left nothing to chance on this trip. With three one-day trips booked online, I knew this wasn't the time to be a warrior princess and attempt to travel independently. Although possible, it seemed unnecessary. I could reign it in this time and be happy as a day-tripper – carted about the various sites by an actual tour guide.

As the sun set I walked back to my hotel along the Corniche, the waterfront promenade. With music playing in my ears, I took in my surroundings. The leisurely flow of day to day life all around; Fishermen's rods patiently posed, couples' strolling hand in hand, joggers and families out enjoying the cool breeze. I felt at ease. Super safe and content - a little invisible, a fly in the wall of their everyday life hundreds of miles away from Scotland.

The world is incredible if we take the courage to leave our comfort zone.

So many people don't get to this point in a trip. They talk themselves out of what could be the most wonderful experience due to following society's blueprint to visit 'normal and safe' countries or listening to their internal narrative shouting loud, "What if something bad happens in Lebanon?" Can you imagine if that negative thought was reframed into, "What if something incredible is waiting for you riding those day trip highs.

As we arrived back in Beirut at the end of the day trip, I knew the sun would set soon. Instead of heading to my hotel, I arrived at a different one to experience their rooftop bar. After reading the amazing reviews online I knew this was the spot to sip on a $$$ cocktail, while enjoying the most stunning sunset over the bay, showcasing the cosmopolitan side of Lebanon.

As I finally arrived back at my hotel a little sleepy after a jam-packed day, I knew if I went near my bed it would not end well. Instead, I grabbed my bikini and went down to the hotel pool, not expecting much to be going on.

Turns out, the local privileged kids use it for their weekly swimming lessons. There I am in my bikini, thinking it would be western hotel guests only. Instead, I am trying to hide my body from the Lebanese youth and not swim into them as they very badly attempted the backstroke. Talk about stressful. After some laps of the pool to wake myself up, I got ready for a night out and found myself back at the same rooftop bar with the day trip ladies sipping more $$$ cocktails.

We formed a gang. Joined by an English Mother/Daughter combo from our tour who were now based in Dubai. Again using Beirut as a weekend getaway. I loved chatting and putting the world to rights with the best company in a very cool setting. It felt familiar. These are my kind of people. What we see as normal destinations, is other peoples 'why would you visit there' nightmares. Only we know why we do this.

The next day I moved to a hotel with a rooftop pool and sweeping panoramic views of Lebanon – free from any local swimming lessons. The nearby Hamra street used to be one of the main places where poets, writers, thinkers, and philosophers would meet and gather. This district now with a young playful vibe, home to International Universities and some very striking urban art murals. Completely up my street – I love this free creative vibe. It is infectious.

When I arrived at the hotel, I noted the free coffee and biscuits in the reception area. These wee gems make any stay a little bit more joyful. Some people miss this stuff as they are chasing the grand gestures. I dumped my bags, slipped on my bikini before entering the rooftop area to find I had the whole place to myself. Perfect.

Soon slapping on the sunscreen for a morning of tanning and reading. I wanted to use the second part of the trip to unwind a little, relax, and explore more of Beirut and Lebanon. A few hours after enjoying the sunshine, and after a quick coffee and biscuit treat at the reception area, I sat perched, waiting for my taxi, ready to see a different and more authentic side of the city from the plush souks I explored on my first day.

My destination the Gemmayze district - the soul of Beirut. A bohemian area with a genuine sense of freedom. No one raises an eyebrow as anything seems to go in this district, with a community atmosphere in an urban setting. Coffee shops feel like traditional houses inviting you in, where the shell of the building keeps its traditional essence, and the young hip owners have layered their creative minds on top to produce some fresh and vibrant venues – a designer's paradise. I sat in one, sipping a coffee, gazing out the massive floor to ceiling glass windows looking onto Saint Nicolas Steps, known as the steps of art, filled with murals and graffiti. Little cafes, shops and even museums pop out onto the steps.

As you walk through Gemmayze, into the neighbouring district of Mar Mikhaël, its young hip bar scene jumps out at you. Local shops, cafes and even churches enticing you in as you feel fortunate to witness day-to-day life unfold in front of you. It reminded me of the Jewish Quarters in Budapest, home to the ruin bars. From the outside, some buildings looked war-torn, then when you peeked in, your eyes greeted with the most stunning courtyards fit for the hipster crowd.

After meandering this district, I felt more connected to the Lebanese people. Now to learn more about their past.

I visited Beit Beirut, meaning 'The House of Beirut'. Once a snipers' lair, now a museum housing Lebanon's war memories. It sits on the green line that once separated the Christian East and Muslim West from 1975 to 1990. As the Civil War continued, it also came to separate Sunni from Shia Muslims. The name refers to the colouration of the nature that grew because the space stood uninhabited during the war. During the war it became commonplace to see snipers on top of buildings. Many of the buildings along the Green Line were severely damaged or destroyed during the war. Beit Beirut is a stand out on the corner of a busy interchange with its blend of Ottoman-style architecture with parts showing Art Deco and Rocco influences.

As well as recounting the tales of the snipers who operated from within its four walls, it also tells the story of the Barakat family, who first commissioned the building. As I wandered into the building, I felt goosebumps. From outside and now inside the building feels like the war only stopped yesterday. Most of the building still looks destroyed and has been sympathetically 'glued' back together to make it structurally safe. But there is no hiding or removing the war scars.

The exhibition focussed on the theme of 'photography as creating technology memories', sharing photos from negatives found hidden in one of the rooms. Acting as clues to pre-war times. Restoring the building and the exhibition was a 23-year project. Truly fascinating. I left with a postcard, the black and white photo of a young Lebanese girl with full fringe, big brown eyes and a gorgeous smile. The postcard sits in my flat, I don't know her past or her story, but it inspires me to continue to be curious and see life as a big game to keep playing as one day I will be all but a memory.

Feeling drained after the museum experience, I was keen to get back to the luxury rooftop pool. I stood across from the museum attempting to flag down a taxi. Easy, you would think. I did eventually find one and of course, like most countries, it became a farce.

I knew what price to expect to pay based on the ride in. At first, he seemed confident he knew my hotel. Then I heard him on the phone asking my hotel location while still smiling back at me with the overconfidence of a typical taxi driver. After a very confusing conversation, he announced the price, and this turned out to be double what I paid earlier. I explained I would not pay that price. He seemed annoyed I wasted his time. The saga rumbled on.

We were bargaining, something I find exhausting and massively awkward. In the end, I walked away dramatically from the Beirut driver. Now feeling even more exhausted. He reversed back and agreed on the price I demanded. "Phew," I thought, "I will soon be back in my bikini at the rooftop pool". That would have been too easy.

As I jumped into the car, he got back on the phone asking someone else my hotel location. By now I am shouting, "You told me you knew my address." He waved me away as if to say, "Calm it, lady, I am bluffing this taxi game."

As we are driving along the expressway, I am muttering to myself, "Why does every taxi experience need to be a challenge?" My train of thought interrupted when the car suddenly stops randomly at the side of the road, and a lady jumps in with her shopping. Then a little further along, an elderly man gets into the front seat. "What is going on?" I thought.

Next thing I witness the taxi driver asking the elderly man where my hotel is. What? Why would a 70-year-old Lebanese man know my five-star hotel? Argh!

With no internet access, I used an offline map to find a Beirut attraction nearby to the hotel that I thought they would recognise. I picked a park that looked like it sat just around the corner from the hotel. There I am in the back of this pretend taxi shouting at the driver, who is in deep discussion with the local man, trying to ignore me. I think I might have been saying, "I'm not paying for their trip too." Referring to the random lady and elderly man.

After dropping the lady off, she didn't pay by the way, I'm next to be bundled out at the agreed park, even though I am paying to be taken to my hotel. What a drama.

As I look around, I expect to see all twenty floors of my hotel. But I didn't. Massively disoriented, I do what I do best and start to ask vetted locals – they were vetted based on how they looked, acted, and in the hope they knew the neighbourhood. All I received were shakes of the head. I felt that feeling again when your tummy is doing cartwheels as you realise you are lost. I knew it was nearby. I could sense it. But couldn't quite place it. The locals now trying to grab my attention to sell me everything and anything.

I kept my cool, pretending to myself it was just around the corner. I just needed to find the right corner. Then that moment came when I glanced down the next corner, and I saw it. There it stood, the modern towering slice of luxury. Super relieved, I scurried off, happy to be inside the hotel and safe from any more energy-sapping local exchanges.

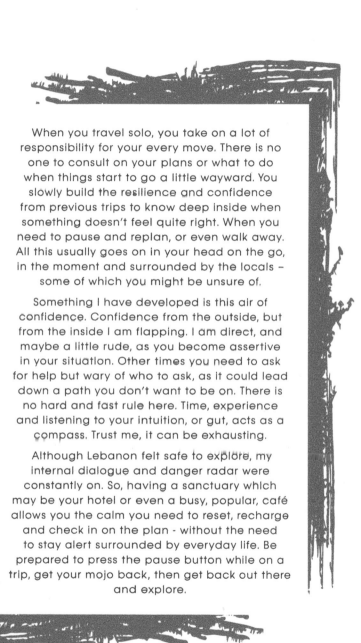

When you travel solo, you take on a lot of responsibility for your every move. There is no one to consult on your plans or what to do when things start to go a little wayward. You slowly build the resilience and confidence from previous trips to know deep inside when something doesn't feel quite right. When you need to pause and replan, or even walk away. All this usually goes on in your head on the go, in the moment and surrounded by the locals – some of which you might be unsure of.

Something I have developed is this air of confidence. Confidence from the outside, but from the inside I am flapping. I am direct, and maybe a little rude, as you become assertive in your situation. Other times you need to ask for help but wary of who to ask, as it could lead down a path you don't want to be on. There is no hard and fast rule here. Time, experience and listening to your intuition, or gut, acts as a compass. Trust me, it can be exhausting.

Although Lebanon felt safe to explore, my internal dialogue and danger radar were constantly on. So, having a sanctuary which may be your hotel or even a busy, popular, café allows you the calm you need to reset, recharge and check in on the plan - without the need to stay alert surrounded by everyday life. Be prepared to press the pause button while on a trip, get your mojo back, then get back out there and explore.

That evening, safely from the hotel rooftop, I marvelled at the Beirut city skyline with the night-time action below. I spent that night at a cool pop-up restaurant near the university campus. I loved the liveliness of the Hamra area. It felt Beirut never slept. This time I only needed to walk back to my hotel. No taxis required. Hurray.

The next day involved my second-day trip, back in the hands of a tour guide ready for more facts, history, and tons of culture. As we jumped out at the first site, I quickly surveyed the day trip crew to check out their vibe. I found myself chatting to an Aussie, around my age with Lebanese heritage. Both his parents left Lebanon during the civil war and headed to Australia for a new life. Although Australian, his upbringing and roots very much Lebanese. In Greece for a wedding, he tagged on some island hopping before a trip to Lebanon to meet the extended family. He cracked me up. Until this trip, he never travelled solo, so purchased a selfie stick for all those candid shots he planned to take on his travels. He turned around, looked me in the eye and exclaimed proudly, "I've not used the selfie stick once." He couldn't believe how exhilarating and fun travelling solo could be. During the Island hopping, he made loads of pals who took his photo. It seemed his eyes were open to another world, and it sounded he would return to Australia a little different from when he left.

My heart warmed at this story. I probably take for granted how easy I find travelling solo and crave it in my life to recharge my batteries, feed my creative and curious mind, and leave a little more inspired from when I started the trip. To share some time with someone on their first solo trip felt special. I felt energised around him.

We walked and talked, sharing stories as we explored the first site, the ancient ruins of Sidon Sea Castle. The crusaders built Sidon's Sea Castle in the thirteenth century as a fortress of the holy land, a castle perched out at sea on an island connected to the mainland by a causeway.

After the castle, we headed to Tyre – this site high on my 'to see' list. Tyre is one of the oldest continually inhabited cities in the world, though so is Byblos remember. That is history for you – always conflicting.

One of the earliest metropolises and the legendary birthplace of Europa - the beautiful girl abducted and seduced by Zeus, the chief of the Gods as believed in the Greek mythology. Excavations have uncovered remains of the Greco-Roman, Crusader, Arab, and Byzantine civilizations, but most of the remains of the Phoenician period lie beneath the present town. Blows your mind a little to think there are whole cities beneath us, some we are aware of, and others left waiting to be found, with tales and clues from eras that appear from the movies.

Founded more than 4,000 years ago, talk about walking in history. Nothing roped off or restricted. When the Romans took Tyre, they built a magnificent triumphal arch and one of the world's largest hippodromes – back in the day would have seated 20,000 spectators. I felt goosebumps as the tour guide explained these are some of the world's largest and most important Roman ruins in the world. Right in front of me. The setting unreal, as you tip toed through the column lined Roman boulevard, over the ancient mosaics, where your eye catches a glimpse of the tranquil sea backdrop. The ruins of the temple tempted us over and we were soon climbing up the steps to where spectators once sat watching the chariot games. The Australian, quickly upgraded to my photographer, took some snaps as I pretended to push down the Roman columns - candidly.

With our tummies rumbling, we were soon presented with the most amazing banquet of fresh local Lebanese food. If you don't like bread or hummus, then don't travel to Lebanon. Over lunch I got chatting to another solo traveller, this time from Canada. I gasped as she told me her job, a librarian. I am a self-confessed book geek. Growing up, I would pretend to be a librarian in my parents living room where I would line up some books, and magazines, then awkwardly I would also become the customer. I always thought I would end up working in a library. The two of us were raving about the joy and benefits of libraries in the local community.

When I first moved to Melbourne, I would visit the St Kilda library every week to borrow and binge all their travel books – some of them planted seeds for future trips. Now back in Glasgow, I am still 100% a library geek. I just love being around actual books. The Australian listened to us geek out and seemed surprised at our enthusiasm for the modest library. I'm not sure he planned to head straight into the library on his return. It seemed a step too far.

The trip continued with a visit to Maghdouche, where a church now stands on the site of a cave believed to be where Jesus and the Virgin Mary visited on their way to preach in Sidon. Legend says that the Virgin Mary waited for her son in a small cave on the tip of the hill. Today, a shrine rises over the site where supposedly the incident took place. The shrine is one of the holiest and most religiously significant Catholic sites in Lebanon. From this viewpoint, you experience sweeping views down into the lush valley and even further out to the sea. My memory isn't of the cave church, but of this view. The site of the permanent Palestinian refugee camp grabs your attention from the viewpoint – the largest in Lebanon and now like a walled-in city for displaced refugees from Syria. First erected in 1948 with a population of over 70,000. A sobering reminder of how delicate this pocket of the Middle East is.

We were soon back on the bus, exhausted after another full day where all our senses were open. This was the last time I saw the Canadian Librarian. Through the wonder of the online community we are still connected today, following each other's travel adventures. Whenever I come across a cool library somewhere in the world, I make sure she is tagged. I think the last was when I visited the Trinity Library in Dublin. Trinity is a library to behold. Add it to the list.

I also said goodbye to the Aussie, but something told me I would see him again.

That night I jumped out of the taxi into Little Armenia and walked into a very Mediterranean inspired courtyard where I enjoyed a dinner date with the ladies again. Sampling the dish 'Manti', a bit like gnocchi. They were maxing out their time here and visited the Cedars of Lebanon, a stunning grove of cedar trees that represent the country. It wasn't on my list but sounded a nature lover's delight.

The next day signalled a special day in my life. I celebrated my birthday. Hip Hooray! It was also the day I would experience the reason I was in Lebanon, to meet Baalbek.

An ancient city 85 km from Beirut that dates back as early as the 3rd century B.C, home to the largest Roman temples ever built. They are among the best preserved in the world, with breathtaking detail and 20 metre high columns still intact. The large temple site, used as a place to worship, is serene and wonderful. Baalbek sits at the foot of the mountain range that separates Lebanon from Syria.

As I jumped on the tour bus, I spotted a familiar face – the Aussie from yesterday. We were back reunited, ready to geek out at Baalbek. First, we visited a site nearby called Anjar, a true gem. In any other country, you would witness a site like Anjar as the star attraction, in Lebanon, this is merely the warm-up act. Only discovered in 1940, it is home to a complex of Umayyad ruins. Umayyad ruins are unique in Lebanon, where the population of this settlement were Armenian. Anjar is close to 1,300 years old with evidence of Greek, Roman and Byzantine architecture, along with the arched Umayyad relics. Although blown away by Anjar, I knew around the corner stood Baalbek – my birthday present to me. As we approached Baalbek you saw a glimpse of the Roman masterpieces from afar, I felt the goosebumps rise on my arms.

This site can only be described as out of this world. After hours exploring and listening to tales from the tour guide - one that stuck was when he explained the locals used the site to fling their garbage bags not realising the significance of the fallen city. Meanwhile, my imagination would consider how the architecture and design stood as a symbol of the strength of the Roman Empire. The Aussie captured some moments on camera which I look back on to remind myself of that day. I couldn't have been happier. As we each snapped away capturing the masterpieces in front of us, we wanted some photos to remember those smiles and that energy. When I look back on those photos taken on my 36th Birthday, I see a girl who experienced the might of the Roman Empire in the deepest of Lebanon, like it is the most natural thing in the world. The scale of the ruins is something I can't even explain. My mouth wide open in awe as I explored. These are the days I travel the world for. Inspiration doesn't come from sitting at home binging the latest TV Series. It comes in the form of what UNESCO describes as "One of the most famous sanctuaries of the Roman world and a model of Imperial Roman architecture."

We finished the day on a tour of the Ksara Caves, a series of ancient caverns used as wine cellars by Lebanon's oldest winery, Chateau Ksara. The huge underground Roman caves were the perfect temperature for wine to mature. After the tour, we enjoyed a tasting – this country is multi-layered. Soon back in Beirut, I said bye to the Aussie and told him to enjoy life like the new world traveller he had become.

That evening I had plans to meet the ladies to experience the Beirut nightlife. The nightlife rivals Dubai, Ibiza and New York. In the end, I changed into my PJs and went to bed early. Not feeling 100%, I felt low on energy. My body telling me I needed rest.

I woke the next day feeling better. With one last day in Beirut, I headed out for a morning of tourist activity downtown, where I found a local market next to the 'I LOVE BEIRUT' art-infused sign. I strolled around without a care in the world, experiencing the blend of new and old architecture, sampling all the local food, and enjoying the art splattered on the streets, knowing very soon this would all be a distant memory - but at that moment, it felt exactly where I was meant to be.

After an afternoon by the rooftop pool, it was time for my last sunset of the trip. I headed back to pigeon rock, the limestone rock formation that I first saw six days before – crazy how you suddenly come full circle. A lot had happened since then. It felt like the right spot to say goodbye to this inspiring country. To pause and reflect on my trip. A trip that was probably two years in the making. Two years of getting myself comfortable, before I felt ready to be unleashed into this exotic gem.

Lebanon turned out to be a melting pot of diverse cultures and religions, delicious food, beautiful weather, fascinating architecture, and enthralling history. Possibly one of the most enchanting places I have ever been to.

A visit to Beirut and Lebanon provided a deeper understanding of the historic and political context of this country and region. Today Beirut is a much safer, and more secure, place with a distinctive cosmopolitan buzz, but there is still a rawness to it. It feels real. You can't easily paper over the cracks from the Civil War. They live amongst it, mending the wounds slowly, ready for a better future.

The people I met along the way were awesome, so vibrant and full of life. An awareness that the world is an open adventure playground and we are the players. Every time I meet someone like me, I smile and realise I am not the odd one out, but just one of many people dotted around the world who want to learn, experience and grow from travelling. I never once take any of this travelling for granted. Experiencing all the mesmerising sites reinforced how I want to live my life – by being curious.

Sometimes when I look at a photo online, I think, "Do I need to spend my savings flying to the other side of the world to witness an ancient site listed on the UNESCO website?" Then I remember how I felt when I first glimpsed the mosque in Beirut, that incredible underground Grotto, or the Ancient Roman site of Baalbek. The goosebumps that jump off your skin when you follow your joy is the feeling I seek out. Lebanon, thank you for making me feel part of your vibrant and exciting future. You have inspired me to want more and keep exploring this vast world, as around every corner is a hidden gem waiting to be found. What ones are you adding to your list?

Lebanon

"Stop acting as if life is a rehearsal. Live this day as if it were your last. The past is over and gone. The future is not guaranteed."

– Wayne Dyer

Sri Lanka: Find joy in the simple way of life, as there may not be a tomorrow

2020 started in Sri Lanka, also known as country number 89. Three weeks spent on this exotic island - a trip I will treasure for an eternity, as not long after life as we knew changed forever.

At the time it seemed like any other trip. I felt free, wild, and untamed. 100% going with the flow of travel life and fully embracing the relative ease you can travel around a diverse Asian country. In 2020, trips were different from my party girl days. Back then I would babysit my hangover around the world. Nowadays I say hello to the chilled life and goodbye to the energy-draining hangovers, you will not be missed.

Trips now focused on maxing out each day by having early nights and early rises, embracing the local community, grateful to be a little wiser and more appreciative of the simple things in life. Each day started with a morning run, some more enthusiastic than others. It's that time of the day, before the sun and heat rise, where you are slowly adjusting your eyes, body, and mind to the day ahead. Your ears are filled with nature, music, or a chatty podcast, with a route planned out, but also open to following what route feels right in the moment. Technically, you can't get lost in a new location you are not yet familiar with. Bliss!

Sri Lanka was truly the dream, and it should have been. I remember the day the dream was a mere speck of an idea. With one free weekend in September, I sneaked off to the Faroe Islands where I found myself sitting in a lovely quaint café, with coffee and cake, letting my mind wander to future travels in Sri Lanka. I felt that feeling, that feeling of excitement when you start to get a vibe about a country. A possible route sketched out, all the 'must-see' attractions pin-pointed and your imagination starts to light up.

During the trip to Sri Lanka, I started to think ahead, into the year called 2020 - not yet known as anything else. How would I reach the milestone I had been chasing? Crazy to think this is the same girl who back in 2015 stepped onto a plane to Japan, for my first solo trip. My ten-year relationship ended that year. Raw, lost, and in need of the world to pick me up and piece my life back together again. I would sometimes tell people I wanted to reach 100 countries by the age of 40. It was never a lifetime goal, but as I ticked off the list of countries to find myself on the verge of number 89, it became a possibility. I like possibilities.

Why wait until 40, when you can reach 100 countries at 38! That was my plan for 2020. A plan that excited me. It was all mapped out.

Then the Covid pandemic happened, and travel life paused for seven months. Thankfully I had the memories from Sri Lanka to feed the desire in my soul as I waited for the travel game to resume again.

After visiting India in 2018, I moved slowly closer to Sri Lanka. Some countries, especially as a female traveller, can seem daunting. I kept this in mind when planning my route around Sri Lanka. From everything I heard, it seemed ultra-safe. If anything, the locals were described as too friendly. Yes, this is a true thing, as they want to make sure you have the best experience of their island – they are a proud bunch.

When I researched the trip, it quickly came together. Probably faster than any other trip I have planned. There is a well-rehearsed route that most tourists head-on. All the blogs described it as the dream – a combination of nature, surf and tradition. For years I secretly kept Sri Lanka as a potential honeymoon destination as many couples combine it with the nearby Maldives for that dream combination. Nowhere nearer finding my Prince, I knew I would need to find a new Honeymoon destination if I ever did find him as Sri Lanka was happening.

Years of uncertainty kept Sri Lanka off many backpacker itineraries. The history of the island is pretty complex. In 1815 the British conquered the Kingdom of Kandy and brought in Tamil labourers from southern India to work in tea, coffee and coconut plantations. One hundred and fifty years of British rule ended in 1948 when, the then titled, Ceylon earned independence. In 1972, Ceylon became a republic and changed its name to Sri Lanka. Buddhism became the country's dominant religion, further antagonising the Tamil minority. Between 1983-2009 the Civil War raged across north and east. After over 25 years of violence, the conflict ended in 2009 when government forces seized the last area controlled by Tamil Tiger rebels. In 2019 Jihadist suicide bombers attack churches and hotels on Easter Sunday, killing over 270 people. The country was slowly stepping out of the shadows of the civil war and that tragic Easter attack.

It's Sri Lanka's 2000-plus years of culture that allures you and quietens any doubt about its stability. Its mystic piques your travel interest. The sheer diversity of the island makes it stand out. Safari tours to feed your nature urge, epic surf days for those adventure junkies and quaint villages with colonial gems. This wasn't going to be just any other trip, not when travelling across Christmas and New Year. I had it planned and booked to the usual spreadsheet level of precision.

The first day started with a 4 am alarm. I arrived late the night before, and after little sleep, I strapped myself back into my backpack and arrived at a crowded train station, nothing to stress about as I expected this. There are whole blog posts dedicated to explaining how to buy tickets to each location, what ticket counter to get to, how to ask for the ticket and any 'watch for this' stuff. Thankful for the travel community while still half asleep, I headed for the train station café with my train ticket purchased for practically nothing - it was so cheap. For the exchange of 10p, I tucked into the staple breakfast of a veggie potato samosa. I was in foodie heaven.

With the train due, I stood eagerly waiting on the platform with the second-class ticket firmly in my hand. There is a big class divide on the trains. 1st class carriages are air-conditioned, 2nd class are unreserved free-for-all chaos carriages with basic seats, then 3rd class is 3rd class - every person for themselves. As the train approached, everyone tried to line up alongside the doors, and some locals started to jump onto the moving train. I felt a bit overwhelmed with the train boarding rules - there seemed none. Feeling out of balance with my full backpack, I caught eyes with a local man. Just as the train came to stop, he jumped on and signalled to follow. So I did. I grabbed his hand and jumped on the moving train. How wild.

As the train stopped and I found my balance, he ushered me into the train carriage, took my backpack off my back and placed it on the railing above our heads, then pointed to a seat across from him. Talk about being assertive and in charge of the situation. A complete legend in my eyes. I smiled, as I thought, "Aww now does he think I am his western damsel in distress?". No way, but I was glad for his help.

The cutest Sri Lankan family of four soon joined us. All six of us squeezed into seats designed for four – talk about cosy. I didn't care. I was the happiest version of myself. The first day in any new country can feel overwhelming and bring some anxious thoughts to the surface. I love the first days. Everything is new and shiny. I'm like a big child. Sitting, watching, learning – being a curious sponge. First time experiences are labelled as such for a reason. You will never experience any of this again. So sit back, breathe and enjoy it.

A six-hour train journey followed where local life passed by or appeared suddenly into view – the train taking you on an adventure into the unknown. I sat with my face out the window, the breeze on my face, letting my mind take it all in, while listening to my music. Something meditative about it all. Knowing you had nothing to worry about but enjoy the train experience until your destination came into sight.

As the only westerner in a jam-packed carriage on my first day in a strange country, you would expect some unease, but I felt like I belonged. This country and its people welcome you in, or maybe it is because I let them in. Open and free to every experience that appears on my horizon.

Each time the train paused at a station, a flurry of activity would happen. It broke up the journey and became a highlight. Passengers would mill on and off the train. Local food sellers would appear with the freshest of food in homemade baskets soon engulfed with hungry passengers. Whatever you wanted, you could purchase from the onboard sellers or even from your window as they strolled on past with a concoction of fresh goodness in wide brim wicker baskets. Hot samosas handed out in newspaper wrappers or some little plastic bags of fruit – pineapple and mango seemed to be the favourites.

Every train station shared a common look from the colonial times, the station name displayed in white handwriting on a wooden board - a clue to my whereabouts. Locals wearing colourful, intricate saris waiting patiently for their train to transport them around the island for the incoming family celebrations. Even the odd Christmas decoration would appear in sight. Some using the train tracks as a shortcut back to the community. Sometimes I would catch someone's eye and we would smile, all before an official-looking guard would signal for the train to leave and the final commotion followed – last-minute passengers flinging themselves onto the already packed out train carriage, and the onboard sellers dashing to leave.

Meanwhile, I sat waiting for the next landscape to slide into view, grateful to have a seat. The local man, my train saviour, sat across from me the whole journey – either on his phone or napping. Whenever I wriggled about my seat to awaken my numb bum, he would offer his seat to stretch out and place my feet on. I declined this lovely selfless act - it just felt a step too far. I know I can be a princess but stretching my legs out onto a local man's seat is a bit out there, even for me.

As I arrived at Anuradhapura, one of the ancient capitals of Sri Lanka, famous for its well-preserved ruins of an ancient Sinhala civilization and over 3,000 years old, I started to mentally prepare myself for the tuk-tuk drivers that would be waiting. As I jumped off the train, I waved goodbye to the local man who saved me a seat, and six hours of standing, and the cutest family, who seemed happy with my departure as they claimed my seat. If this was anything to go on, I was going to be well looked after.

As expected, I was greeted by the freshest and friendliest Mr Tuk Tuk driver the minute I stepped one foot off the train platform into the road. Dressed smartly, he flashed his dangling tourist badge in my face. Something strange then happened, After a quick introduction, we immediately agreed on the price to my hotel – no haggling, bargaining or game playing. He named a price, I considered it and nodded. The start of a lovely arrangement. After I checked in at my lakeside hotel, we agreed for him to return and collect a refreshed Jacquelyn an hour later. Yes, yes, yes! This is travelling – after no sleep, an early morning start, a long six-hour bum numbing train journey, I appeared like an eager beaver wearing a 'Be Happy' tee shirt, of course, ready for my first day trip in Sri Lanka.

Anuradhapura is built to be explored. The immense archaeological ruins and impressive religious sites declared a world heritage site because of their status and significance as a major centre for Buddhism. As one of the oldest continuously inhabited cities in the world – my inner geek high fiving herself - it truly transports you to an entirely different era. Mr Tuk Tuk driver was instructed to deliver the top sites to my eager eyes.

A sacred city, hidden away in dense jungle for many years, now a tourist attraction that would rival Angkor Wat in Cambodia or Bagan in Myanmar with its palaces, monasteries and monuments. With limited tourists, I felt the only westerner in the 'City'. Every site felt special, a nod to the Buddhist religion and many overrun with cheeky monkeys. Monkey fear is real. I developed it from a visit to

Ubud in Bali where the monkeys would roam freely and attack if they sensed you carried food. I once saw one manhandle this girl for something in her handbag. Terrifying – all while her boyfriend took a photo, probably for social media. Crazy.

After my initial eagerness to explore, I could feel my energy levels start to drop. With the Day One sites ticked off, I arranged for Mr Tuk Tuk to take me back to my hotel, not before he booked me in for Day Two. He knew we were the best double act.

After an early night, I woke early feeling fresh and ready for a sunrise run around the neighbouring lake. I soon spotted some sort of blessing by the shore involving a group of locals and monks wearing their colourful robes. I'm not sure what they thought of my short running shorts as I tried to discretely run past without being spotted. After a swim back at the hotel in the most tranquil nature-filled setting, I felt energised and ready for Day Two. The day started exactly how I wanted, in nature – alone and present - enjoying the stillness before a full day crammed with more history and culture.

The tuk-tuk zoomed out of the sacred city as I snacked on a breakfast samosa purchased for a grand total of 15 pence. It became my daily go to snack. We were heading straight for Mihintale - a sleepy village and temple complex - a special place in Sri Lankan folklore. Back in 247 BC, the King of Anuradhapura was hunting a stag on Mihintale Hill when he was approached by the son of the great Indian Buddhist Emperor. The son tested the king's wisdom and, considered him to be a worthy disciple, promptly converted the King on the spot. It is believed that this area is the specific birthplace of Buddhism in Sri Lanka.

You access the sacred complex by climbing hundreds of energy-sapping steps, as the sun beats down, where a giant white Buddha statue and a magnificent 40ft stupa, dating back to the 1st century BC, awaits. I felt part of a very sweaty pilgrimage.

Mr Tuk Tuk told me about another site, a gorgeous lake. As we explored the lake together, he decided he wanted to become my photographer. I encouraged it until he started to get a bit too big for his boots and directed me like we were on an actual shoot. As I giggled to myself, he picked a fallen flower from the grass and handed it to me. As I accepted his gift, he signalled to wear it in my hair. "Oh right," I thought. I didn't want to encourage him, so accidentally dropped it!

As quickly as I arrived in Anuradhapura, it became time to head South where I would be spending Christmas. Mr Tuk Tuk and I waved to each other as I sat back in the minibus safe in the knowledge that my next destination waited on the other side of this bus journey. The epic Sigiriya. What a whirlwind couple of days and a mad departure. He practically flung me onto a departing minibus the minute he worked out it was heading South. Talk about service. My Tuk Tuk tour done and flung out of the city.

Sigiriya is an ancient rock fortress built nearly 200 metres high, which dominates the town of the same name. I remember when I first saw it, sat in the back of a second local bus heading towards the village. A 30-minute journey from the main town of Dambulla out to the remote backdrop. As I sat chatting to a friendly German, it appeared on the horizon, I stopped mid-conversation to take it all in. I ditched the pool and hotel vibes from Anuradhapura to enjoy a local homestay for the night. Greeted by a father and son combo. We walked beyond their house where they had built two apartment-style villas each with a balcony overlooking the gardens. The son asked my plans in that Sri Lanka 'we are here to help' friendly manner.

I explained my well-thought out plans and my optimistic mood changed when the son glanced directly at me, then his watch, then back at me, before he explained I must leave now to hike the Pidurangala Rock as there is an entry cut off time. The rock described as the best viewing spot of the awe-inspiring Sigiriya Rock and a popular spot for sunset with 360-degree views of the valleys. I planned to climb the actual Sigiriya Rock, known as Lion Rock, the next morning for Christmas. Nothing would get in the way of my plans. I jumped up and grabbed the essentials for a hike and two minutes later stood ready – no excuses here!

This Christmas eve hike was one of my Sri Lanka travel dreams. I felt excitement bubble away, this is when you feel the freest – floating about a country open to new adventures. After a frantic tuk-tuk journey, I found myself at the foot of Pidurangala rock where you enter through a sanctuary leading you to the paved, rocky passage. At times deep in lush greenery, before you tiptoe over rocks until you hit the boulder. This is where it gets a little tricky. You need to climb up onto it then 'leap' up onto another boulder above you where some lovely traveller (the last person from the group in front) would wait to grab your hand and help you up. All slightly terrifying if you overthink it. I made it up in one go without making a scene, thanking the hand holding guy in front of me. What would we do without the amazing backpacker community!

As I turned, I caught my first glimpse of the sun setting over Lion Rock. I genuinely don't think I have seen anything like this in my life. Sigiriya, sometimes described as the eighth wonder of the world, sits mystically rising through the vast green canopy of the jungle. The stillness echoes out and the sheer scale is hard to comprehend. All around the sky changing colour as the sun lights up the surrounding jungle, showering the vast landscapes in golden glows with the whispers and cries from nature. It was a goosebumps moment, how wonderful is nature? After an hour of taking all the photos, I sat pondering what my eyes were witnessing. Sometimes you just need a moment. To pause and be truly grateful.

I quickly worked out that navigating the slippery boulder and the rocky path wasn't an experience I wanted to try in the pitch black. After the sun fully set, I set off for the boulder exit. It seemed so did everyone else. After a scramble, at one point sliding down some rocks and holding on to branches to make my way towards the path, I felt relief to be heading back to the tuk-tuk. Safely back at the homestay, the dad arrived to work out my plans for the morning. What a service.

I explained what I thought were more well-thought-out plans until he shook his head and took over, first his son and now him. He soon outlined my breakfast time, and the time I should leave for the rock. His reasoning, "The Sri Lankan people treat Christmas Day as a sacred day to climb the rock. There will be crowds of them and they walk slow. There is no getting around them, so get there early for opening and you will enjoy it more." Noted.

I hate 'slow coaches' and for once knew when I should listen to someone else for advice. With that in mind, I went to sleep knowing in the morning it would be Christmas Day when I had a date with an incredible natural beauty to look forward to. Sri Lanka was living up to my expectations and more.

I woke on Christmas Day 2019 to find a Sri Lankan breakfast served on the balcony of the homestay delivered by the father. I spotted my new favourite food from the world of traveling. Pancakes rolled and packed with coconut and honey. So sweet and light, but also mega filling. With this in my tummy, I was ready to be an explorer. Next stop, Lions Rock.

With low hanging clouds floating over the site, I gasped as I witnessed the rock close up. It looked like it rose dramatically from the central plains. Near-vertical walls soar to a flat-topped summit. From afar the rock looks impossible to hike and your mind is trying to work out how you ascend this mammoth rock. There are a series of staircases attached to the walls to reach the top. On the way up, you pass a collection of extraordinary frescoes and a pair of colossal lion's paws carved into the bedrock, hence the name Lion Rock. The surrounding landscape, where you catch glimpses of lily-pad-covered moats as you glance back down, adds to Sigiriya's royal mystique. This would be a Christmas I would remember for a lifetime.

As I reached the top, I gasped. You feel welcomed into the Sri Lankan secret - the enigmatic rocky outcrop of Sigiriya is Sri Lanka's single most dramatic sight, from afar and on top. The summit contains the ruins of an ancient civilisation, thought to be once the epicentre of the short-lived kingdom of Kassapa. There are spellbinding misty views as the sun is burning through the clouds. I spent time exploring the ruins and enjoying the views, taking lots of photos and making memories for when I want to go back and relive that day again. Standing in my colourful yoga pants, I treasure one photo where I am performing a pretend star jump move. No idea who took the photo, but I think they encouraged it. I love it.

As I returned to the ground and reality, queues and local people were swarming the site like eager bees. Lots of locals - all taking their time. I smiled as I thought how accurate the advice provided by the dad was. No one wants to get stuck amongst the slow walking locals.

I returned to my homestay, ready to move to a new plush hotel for Christmas Day.

After lots of goodbyes from the dad and son, they dropped me and my backpack off at my posh new hotel. I felt like a feral backpacker arriving into a slice of eco-luxury deep in the jungle. I picked the hotel for the outdoor pool with views of Lion Rock, where I spent Christmas swimming laps and with each lap I caught a glimpse out towards the rock – what an unreal Christmas evening. I felt so at peace, surrounded by the energy of this enigmatic natural wonder as the backdrop to the lush green hotel gardens with tea lights that lit up the pool area. I sat in the outdoor lounge bar sipping on a honey and ginger tea, listen to me – the gin girl is long gone, when I called Scotland to check in on the family Christmas. Their day just getting lively, while I was in full wind-down mood. Christmas 2019 done.

Over the next four nights, I experienced the trio of Kandy, Nuwara Eliya and Ella. All connected via the most scenic train ride, maybe in the world. The train journey starts from Kandy where I spent one day and night exploring the Buddhist temples, the central lake and eating cake. The next day I arrived early at the station to get in line and queue for the train tickets, they are like gold dust. Before I flew into Sri Lanka, I tried to buy tickets online, but they were long gone. In the end, after queuing with the rest of the backpacker stragglers, I had in my hand a 2nd class unreserved ticket – only entitled to set foot onto the train, nothing else. Even that would be challenging as I glanced at the mobbed platform, feeling a little uneasy.

When the train finally arrived, late, madness followed. Everyone was on tenterhooks waiting to poach any unreserved seats as soon as the train stopped, and it was tricky to work out where the train would stop on the platform and how to position yourself. When the train finally stopped, the chaos began. Sometimes it is best to travel solo as you only need to look out for one person – that person you. I ended up on the train – hurray and in a carriage that appeared to be the reserved 2nd class carriage. I knew this and knew this wasn't my carriage, but from what I could see of the unreserved carriage, you couldn't breathe in there.

My newly adopted carriage seemed chilled with everyone taking their designated seats. I took a seat, like a complete opportunist, and waited to be moved. I did that thing where you look out the window, pretending this is clearly your seat as you are so comfortable in your surroundings. No one came to move me along and claim the seat, so I claimed it. I sat expecting to eventually be moved as more people came into the carriage - it never happened. As I glanced out the window onto the platform, there seemed to be a panic infused scene as the unreserved carriage stood jam-packed. People with their backpacks still trying to timidly get on, some were trying to launch onto it and others had admitted defeat.

Meanwhile, I sat feeling a little guilty but also a bit smug. The train started to depart, rolling past lots of people who hadn't made it. Even now I don't understand this. Why didn't they make it onto the train? In the end, I sat across from a local man and an English couple. Turns out they paid $30 for their tickets. I think I paid £1.40. They looked at me like I had magic powers. I shrugged – clearly they were scammed. But at least they were on the train.

As for me, I am a chancer. The ticket attendant who eventually appeared did, at every opportunity, tell me I wasn't supposed to be in that carriage and that seat, but never ever told me to leave. So, each time I would sit, nod and smile in agreement – as he was correct.

The train meandered through the countryside with manicured tea plantations, where tea pickers popped up like little dots on the horizon, and cool misty mountain backdrops were the norm. It felt such a unique journey. Never quite sure what the next turn would bring, it never failed to amaze though as sweeping views of valleys packed with lush greenery popped into view. I stuck my head out the window to quickly spot legs dangling out the carriage doors and cameras poking out every window taking it all in. The train follows the twists and turns of the track into the never-ending distance. I broke up the journey to Ella with an overnight stop at Nuwara Eliya. It felt like a slice of the British countryside tucked into the middle of Sri Lanka. What a country.

From the start of the trip, I plotted a vague plan with the hope to arrive in the wilderness of the South for New Year's Eve. As I made my way South, I would hear a whisper from inside – my inner critic – "You should be around people in some strobe light-infused bar for NYE." Instead, all I wanted and longed for was the peace of nature. To be alone. To simply be.

The thought of ending and starting the year in nature was my new high. After navigating the bus system across Sri Lanka, I arrived at my NYE homestay. I felt this little buzz of excitement as I met my new local family. They welcomed me into their home deep in the outskirts of the National Park.

As I was shown to my room, I heard myself mutter, "Wow." It felt like an eco-village lodge. The room looked brand new, with a massive walk-in shower, and King size poster bed. Then I turned and gasped a little. The bedroom led out to an enormous balcony overlooking a lush green garden with a jungle vibe. I could hear the animal calls in the distance and the sound of the leaves falling. I knew this was the reason I came to the South – to feel the stillness run through my body.

I had arrived at my dream destination for NYE. And, again, felt a bit smug. This was all planned and made possible by me. High five to that.

After some confusion, the homestay confirmed in the next hour I would head onto my first ever elephant safari. Until now, I had been feeling quite casual about it all. That changed when the jeep arrived with the local guide to collect us. An English traveller arrived just after me and her arrival made the NYE safari trip possible. The thought of experiencing elephants in the wild had us buzzing with excitement and I felt her energy rub off on me. I remember thinking, I wonder if we will see any elephants?

The UdaWalawe National Park felt special the minute the jeep drove through the entrance gate - we instantly drove alongside a herd of elephants. I felt goosebumps and the biggest smile appear on my face. "Unreal," I muttered. It continued, elephant after elephant strolled into view. Some moving as a herd, others looked lost at the back doing their own thing, then I spotted the cutest sight of the day - a mother elephant and her calf! Strolling through the greenness – the animal kingdom definitely makes you stop and ponder life a little.

They had us "Ooohing" and "Aaahing" for ages until our driver decided it was time to carry on. A truly breathtaking experience. My fellow traveller was great fun. We were nearly wetting ourselves laughing as we both got the fright of our lives as we turned the corner to be greeted by, well, more elephants. But this time they were right there in front of us. Inches away from the jeep. Maybe three adult elephants. One less than an inch away from the Jeep door, where we sat as still as statues. The local driver didn't warn us on how we should behave, you could feel the elephant's breath and every movement made you sit still with fear it would use its trunk to toss the jeep over. As we enquired about our safety, he explained we were safe unless there is a sudden movement to disturb them. Eek. No sudden movements, please.

As we were so close to these amazing creatures, we had to get some candid shots. I went first and sat poised with the breathing elephant behind me. As I smiled at the camera, I whispered, "You will tell me if it looks like it is on the attack". She nodded. Then we slowly and bravely switched seats, I kept my attention on the elephant while trying to snap away. What an experience, slightly terrifying but wonderful! Of all the photos of that trip, that one makes me smile the most. Sitting like the queen of the safari with the elephant in the background, inches away. Pure joy on my face, hiding the fact I was terrified.

As the sun started to set, we spotted a herd of water buffalos, you guessed it, in the water. We sat watching them mesmerised. There is something about being a little lost in the world and nature - in the presence of the animal kingdom as the sun set on 2019 - to invigorate and inspire you into the New Year. The year 2020. That night we enjoyed a local curry at a nearby restaurant - nothing grand or glamourous. Soon in bed by 11 pm, I fell asleep ready to dream about the next adventure that waited for me.

New Year's Day started with a refreshing run followed by the most amazing home-cooked breakfast. My favourite coconut and honey filled pancakes were presented - yippee - and I experienced my first hopper of the trip. Egg hoppers are a staple in Sri Lankan cuisine, essentially a nested egg cooked in coconut milk and a rice-based crispy crepe. Served with curry. Yes to that!

We spent the morning back at the Udawalawe National Park, but this time it felt a little different. We arrived to watch the morning feed at the Elephant Transfer Home. Its primary objective is to rehabilitate orphaned elephant calves for ultimate release back into the wild. Seeing them at feeding time from the viewing platform made my day. At one point, I couldn't stop laughing. They were all lined up in a single file, and when the keeper allowed them to walk up to where they are fed, each of their personalities would come out. Some played it cool, others started by playing it cool, then went for a last-minute sprint and lunge for the milk, then others bolted for the milk the minute they were allowed to. The joy.

As we said goodbye to the elephants, we also said goodbye to the best Sri Lankan family ever. I felt sad to say goodbye but knew the next adventure was around the corner.

A bus journey later, I arrived at the beach with no real plans other than to slow down and chill. The first two weeks had been full-on, travelling continuously with no real base for more than a couple of days. I knew I wanted to learn to surf - you know, become that surf chick at the grand old age of 36. With a little list of coastal villages and beach areas to decide on, I based myself in Weligama for six days.

I got into a little beach town chilled routine.

This girl 100% ready to live the chilled life. I would wake early and run, sometimes at sunrise, sometimes later. Head to the local rooftop morning yoga session, then stroll one level down for the smoothie bowl goodness and real coffee bean fix. Followed by a surf lesson! Whoop. Then maybe some reading or an afternoon exploring. Before an early dinner and bedtime. It probably sounds boring to a lot of people, I would have been one of those people. But I've partied all over the world and suffered the epic hangovers. Now I am deciding how to live my life every day rather than allowing the booze-fuelled life to takeover, and well ruin these experiences! There are epic experiences to enjoy, and they do not need a hangover.

I remember walking to my first ever surf lesson. I felt that mix of nerves and excitement bubble inside. Not quite sure the last time I tried something completely new where I would be taken so far out my comfort zone. The eternal learner excited for what could become of this surfing thing, it looked so free and wild, but also I knew the reality could be very different. Then I noticed the voice – that inner critic that lives inside my head, in all our heads, and if I don't control it, it controls me. It started to say, "Oh do you think you are going to be any good at this surfing?" followed by, "Of course you won't. You are always terrible at new stuff". I could feel the nerves take over from the excitement and a bit of dread seep in that I would be terrible. Then I woke up, metaphorically, and realised I didn't need to listen to the made-up thoughts swirling round my mind. Thoughts that our ego likes to pump into our head to protect us from failure, from trying something new. I slowly heard the other voice in my head rise and take charge - my cheerleader! Explaining to my inner critic, "Is that not the point in lessons - to learn, make mistakes and grow. To try and experience new things, take ourselves out of our comfort zone?". One of my favourite quotes in life came to mind, "What if I fail. Oh, but darling, what if you fly". I quietened that little self-doubt voice and felt ready to fly. Don't allow the self-doubt, that lives in us all, hold you back. Free yourself and have the most amazing experience.

Of course, my first lesson and the three I eventually had were a rollercoaster. At times I was terrible. Sometimes I genuinely fell face-first into the ocean sliding across the sandbank, holding onto my bikini bottoms while spitting out the salty sea that made it up my nose. But I kept dusting myself off to get back on the board, ready for my instructor to shout, "start paddling." The feeling when you judge the incoming wave, jump up and stand surfing the wave. That feeling is something else. Sometimes I would ride it out, other times I would jump up to immediately nosedive as I mistimed it or start to doubt the wave and jump off the board. But when I caught the wave, it felt effortless. You felt your body and the board rise in unison.

At the end of the third day, I told my surf instructor I felt ready to go solo. He smiled and never questioned my choice. He had been amazing - these guys have all the patience in the world and a way of delivering feedback in such a way you don't feel like a terrible surfer, but more encouraged to keep trying. My instructor - the typical Sri Lankan surf-dude type, with the most striking eyes and stare, long shoulder-length hair and the full hipster beard. Handsome but full of nonsense. What a way of life. Late-night partying and early morning surfing.

My last lesson turned out to be my favourite - I surfed at sunset. What an amazing experience, pretty difficult to explain - it felt like the energy from the sun transferred into the water as it started to set on the horizon. A mix of urgency and calm. Everyone knew this was the last of the day's surf as the light dimmed, the beach busy with backpackers taking photos and sitting reflecting, locals playing cricket. If only you could bottle up that feeling.

The first time I went out myself to surf, I felt nervous again. I waited for ages out at sea lying on the board - I couldn't catch a wave. I could feel the frustration set in and my newly earned surf confidence start to slowly decline. Then I spotted a couple of young local boys who were on fire. They would lie on their boards waiting for when they saw the surf start to bubble, then their arms would start to paddle frantically. I decided to use them as my nudge. I swam nearby and lined my board with them and waited, then when they went, I went. And I grabbed my first wave solo – what a feeling.

That feeling of accomplishment – this is why we try new stuff.

Remember that quote, "but darling, what if you fly." I flew. Of course, there were constant up and downs, high and lows, but I surfed all by myself!

That night I celebrated my solo surf achievement by heading out with a German backpacker staying at my hotel. We met at the pool, he found himself solo after his friends flew home earlier than him. We jumped into a tuk-tuk towards the spot everyone spoke about. The Doctor's House is a 200-year-old former Dutch and Ayurvedic hospital that sits just off the beach. What a setting. The brainchild of a couple of Australian guys who brought an insane vibe to this pocket of the west coast. Everyone seemed to be there - I even saw the local surf guys! Live music blared out as everyone chilled. A mix of hippy and hipster types.

As the Doctors' House closed, we moved over to the opposite 'Chill Bar' on the water's edge where everyone danced on the sand. This place summed up my Sri Lankan experience. A collective energy and vibe. Everyone chasing the same wave, that wave of energy you get from travelling and freeing your mind. A feeling of bliss circled this place. We were wholly present in the moment.

On my last day at the surf beach, I waited a lifetime to catch a wave during a sunset surf. I felt that frustration again. I wanted this surf to be as magical as the one with my instructor. Then, as I started to think maybe I should call it quits and return the board early, I caught a wave and felt the euphoria, the surge of energy from the wave moves into my body. I went back for more, and in the next 20 minutes, got another handful of waves in.

Sometimes in life, we need to let go of the expectation created in our mind and go with the flow. Stop forcing the outcome. Surfing felt intense, but so is any new skill or activity. We want to jump from 'never tried' novice to an expert within minutes. To even consider I would one day surf blew my mind. To then go on and do it, felt next level. A little proud that I silenced the inner critic voice, and just went for it – nose-diving and all. The day I first surfed myself, I could hear the voice. It is normal. It is there to protect us, even reign us in. But sometimes, we just don't need it and need to gently thank it for its words and hush it calmly.

After five days in Weligama I got used to the slow paced way of life - running, surfing, lying in the yogi child pose, reading, catching sunsets and day-tripping to the neighbouring area. Galle is up there as the jewel of day trips. The whole historic town is a World Heritage Site with imposing Dutch-colonial buildings, ancient mosques and churches, grand mansions and museums. With laneways to get lost down, hipster cafés to entice you in, all the quirky boutiques and colonial architecture around the imposing Fort. Koggala, home of the Sri Lankan stilt fisherman where men sit perched far from shore atop crude crucifixes of sticks and twine, dangling fishing rods into schools of fish. Most of them staged for the backpacker tourist photo opportunity – I sneaked in a photo. And Mirissa Beach - a vision of tropical bliss with powdery pale sand, cobalt blue water and picturesque coconut palms, where the Instagram crowd descends on for the candid travel photoshoot.

This pocket of Sri Lanka has you hooked, but sadly nothing is forever.

And just like that, I arrived back in the capital Colombo, where my trip started. I spent one last day ticking off all the sites. That evening I strolled down the promenade where an electric atmosphere was in full flow as local families enjoyed the full moon holiday. An energy whirling around. I enjoyed some fresh chopped pineapple from a food stall, living life like a local now. When I first arrived, I felt wary of this unfamiliar country, but now I felt the warmth from the people. Respectful, playful, gentle, and a little curious. They took me in and treated me like one of their own.

As I jumped into the pre-arranged taxi to the airport I knew I had once again completed another new country without any dramas or scams, a little more tanned and enlightened than before I arrived. There is always a feeling of relief when you know very soon your potential travel danger radar will switch off and I will back in Glasgow.

Yes, in everyday life there are dangers of being knocked off your bike, missing the train to work and being late for an important meeting or locking yourself out of your flat, but the potential travel danger is next level. I certainly didn't plan for this taxi ride to be a potential danger. Always expect the unexpected, until the bitter end.

The driver seemed standard Sri Lanka friendly - very chatty. His English wasn't amazing, but I understood everything he told me, which turned out to be a lot. I learned about his family, where he lived, the house he was building, how he likes to be a taxi driver. Then, as we continued on the journey, he started to tell me I seemed a nice girl, and I was long.

Listening to my music with one earbud in, at the description of 'long', I sat up a bit in the backseat. Turned out he liked how I was tall but kept saying long - I chuckled a little. He would try and catch my eye, smile and ask if I was ok. By now, I felt I had to be a bit more assertive. I paused my music. He asked if we could go for dinner. "What!" I screamed in my head – now super alert. People baffle me most of the time. I became very confused about this taxi exchange. Why, when in a taxi to the airport, would I want to go on a dinner date with my driver. I paused my music to explain I wasn't hungry as I had recently eaten some food, so if we could just head to the airport - you know - for my flight. We drove some more. More compliments flowed - mainly he kept with the "you are long" line. I've had worse.

Not done with the prospect of a dinner date, the next thing I know he is explaining how there is a nice beach near the airport, we should maybe stop off there. At first, I tried not to laugh out loud. I generally thought someone must be winding me up here. Why would someone in a taxi on the way to the airport, suddenly have all this extra time for some dinner and a late-night random visit to the beach? I am usually sweating at the airport after seeing all the queues when I realise I haven't calculated the time for this. I certainly didn't have time or the incline to entertain this local's friendly suggestions.

Instead of laughing, I looked him sternly in the eye, through the rear-view mirror, and explained after spending three weeks in this amazing country, I didn't need to see another beach in the pitch black - so if we could just drive directly to the airport that would be amazing.

He looked insulted that I turned down the best night of my life.

I felt a sense of relief when I saw the lights at the airport. Hopefully, I would soon be walking through the departure terminal free from the intense stare of the driver. He had one last suggestion. He knew a nearby petrol station that sold cigarettes. He asked if I wanted to leave the airport drop off lane and head to the petrol station. I nearly choked on my words, while again trying not to laugh at the absurdity of it. Once again, I explained all I needed him to do was to keep driving forward into the lane labelled 'Airport Departures'. He shook his head and said it is busy. Mr Driver, I have a flight to catch. I don't care if the airport, the queue into the airport building or the queue into the airport carpark is busy. I have something really important to make sure I am not late for. This was becoming exhausting.

As we drove through the airport carpark barrier, I felt relief surge back into my body. As I jumped out, he scurried around to hand over my backpack from the car – like the friendliest local man ever. I quickly flung it on my back, waved him goodbye without looking him in the eye, soon safely inside the airport building. Exhausted, mentally exhausted.

If taxi drivers aren't trying to scam you for cash, they are trying to get some backpacker extras from you! What an opportunist. The rules of the travel game are clear - be nice, smile but always remain alert, and be prepared for opportunists. Don't let them ruin your day, or trip, though. Although this is my last experience in Sri Lanka, this is not my lasting memory. Breathe, smile, and wave goodbye to the opportunists as nice people and fun adventures are waiting around the corner. And that is the end of Sri Lanka.

Sri Lanka takes you on the ultimate journey if you let yourself experience everything to your core - the good, the bad, the difficult, and the exhilarating. Let yourself feel it and be changed by it. Shaken, terrified, and inspired by it. Let what you feel change your life. Let it make you a person who isn't afraid to be vulnerable, isn't afraid to love, isn't afraid to face the world head-on.

I am forever grateful for being a wanderer and experiencing all the lessons this amazing world provides. To every local person who takes me under their wing and makes it their mission to turn a moment into a memory. I am forever grateful.

To the tuk-tuk driver who held my hand as we chased the highs of walking through waterfalls in the highlands, to the elderly man who motioned on the bus to take one of my bags onto his lap to give me space, to the boy who worked the local bakery where I would buy the most amazing banana bread, to the young boy who carried my backpack across the train tracks and waited for my air-conditioned minibus to arrive, and to every homestay owner who treated me like a princess. And lastly to the man in his 80s, with no teeth, who sold me a collection of postcards on the beach. He proclaimed I was rich, and I let him into a secret, he was – to live in a country like Sri Lanka.

We may not share the same religion, culture, or skin colour. We may live on completely different sides of the world and have different day-to-day routines. But we share the same outlook on life. Your warmth will forever stay with me. We are all part of a bigger greater good. You welcomed me into your community, and I will pay it forward by living a life with no barriers, boundaries or borders, driven by human connection.

Sri Lanka reminds you that life is a gift. 35,000 Sri Lankans died in the 2004 Boxing Day Tsunami. While staying on the coast, I visited a memorial where the 18 meter Buddha statue, donated by the Japanese, is the same height as the destructive wave which devastated the nearby coastal village during the Tsunami. This spot saw true horror in 2004. A train passing by, hit by the tsunami wave.

Life goes on, but they will forever live in the shadows of this terror. I ran to the memorial and on the run back, I paused on the beach to take it all in. Life isn't fair, tragedy happens and there is no explanation. There is no going back. We can only move forward. There is no divine intervention, we can't rewrite what happened but live a full life for anyone taken too soon. The universe is a complex system, far too complex to predict at times. We need to surrender and, while we can, enjoy the ride of our life. Find joy in the simple way of life, as there may not be a tomorrow. So don't wait for the big things as they may never materialise. Sri Lanka taught me how precious life is. I will forever live it to its fullest.

Sri Lanka

"We don't stop playing because we grow old; we grow old because we stop playing."

– George Bernard Shaw

Ethiopia: Introduce playfulness into your life and let the wildness flow in

Africa is the one continent I need to explore more, so much more. I have a list and, if the Covid-19 pandemic didn't happen, a few more African countries would be ticked off by now.

Instead, I will always have the two weeks I spent in a country that opened my eyes to creating your own opinion of somewhere and appreciating what you have.

You can think what you want on coincidences, or whether we are all part of a grand masterplan. I believe in a bit of both. I believe we are all walking on our own invisible paths where along the way you will, not knowingly, encounter a crossroads – a decision point. If you are awake to it, you will be a participant in the decision at the crossroads. Other people will be walking along their path on auto-pilot, letting life drift by. Unaware of the choices being presented to them.

For a couple of years, I followed an Irish guy online, a mad traveller on a mission to step foot in every country. I felt invested in his journey, and along the way, would become inspired to travel to some of those same countries. I can thank Johnny for writing a blog about the Faroe Islands, one of the few people who have, which became the basis for my trip there. I knew he also ran a non for profit adventure tour company with his friend where you spend a few days supporting a local community before exploring the country as a group. I signed up for his newsletters back in 2016, not realising I planted a seed that would bloom three years later.

At the start of the year, I always plan my travels for the year ahead. In 2019 I received a newsletter listing the future adventures offered by his company. My heart skipped a beat when I glanced at the newsletter and read 'Ethiopia'. The trip involved providing a water well to a local community. Back then, Ethiopia sat high on my travel list, but for whatever reason, I hadn't made any plans to travel there. Any time I glanced at an organised trip, I would close the web browser. None of them jumped out at me.

Things soon started to happen to make Ethiopia become a reality.

As I looked again at the newsletter I felt this intense excitement, where I stood at the crossroads of a trip of a lifetime, the Ethiopia trip was planned for October – my birthday month. Everything would be arranged, all I had to do was click the apply button and figure out flights there. I felt that feeling, a mix of anxiousness and excitement – the universal sign that greatness awaited around the corner. After sleeping on it, I knew the decision. A week later, I pressed the apply button and sent the application form off for what would become the star attraction in my 2019 itinerary, the year I also visited Slovakia, Azerbaijan, Georgia, Armenia, Kosovo, Sicily, North Macedonia, Albania, Spain, Italy and Faroe Islands. Ethiopia added to the end. What a year. As I type this, it is the year 2021 and I'm not even sure when I will travel again. I am jealous of that travel year – 2019, I went all in.

A full nine months to wait and overthink a few things. I wouldn't say I am a massive overthinker, or if I do, I don't let it prevent the thing I am thinking about. It feels like part of travelling the world. Considering everything that can go wrong, making sure whatever you can do to prevent it happens, or at least plan for it, otherwise let it go.

Weirdly for someone who, on the surface, looks outgoing and can get on with most people, I worried about the people on the tour. A trip to Ethiopia isn't standard, so there is the risk of some oddballs – no one wants to be stuck with oddballs. Plus, I love my own space and that feeling of freedom. I know from the other group tours I have done – Jordan, Israel, Kosovo, India and Nepal – you can easily get booked up with a strange group. I have always been lucky. I felt it bubble away though, the feeling of unease. As I couldn't do much about it, I let it go and hoped they would be normal like me. Well as normal as normal is nowadays.

With all my trips that year, October suddenly arrived and I flew overnight from London direct to the capital Addis Ababa.

Ethiopia, as the only African country to have escaped European colonialism, kept much of its cultural identity – leading to the potential for an experience of a lifetime. A landlocked country in the Horn of Africa where archaeologists found a trace of life dating back 3 million years ago. Lucy is the common name of several hundred pieces of fossilized bone representing 40% of the skeleton of a female species – the species thought to be a small-bodied and small-brained relative of the human species. With this in mind, I felt ready to step foot on the same path as my ancient relative. What a gem from Ethiopia - 3 million years. Blows your mind.

Eight hours later, I arrived in Addis Ababa, not 100% ready, but at least I made it.

I booked the same hotel where the tour would begin the next day. I slowly made my way out of the airport terminal, walking away from the swarm of taxi drivers waiting for eager travellers to collect. As I glanced at each name on their handwritten sheets of paper, I felt that anxious feeling bubble away as you are trying to appear calm and in control but as each card displayed another name, I could feel that sinking feeling. Then from nowhere, I suddenly spotted a small Ethiopian man rushing up waving a name card as if he knew me – as I glanced at it, I felt relief fill my body and my shoulders drop. There in front of me, my name shining in the daylight sunshine, scribbled with a black marker.

The hotel minibus driver brought back another solo traveller, and we soon discovered we were both signed up for the same tour. Result. I suddenly felt more relief flood in. She seemed perfectly normal – like my level of normal, I knew we would be ok together if everyone else turned out to be strange.

After checking in and enjoying the free breakfast offered to us, we were soon dropped off in the heart of Addis. The hectic capital, a complete maze - new skyscrapers on dirt roads next to traditional markets where rural customs are preserved. The name Addis Ababa translates as "New Flower" in the Amharic language and is the pulsing heart of this eclectic nation. I had my face up to the window, never quite sure what to expect from a new country - this felt chaotic and calm. I know, surely a contradiction.

Our first stop, Tomoca - the famous coffee spot. As one of the oldest coffee spots in the city, we were surprised to experience a fully authentic Ethiopian café, not ruined by the Instagram tourists as, well, I don't think they visit this country, serving up mainly locals and a splash of tourists. This is the land of the finest Arabica coffee - as legend would have it - discovered by an Ethiopian shepherd boy and his goats sometime around the sixth century. It became a staple of the trip – "macchiato coffee, please".

We felt brave enough to wander the streets, exploring with all our senses, and see what local food we could find. There were playful fruit sellers, young boys trying to impress us with their orange juggling skills, and locals insistent on helping us out as we looked for food. One local insisted on giving us his phone number in case we needed any help, we explained we had no connection. When I'm with others on my travels, I let my guard down a little as you feel safer in numbers but as two western females deep in the heart of the city the danger radar was ON.

I read about The Taitu Hotel, built in 1905 when the Ethiopian Empress established this hotel to provide foreign guests with a place to rest and dine. It soon became our sanctuary from the baying locals, all ready to help us. It provided our first experience of what we would know Ethiopia for, terrible service and general confusion. We sat at a table and waited, waited for the menu. And waited some more. It finally arrived. We waited for the server to take our order. We waited for the food. They don't seem to understand any kind of service, like the basic 'this is a restaurant in a historic building that tourists will come to visit' type of service.

As a vegetarian, I'd been looking forward to the Ethiopian cuisine - the blogs raved about the veggie options. It's a rite of passage to try the local staple injera - a spongy pancake-like bread piled with various vegetables and delicious spicy sauces. When it finally arrived, I took my first mouthful of injera and, well, it didn't blow me away. I so hoped to love it. Sadly, there is no flavour in Ethiopian food and I would soon find out it is best to stick with bland tomato pasta - for you and your tummy.

We managed to make our way back to the hotel with the help of a local called David who we bumped into outside. After a word with his driver, they welcomed the opportunity to return us safely to the other side of the city. He was a diplomat and showed us how welcoming the Ethiopians are. He even shared his phone number so we could reach him if we needed any help. The world of travelling needs more David's.

That night we bumped into some of our group at the hotel reception area. After a quick outfit change, we were soon jumping into taxis to the lively area of the city. You don't imagine Ethiopians like you and I in the Western world. Sitting in bars with music playing or football shown on the screens mounted on the wall captivating the crowds, sipping pints of beer while eating pizzas. But they do. They are like you and I. Well not everyone in Ethiopia, since there is a class divide and real poverty. But likewise, not everyone in Scotland has the privilege I have to travel the world.

As I sat in amongst the tour group, everyone trying to suss each other out, discovering what country they were from, their route to

Africa, how they found out about the trip, any first day experiences - I knew I had a decision to make. A decision on whether I was going to have a drink with the group. That January I had stopped drinking. With no big grand plan, milestone, or challenge - I just knew I wanted my life to be different. In the end, I stopped quite organically.

I felt my life was more difficult than it needed to be when I drank alcohol. Cradling a hangover around most of the next day, maybe even into the day after. Then not feeling 100% again until Thursday, that old cliché, to start over again on Friday. Stuck in a vicious cycle where I would be the party girl at weekends - eat all the rubbish food, wander about with no sleep, then train and be all healthy midweek - even accomplish things like a marathon. I achieved some amazing running goals as a party girl, but I made it harder for myself trying to train around my hangover. Way harder than it needed to be.

At the end of 2018 whiling hiking in Nepal I didn't drink for ten days. I felt amazing. More present, connected and completely inspired to change my life. Maybe surrounding yourself in nature is the trick to challenging years of ingrained behaviour. I started to feel that I didn't need alcohol in my life to have fun. After the trip to Nepal, I flew back to start a new 12-week marathon training programme, where I committed to using the run, partly as an excuse, to not drink. It made it easier to explain to others why I choose to stop when they constantly questioned my decision.

Fast forward ten months and I still hadn't drank. This my first real 'should I just drink' challenge. We use alcohol to socialise, connect and fill any social awkwardness. It is the instant 'I can talk to strangers' or 'I can do anything' confidence booster. As everyone gave the waiter their boozy orders, I paused as I could feel it, the itch and little voice in my head whispering, "Just join in, have one drink. Go on – you won't single yourself out that way." The temptation there, I also know the reason why I continue not to drink. That reason needs to be stronger than that little voice in your head.

As I felt myself swaying between remaining sober and having a drink, I explained to those sitting near I hadn't drank since January. Just like that, Johnny turned and explained the guy next to him, soon to be introduced as Jordan, had started a sober challenge – thankfully they all got it. I felt that ease drift away as I looked the waiter in the eye and asked for an orange juice. Phew.

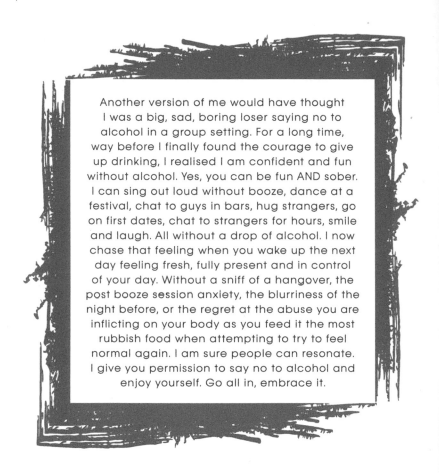

Another version of me would have thought I was a big, sad, boring loser saying no to alcohol in a group setting. For a long time, way before I finally found the courage to give up drinking, I realised I am confident and fun without alcohol. Yes, you can be fun AND sober. I can sing out loud without booze, dance at a festival, chat to guys in bars, hug strangers, go on first dates, chat to strangers for hours, smile and laugh. All without a drop of alcohol. I now chase that feeling when you wake up the next day feeling fresh, fully present and in control of your day. Without a sniff of a hangover, the post booze session anxiety, the blurriness of the night before, or the regret at the abuse you are inflicting on your body as you feed it the most rubbish food when attempting to try to feel normal again. I am sure people can resonate. I give you permission to say no to alcohol and enjoy yourself. Go all in, embrace it.

That night, and many nights on this trip, I sat in the company of a group of strangers, who eventually became friends where we shared stories, made memories, laughed a lot – all without a single drop of alcohol. They would sometimes proclaim, "We wish we met you when you were on the booze." I told them the truth – "I'm the same".

We are our own energy, vibe, and buzz. Strip away the alcohol and many people will feel lost - I felt more alive. Way more in control, present and appreciative. Yeah, me and alcohol have a history, we had some ride together. But that rollercoaster ride, for now, is on pause! I am on the nature and chilled ride instead.

Following another day in Addis exploring some of the attractions, and getting to know each other, we were soon on a minibus heading into the rural plains of Ethiopia. It felt dusty and well, very African. Which I know sounds silly – of course it would feel African. But that is the thing, some countries don't feel how they should. If anything Ethiopia was more African than I thought.

Before I flew out to start the trip, we received an email from the company explaining the project coordinator had sourced a village to receive the new water well about a year ago. However, recently following some tribal warfare in the community, they decided to play it safe and move to a different community.

Leading up to this, I didn't feel any unease about travelling to Ethiopia or visiting a rural part of the country. Suddenly I found myself re-reading the email, in particular, 'tribal warfare'. "Oh well," I thought. I am sure it will be ok. The answer to all worries.

Our group of seventeen, from all around the world, spent three days in the local community where our donations funded a water well. Previously the community walked 1.5 hours on a round-trip every day to source water from the river. The water in the region tainted with high levels of fluoride, killing the kid's teeth and the adult's bones. A local African based charity made it happen. With our donations and help from the village leaders, the project started. Following our visit, the well provided irrigation for farming and, more importantly, freshwater for 140 village households! Of course, we weren't involved in the drilling, can you imagine, so instead, we were welcomed by the villagers who opened their school doors so we could give the school a little facelift. It felt a privilege to access the local community life to see the 'real' Ethiopia and give back.

That is what I realised life is about. Giving back to the community, either in your own country or right here in Africa where they need our support. There is a Chinese saying that goes, "If you want happiness for a year, inherit a fortune. If you want happiness for a lifetime, help somebody." Even Winston Churchill knew happiness is found in helping others, "We make a living by what we get; we make a life by what we give." Giving back activates the feel-good vibes inside our brains. Whatever the reason, it does feel good, and of course makes a difference, regardless of how big or small the act. I much prefer being hands-on, experiencing the community I am supporting. Something that this trip allowed me to explore.

As we were introduced to the school kids, I felt a sudden surge of emotion. Relieved for my sunglasses to hide the tears that would well up while I tried to compose myself. The community had no idea we were coming. To witness their faces gazing quizzingly at us, to then slowly warm to us and in the end welcome us in like their own, broke my heart. After getting over the idea that a bunch of westerners were roaming about, splashing colour on their school walls, they soon had us all under their spell. These kids have nothing, so to give a little back was special and something I'll remember for a lifetime.

I probably use travelling as a release, an escape from the daily grind. It is a chance to reset - let my mind wander, shoulders drop from the daily stresses that build up and provide perspective to bring back into my day to day. We are conditioned in the western world to strive for more: a bigger house, the latest car, job promotions, and all the designer gear. Everything is disposable - your dinner one click away. We chase likes and followers, selfies layered with filters as everyone tries to out-compete. In Africa, life is simpler - meals made from the food grown from the land, things happen when they happen. There is an appreciation for each day. What will be, will be. No one seems in a rush - they are living in the moment. Or the truth, the real raw truth - they have no other choice but to live in the moment. In the west we live so far in the future, we miss so much from life.

At one point, some of the local boys were playing with a football made from rubbish all mashed together into a ball. There are no toy shops in rural Africa. On the last day, we presented them a collection of footballs, alongside some other essential items, and their faces lit up. Each of them looking mischievous, eager to use their new football. As soon as they could, the football kicked onto the playing field where a game played out. The pure joy on their faces.

I've seen real hardship and poverty on my travels. On some trips, you notice they have nothing, but they are happy. It can be confronting, shining a light back on your own life. I've realised we place burdens on ourselves and manifest our own stress with the expectations we associate with life when all we need is very little. Travelling taught me to enjoy the small stuff. The fresh cup of coffee, the smile as you catch someone's eye, a sunset run as you feel the energy of the day disappear.

As we painted the school, we blasted out the tunes to share those playful vibes. The locals didn't seem overly impressed with our choice of music. I spotted a group of boys standing on the side, watching us. As I approached the group, I put on my playlist to invite them to a bit of a dance-off. They looked at me like I was mad, until the eldest boy, who I think was more a man, decided to enter the dance-off. It went from a bit of fun to quite a serious competition.

A small circle of locals formed the dance-off stage. I would show off a couple of moves - completely made up on the spot - then the circle would switch focus to the local where he returned a dance move. It was wild, I was squealing with laughter. It may have been my avoidance technique to get out of the painting work! Sorry group, just entertaining the locals!! I've realised people can be serious – way too serious, always fearing the worst. I like to be playful. I've trained myself to expect little and be surprised by what you do experience. We couldn't communicate as none of the locals spoke English, but where there is music, then there is the opportunity for a Scottish inspired African dance-off. The dancing theme continued into our last day.

They loved to get their photos taken so they could see what they looked like as they don't have any mirrors. One girl was absolutely striking, her personality and smile infectious. The definition of sassy sprang to mind. She would follow me around pointing at who she wanted her photo taken with, like I was her personalised photographer. After a small group of them formed, I again switched on my playlist. It is so difficult when you can't share a conversation. Music seems to connect people across language boundaries. I again stood in the middle of a small circle dancing to some Western music. Miss Sassy looked on in shock while howling with laughter. She was having none of my dance moves and made it clear.

After a while, she shouted some young boys over, signalled over to switch off my music then brought out this tiny and very used-looking phone. From what I could tell, she had two songs on it and demanded one of the young boys show how they dance in Africa. Wow, did they teach me a lesson – I surrendered. I caught the eye of Miss Sassy and we giggled. As I glanced around at the circle of youngsters, my heart broke again. They were standing in a mismatch of clothes. Some torn, some soiled, some missing but no one seemed to care. The displayed the boldness and strength of the African spirit. Life goes on.

The kids were amazing, their big brown eyes curiously watching our every move. Only one person could put fear into them. The village elder. The elder, not like any other elder in Africa. He wore a two-piece suit and walked with an actual spear. He had the authority and charisma of a man in charge of a village. Of course, the playful me took a shine to him. I like a man with authority. I met my match, though.

I stood chatting to him, as he couldn't understand English he would answer in the local dialect, then look at the young boys who were all rolling about laughing. As one guy in the group took our photo, I pretended to lean in for a kiss on the cheek and, wait for it, he turned quickly to receive a full kiss on his cheek. Massively shocked, I tried not to overreact or lose it by giggling. The boldness captured in a photo. That kiss. Would it be my last kiss in Ethiopia? To be continued.

We soon packed up and waved goodbye to the community. At the last ceremony, I glanced around at the faces of the locals and felt this rush of emotion again. I slipped on my sunglasses as I once again felt touched by this experience, and tears filled my eyes.

When you realise where you are born is the main decider of your quality of life, it is difficult to process. So many people around the world don't have the privilege of what we take for granted. Their smiles would break your heart as you realise people in the west have forgotten how to be happy. I practice gratitude each day, every morning listing ten things I am grateful for. It balances you and grounds your expectations from life. Stops you from chasing the big stuff and living in the future. It focuses your mind on the present and what you do have. I always list my travel memories as one item.

Those feelings I felt during the three days, a constant reminder to live a full life.

Back in Addis, we were booked on an early morning flight to start our next adventure, but first, we popped into our local bar. The bar with grass on the floor. No, not a beer garden but a bar with a ceiling and cut grass sprinkled across the ground. A local would appear and water the cut grass. The grass is a local tradition to bring happiness in – it certainly made me happy watching him undertake this little ritual. We would sit in tiny plastic seats amongst the locals. The waiter wore a white slaughter jacket – I think it might have been a butcher shop as well. Very confusing.

They served a yellow concoction in a Johnnie Walker bottle, usually storing the world-famous Scottish Whiskey. When I enquired about the cloudy looking potion, the man, wearing the butcher coat, poured a shot of what he described as a honey wine, known as Tej. I took a sip. This is Africa, a bar serving their own homebrew. No rules. Only happy green grass vibes.

The next morning, we boarded the small plane taking us to our first destination on the tour itinerary, I knew this next part had all the hallmarks of an epic adventure. Lalibela awaited us. The complex of churches built into the ground out of volcanic rocks.

As everyone took their seats, I sat next to a local. I remember thinking, "Only you." Everyone else sat next to someone in the group. We got chatting, naturally, and it turned out he was an established photographer heading back to Lalibela, his hometown. Can you imagine this as your hometown? Home to eleven medieval monolithic churches of the 13th-century 'New Jerusalem', a high place of Ethiopian Christianity, still today a place of pilgrimage and devotion.

We shared a few stories on the plane. He showed off his portfolio of work – I sat jaw to the ground at his photos, mainly of the Ethiopian wilderness and nature, knowing his shots would soon become my reality. He even wrote my name in the local language on the airplane napkin. We crammed a lot in on the one hour flight.

As we landed in Lalibela, you instantly felt the magnetic pull. We had to wait until the next day to experience the full magnetic pull of energy of the complex of churches. That day soon turned into one of the wildest days in my travel life, the result of my playfulness and I think the universe flinging wildness my way.

Where we stayed had this makeshift gym. As I recovered from a running injury, I used the gym to keep my body ticking over. That morning I ran a couple of km on the clunky treadmill, followed by some stretches and yoga moves. As I moved into the yoga sequence, a couple of local 'lads' arrived to workout. I wasn't sure if they were guests or lived in the town. During my workout, we exchanged no dialogue. So I was surprised as I left when one followed me outside into the morning sunshine. He asked about my plans for that night, then invited me to his birthday party somewhere in the village. He explained he owned a tuk-tuk so could come collect me from the hotel. Sounds like he thought it all out. I wasn't sure what was going on. Was this a VIP invite to his birthday party? I explained we were a group of 17. He mistook this response as my age. After laughing out loud, we cleared up the fact I was not 17. He seemed insistent all 17 of us come to his party in his tuk-tuk. Like that would happen.

He wanted a pickup time, meanwhile I wasn't even sure I had agreed to the party. He suggested 8.30 pm, and explained that he would be waiting at the reception. I shrugged. Had I just agreed for all 17 of us to attend a local's birthday party? No idea, but I knew we had dinner plans. I giggled at breakfast as I announced to the group we had a birthday party invite for that evening. They didn't believe I hadn't encouraged this interaction. I don't think I did.

That morning we set foot inside the wonder of Lalibela. It is so hard to explain what I saw, felt and experienced. Lalibela is history and mystic captured in stone, alive with the rites and awe of Christianity. No matter how many photos I've seen of its breathtaking rock-chiselled churches, nothing can prepare you for the reality of seeing it for yourself – through your eyes. With white-robed pilgrims in their hundreds crowding the courtyards of the churches, reading from the scripture and chanting, it is raw and powerful. It stops you in your tracks.

Lalibela, King of Ethiopia, sought to recreate Jerusalem and structured the churches' landscape and religious sites in such a way as to achieve such a triumph. The churches at Lalibela are clustered in two major groups, one representing the earthly Jerusalem, and the other representing the heavenly Jerusalem. Located directly between them is a trench representing the River Jordan. If the Ethiopians couldn't visit Jerusalem, they built their own version. Mind-blowing.

As the guide walked us through the gigantic site, I would stroll off observing the locals reading from the scripture, sitting chanting, or standing touching the stone churches inhaling in the spiritual essence of what this represented to them. You felt you were witness to something special, a modern-day pilgrimage. All the locals wearing white robes, at times you would tiptoe over them through the churches trying not to disturb. You sometimes caught their eye but it felt they would look through you as they connected with a higher purpose.

We arrived at the last site of the morning tour, the Church of Saint George, the main monolithic church carved downwards into the volcanic rock referred to as the Eighth Wonder of the World.

We all wandered off in various directions trying to take in what we were witnessing in front us. I found myself sat on the edge of the volcanic rock glancing down, where I was involved in a photoshoot - with my airplane photography buddy. Yes, I know. Talk about a chance encounter. I quite literally bumped into him as I strolled the monolithic site a little open-mouthed, taking it all in, not expecting to know anyone other than my tour group. I didn't fully recognise him at first until I did that "Omg look who it is" reaction when my brain finally caught up with who was standing in front of me. Seizing the opportunity, I used my new friend with his pro photography skills to capture the essence of this site from all angles. He loved it. While involved in the photoshoot I spotted someone, someone who, let's just say, caught my eye. I noticed him earlier at one of the other sites - he seemed different. As I made my way down to the base of the church, I noticed him again. He was a local tour group leader. He stepped into the church with his eager group.

I followed them inside and stood nearby. He was the most handsome man in Ethiopia. I remember whispering to the girl I shared a room with that I fancied him. She confirmed his handsome qualities with a nod. As he walked past, I caught his eye and while looking deep into my eyes, he said "Salam." There seemed an intensity to him. My roomie looked at me and I gave her the nod as if to say, omg – did you see that. I suddenly felt like a teenage girl. When most tourists left the majestic church, I took the opportunity to stroll around, to feel the worldly presence of this site. As I walked back up towards the group I saw the handsome tour guide again. Standing alone, nearby. I suddenly found myself boldly approaching my love interest.

I remember feeling a bit nervous and this voice in my head asking, "What is the plan Jacquelyn?" They were zero plans. We exchanged an initial awkward greeting, then some small talk, and he moved things up a level and asked for my phone number. He suggested we could meet later – you know, while in Ethiopia, secured a first date. Yes to that!

The phone number exchange made, I giggled like a teenage As I turned to check on my group, they were all standing looki on. I felt a bit mischievous. I waved him off, soon back on minibus, slightly cringing at my flirty chat. Next we headed to lunch stop. As you would expect with a group of seventeen op minded travellers, there was lots of chatter about my future date in Ethiopia. When I switched on the Wi-Fi, my phone started to beep and beep. I had five messages waiting to be answered. I started to feel nervous, what had I started.

After an afternoon exploring more of the vast and impressive site. We were back at the hotel, and my first date was in touching distance. I felt even more nervous. We were given a couple of hours of downtime before dinner. Some people went for a nap, some to freshen up and others sat at the hotel reception with a drink.

I sneaked out to meet my date.

I didn't even really allow myself to overthink it and went with that feeling of excitement, I felt it deep inside. What is that saying I live my life by, 'Follow Your Joy'. He seemed full of joy. I scurried past the guys in the group, who at first looked on quizzingly while I announced - got to go, got a fruit juice date. I'm pretty sure they shouted to show him a good time. Not sure what they meant!

He stood waiting outside the main gates of the hotel; I felt the awkwardness of it all and tried not to giggle. We walked through the village, the village of one street. Everyone seemed to know him. As we walked by the locals, they would exchange the local greeting and cast a side glance towards my direction. I tried to make myself invisible, as I felt they would show their judgement.

Five minutes later, we were sitting in tiny plastic chairs on the main street sipping our fruit juice – it was an actual fruit juice date. I checked out this place, now the date venue, the day before after reading about it in a blog. When I strolled by, I realised a fruit juice café in Ethiopia differs from the standard juice bar overrun by the clean-living travel hipsters in any other country. Here it looked like a shack, selling two juice options: Banana or Avocado. I played it cool and told him to choose – listen to me. Soon I slurped on a banana delight, while the small talk continued. Fluent in Italian and English, university educated and currently building a home in the outskirts of town, he sounded the absolute catch. As we made eye contact, I could feel myself mutter inside, "So Handsome." I was also secretly giggling away inside my head at how wild this all was. I felt free and untamed, a little sassy - enjoying the boldness of our first encounter which translated into this cute date.

He seemed keen we go a walk. When we met at the hotel entrance, explained we had 45 mins to enjoy our fruit juice date as I had to be back for my group dinner. You could sense him watch the time tick away. Adamant the date required a stroll to the local viewpoint, we soon finished the fruit juice, which he treated me to - what a gentleman - and were next walking past all these local kids playing football.

As we walked past the kids, constantly aware of my surroundings, the viewpoint came into view. It seemed a little romantic. Stunning views looking out towards the lush green valley surrounding the religious site waited for us. As I glanced out looking at the views, he took the opportunity to get close and there may have been a viewpoint smooch, only interrupted by a local mischievous kid. When I asked what the kid shouted, he just laughed. I could sense my love interest wanted to continue to smooch, and I also sensed his excitement. I turned away to enjoy the view explaining we should head back. With one last smooch, I knew my fruit juice date was complete. He wasn't quite done. He attempted to plan our second date for that night. As we strolled back through the village, I again avoided all eye contact with the locals, very aware I was probably one of many female travellers he takes to that viewpoint. At the reception gate, he insisted we try and meet up later after dinner. I smiled, knowing this wouldn't be happening. This girl was quite happy with her day date. As I walked back into the hotel reception, all the guys were still sitting there. I avoided eye contact, feeling like a naughty teenager.

That night we had dinner at the most amazing spot. I first heard about the Scottish inspired hidden gem by the photographer on the plane ride – I told you the universe lined up for us to be sitting next to each other.

The mesmerising design of the restaurant called Ben Ababa stands overlooking the most breathtaking landscape. It is one of the most inspirational places I think I have ever dined. Layered like a maze of different sized terraces, curved sloped walkways, upside down pods, all grabbing your imagination. The unusual designed open-air restaurant is surrounded by 360-degree views taking your gaze deep into the valley out towards the mountains of Lalibela. On reflection, it made the viewpoint earlier on during the fruit juice date seem a little lowkey now. Ben Ababa is built on a hill, the brainchild of a retired Scottish school teacher who first fell in love with this region when she spent some time teaching here. She partnered up with a local and they now co-own this incredible restaurant where the name is a symbol of the blend of

Scottish and Ethiopian cultures - also a focus of the menu.

The interaction with Susan, who runs this epic creation, made the evening special. She sat sipping some red wine while greeting us into the restaurant. Her face lit up when she heard the accents from the Scottish in the group – shout out to Scotty and Ali. We turned Susan into a celeb that night, listening as she shared her tales – she recently filmed with Ben Fogle for a UK documentary series called 'New Lives in the Wild'. What a character. Full of life, with a playful nurturing side. On the verge of stardom, she liked to remind us that if this booking happened in a few weeks, she would be too famous to chat with us. All the UK newspapers wanted an interview with her. Love it. She loved us.

One of my favourite moments of this trip followed - standing with Susan, Scotty and Ali as we embraced in a photoshoot with the valley and mountains rolling behind us, as we 'belted' out the Scottish National Anthem - the most surreal experience. We even told Susan about my fruit juice date earlier that day with the local guide. She smiled and told me she might be seeing me back living here. "Calm it, Susan," I thought.

With good food, non-alcoholic beer - yes Susan - the best company and the most stunning setting, I felt grateful, inspired and part of a wider travel community. Each on a journey, leaving our own footsteps in the world.

Back at the hotel, my dating life soon caught up with me - listen to me. As we sat at the hotel reception, my fruit juice date messaged, expecting a night-time date back at his. I remember seeing a video call appear on my phone - I think I did that thing where you hide your phone in a panic like they can see your reaction. The group weren't sure why I wasn't keen on the night-time date. If I am being honest, I enjoyed the flirtiness of the first exchange, the playfulness of the earlier fruit juice date, the passion of that viewpoint smooch, but my fun for the day was done.

At this point, I am trying to let down the fruit juice date when I feel a nudge and someone points up to the reception. A local is standing, pointing down at me. At first confused, I then felt that feeling of dread. It wasn't the fruit juice date but the guy from the gym this morning, the guy who invited me to his Birthday party, enticing me with his own tuk-tuk like the don of Lalibela. "Oh no," I whisper, as I see him walk over, "it's the birthday boy." Next thing I know, he is showing the keys to the tuk-tuk ready to escort us to his Birthday party. I couldn't bear the awkwardness of the situation.

While politely explaining I didn't think I could make his party, I felt the pressure of the group watch our exchange. They were winding me up, telling me I should go to the bash and not be rude to the birthday boy.

I kept shooing them. He seemed insistent, especially as his own tuk-tuk would escort us there. I could feel the eyes of the group on me, as it to ask, "Why wouldn't I want to go to his birthday bash?" I later found out this is a bit of a scam where they use their 'birthday' to get you into their friend's bar to spend money. Thankfully he got the message and left. The group weren't convinced this was the end of my night, and the next day at breakfast quizzed if I sneaked out to see my fruit juice date. Even now, I am pretty sure some of them thought I went after those late-night date vibes.

What an experience Lalibela turned out to be – this level of excitement doesn't happen in a whole year in Glasgow... What next did Ethiopia have install for us?

We were off in the minibus direct to the next destination, Bahir Dar, where we enjoyed a mini trek to the famous Blue Nile Falls. Bahir Dar, the start of our hiking and camping adventure in the Simien National Park – another world heritage site. This part of the tour had the potential to be epic – an escape into the wild, chasing those nature highs. Ethiopia still thought of as a country in drought, due to the devasting famine in 1984 that led to hundreds of thousands of people starving to death. The droughts repeated in future years, in a cycle, leaving a devasting legacy. A cycle linked to the ecosystem that we are all prisoners to its force around the world. With this in mind, I didn't expect the trek in a country renowned for drought and famine to be that memorable.

Packing for the trip became complex because of the varied itinerary, weather, and activities involved. I did, however, manage to fit in a sleeping bag, all for one night in the Simien Mountains National Park. While we sat in the minibus, in the last town before the valley, a group of local men with AK 47 rifles jumped on. I sat looking at them, then my group. Waiting for some reaction or explanation. We spotted lots of men with rifles on the streets of this region but didn't anticipate them to be on our bus. They started to look for a seat in our already crammed minibus. Nothing fully surprises me anymore on my trips, especially in a country like Ethiopia, where what you expect to be wild or dangerous is Africa normal. This turned out to be one of those scenarios. It transpired these guys were our security for the trek. What!?! Why do we need to have security?

I am not sure we ever received an answer that wasn't vague - part to support the local economy, part to protect us in the very extreme scenario there would be any 'issues' between bordering regions, or from any wild animals. "Oh Okay," I thought. I, of course, ended up sitting next to one of the AK47 wielding men. He seemed a gentleman – quite literally an old gentleman with the kindest of smiles. We smiled and shared some selfies. The photo to me is normal, but if someone stumbled on my photo album, they would probably think I am being held hostage. The men, with the rifles, wore those plastic 'jelly' shoes as the tour group all jumped out the minibus wearing the latest adventure gear. I felt a little guilty.

We started to hike in the Simien National Park, surprised to discover no signs of drought. Instead, a vast valley with lush green scenery came into view. The greenness blew my mind - no one would have thought this was Ethiopia - with one of the most spectacular landscapes with jagged mountain peaks, deep valleys and sharp cliffs dropping dramatically. The Park also home to some extremely rare animals: Gelada baboon, Simien fox, the Walia ibex, a goat found nowhere else in the world, and the Ethiopian wolf. After hearing about the wolf, I felt thankful for our guards. We followed the rifle-wielding locals along the winding trails that meandered through the park. Stopping to appreciate the beauty, gasp at the tall peaks and enjoy the standard candid, jumping in the air, photoshoots. The tallest peak stands at 4,550m, with other mountains in the range over 4,000 metres, all of them with sharp, jagged tops, making for a truly dramatic landscape. Ben Nevis, the highest peak in Scotland, is 1,345m in comparison.

It felt we were the only hikers in the park. After a few hours hiking, taking our time and enjoying everything there is to life in the great outdoors, we reached the campsite. Along the way, the plans changed from camping outside to sleeping inside the camp bunkhouse. If you were a prince or princess, you would have been shocked by the basic facilities. I accepted it for what it was. I also knew my sleeping bag would protect me, I planned to cocoon myself from the elements. What followed soon became another highlight. I'm not sure the gun-wielding men were ready for what happened.

The group knew the rules to survive a night in the wild, in dropping temperatures that hovered over freezing. Bring all the booze to the campsite party. All layered up, thermals on Nepal style, we made a campfire where we sat around on a mixture of chairs and logs, soon enjoying a chilled evening with tunes playing in the background, drinks flowing. A sense of accomplishment. No signs of the wolf.

As the night turned dark, we moved indoors to the bunkhouse, where some of the best food I've eaten the entire trip was served up. I loved this feast, convincing myself as I didn't have the warmth of the booze to heat me, I would eat all the food to bring warmth to my tummy. Some of the guys went all-in on the booze and saw the food as an optional interruption. One guy, who shall remain nameless, seemed particularly tipsy.

The night continued outside around this massive campfire set up by the guards. At times, the fire felt out of control but the riflemen kept an eye on it. With the tunes blaring, we all sat enjoying the sense of connectedness, chatting and laughing. Sometimes I would sit listening to the mix of music, laughter and chatter gazing into the fire. Completely grateful for that moment, and every action I have taken in life to bring these experiences into my life.

Things escalated a little - we can blame the Vodka. The infamous Scotsman in the group decided to dance around the fire bare-chested. The riflemen looked on as they were encouraged to join in. They kept their clothes on but amazingly joined the 'around the fire' dancing in an awkward shoulder shuffling manner. At times I cried with laughter, stood open-mouthed or signalled to the less tipsy guys to intervene. To think I worried about the group being full of boring people. In the end, some were way too wild! What a mix - Irish, Canadian, English, Scottish, Greek, French, Norwegian, American, South American and German.

The next day I woke to watch the sunrise, thankful to be fresh as a few nursed their hangovers - never joyful with another half day of trekking in front of us. We stopped to witness a pretty cool waterfall where we shared some group memories from the campfire chaos. As we drove out of the park, there waited in front of us one last treat. The Geladas baboons, known for their bleeding heart symbol on their chest, were marching through the valley as a playful tribe. It's hard to express the mesmerising sight of seeing hundreds of them stroll past within a couple of metres of us. They were totally untroubled by our presence. It seemed they didn't notice us, or maybe they thought we were part of the troop. They were the most intriguing creatures - I could have sat and watched them for hours. The Animal Kingdom is enthralling. And just like that, we drove through the gates of the Simien Mountains National Park back towards Addis Ababa - not before we dropped off the AK 47-wielding security guards. The tour officially done. Flashed by in the speed of light - full of life experiences. Too many to list, but I will give it a go.

First up, serving a local community providing a new water supply. That overnight stay at long-distance running legend Haile Gebrselassie's hotel, where I sat reading the book of his life provided in the hotel room - flicking through the pages in awe. I ran on the banks of Lake Tana, surprisingly linked to Scotland, where the Scottish explorer James Bruce traced the source of the Blue Nile to the Lake. We took a boat onto the lake to visit the mesmerising ancient monasteries dating back to the 16th century, before spotting some hippos who casually popped up. Trekked to view the enthralling Blue Nile waterfall followed by a dreamy sunset boat trip. To then witness that wonder known as the Ethiopian Jerusalem – Lalibela - is something that will stay with me forever, hauntingly spectacular. To the many coffee ceremonies we experienced, where they began by spreading fresh flowers and grass on the floor while burning incense to make the air even more fragrant. Always a site when it happens in your hotel lobby. And how can I forget all my guy friends – Mr Photographer from the plane ride, gym birthday boy with his own tuk-tuk and a special shout out to my fruit juice date for being a gentleman and paying for that juice.

Well, Ethiopia. What a country and what a trip.

This my first time in sub-Saharan Africa jam-packed with beautiful landscapes, random 'African' experiences and so, so much culture. It's beautiful, chaotic and warm. The reaction from the kids to a smile or wave will stay with me for a lifetime. My heart opened and my mind blown a little, with lots to consider. The world is full of adventure and eye-opening experiences. Ethiopia, you've been one big adventure playground. I believe every morning you have two choices: continue to sleep with your dreams or wake up and chase them. I'm awake to living out my dreams. Ethiopia reminded me to be playful and live in the moment. If you want to enjoy a fruit juice date, why not. If you want to trek in silly ballerina slip on shoes, do it – but expect to slide about. If you want to continue to feel fresh and be present in every moment, then say no to the booze. Make the choices that will lead to a fulfilled life and have wild experiences along the way.

One morning I sneaked out of my hotel to run around Lake Tana just after sunrise – my first proper run in weeks after the odd run on hotel treadmills. As I walked towards the lake, I stumbled into an outdoor fitness class attended by about thirty locals, performing stretches and high kicks while techno tunes were blaring out of a makeshift speaker. I stood open-mouthed, naively thinking I would be the only person on the streets enjoying the early morning. This fitness group were the definition of playfulness. You can hang around a high tech gym looking in the mirror, being seen to work out, or you can move around jumping about to a boom box in the fresh air. We make our own energy, and the more we make, the more we attract.

It is difficult to fully understand a new country and culture. From what I experienced and felt, it seemed the Ethiopians didn't have all the external distractions that we are consumed by in the west. Maybe summed up by the experience in the community when I realised they had no access to a mirror. They didn't know what they looked like. The eyes of another can be a mirror. If they'd looked in mine, they would see pure joy as my reflection of them.

Ethiopia also taught me not to worry about the people I meet on my travel journey. Not everyone will be your cup of tea, but generally, you can find something in someone to connect over. I knew I would keep in touch with some of the group, as we formed a common connection. A shared desire to travel the world, developing a greater understanding of how it connects us, leaving a lasting impact on us that we share back into our daily lives. If you trust in serendipity, the occurrence and development of events by chance in a happy or beneficial way, then you know that nothing that is meant for you will pass you by - as long as you are putting yourself out there and actively seeking opportunities. I think I made the most of my opportunities in Ethiopia. They led to the wildest time - forever grateful for having a playful mindset. I encourage you to play more, why not.

Ethiopia

"You only are free when you realize you belong no place — you belong every place — no place at all."

– Maya Angelou

Nepal: Hello to the natural high of life

I will always remember flying into Nepal. Glimpsing the Himalayas as I stared out the window eager for my first glimpse of this magical part of the world, contemplating that I would hike in the same mountain range. That goosebump moment. As I landed, Nepal felt less serene and more chaotic on the ground than up in the sky. Soon standing in line to complete a visa on arrival form, a different queue to pay the visa fee, then finally another queue to receive a stamp. All a little draining but necessary. Next thing I find myself hassle-free and safely in a taxi heading into the capital, Kathmandu.

Nepal felt grey, dense, and claustrophobic - everything built on top of each other. With no real pavements, everyone seemed to walk everywhere. From everything I heard about Nepal, I expected this dreamland, the gateway to some of the highest peaks in the world, home of the Gurkhas and the colourful peace flags fluttering in the wind emitting positive spiritual vibes. Talk about false expectation setting. I expected gold brick roads and the purest blue skies. Instead, greeted with a city filled with smog from a steady stream of mopeds polluting the air. Forgetting this is also a third world country, and a city recovering from that devastating earthquake of 2015.

I flew into Nepal following a tour in India which exceeded all expectations. A trip filled with many unreal day trips, the wonder that is Taj Mahal ticked off my bucket list. I felt lucky to have shared India with the best group, each day packed with epicness. I was tired, though. Mentally and physically. I needed a couple of days of 'Jacq' time to re-energise ahead of meeting my Nepal trek group where we would spend ten days together. The taxi driver could spot my newbie status, with my face practically stuck to the window thinking to myself, "I am in Nepal." Each new country has a way of sneaking up on you.

I dated a guy in early 2018 who was a little obsessed with Mount Everest, the highest peak in the world. It rubbed off on me. Although our relationship ended, he planted the seed. And the minute I made plans for a Christmas and New Year adventure, I felt excited when I found a tour to the Annapurna Basecamp, which started on Christmas Eve. The basecamp sits surrounded by a ring of mountains – next level adventure awaited. The thought of waking up on Christmas Day knee-deep in the Himalayas filled me with eagerness, and the thought of starting a New Year in this dreamy country filled me with joy. I read, researched, and studied the proposed itinerary with a magnifying glass. I could feel the fire inside grow into a flame. This trip would not just involve Nepal. An idea emerged as I plotted the end-to-end trip. Alongside India and Nepal, I added Oman and Dubai. Of course I did. I knew I was chancing my luck, but as a complete opportunist, it would have been silly to rush back to work after trekking in Nepal when I could enjoy some sweaty luxury in the Middle East. Why not was my attitude back then, and still is. I am not here to go half in. It turned into the most majestic six weeks - a little life-changing.

Back in Nepal, I needed to unwind, recharge, wash some clothes then mentally and physically prepare for tour group round two.

With no real plans, I walked, wandered, strolled, and meandered the maze of interconnecting streets and lanes, taking it all in. As I turned the corner, I looked up and smiled, I took my first steps under the red, blue, yellow, white and green Buddhist prayer flags representing the elements. Calmness washed over me. White symbolises air, red is fire, green is water, yellow is earth, and blue is wind. The flag mantras carried by the wind like silent prayers. Too busy gazing towards the flags, I nearly walked into a monk wearing traditional clothes. I started to feel the energy Nepal is known for, the warmth of the locals and the spiritual air. I felt my funk fade away.

That afternoon I booked in for a much needed deep tissue massage. Talk about what the doctor ordered. It soothed away any underlying aches and pains and took my mind off the incoming trek. After washing off the massage oil, I found myself in the 'place to be seen' in the heart of the nightlife area of Kathmandu, sipping on a hot rum in a cool music bar. I eventually left to find a foodie place that popped up in every blog I read. After getting slightly lost in the maze of Kathmandu, not ideal at night time, I soon sat with a plate of moo moos - the Nepalese dumplings. The dumplings tasted so yummy and were so cheap. I knew I wanted more but reigned it in. Moo moos are one of my favourite travel foods. The day I left Nepal, I felt sadness at saying goodbye to the moo moos.

Back at my hotel, I started to think about the future. The next day I would come face to face with my tour group. I felt nervous about meeting them. What happens if they are boring, intense or unfit?

I put this to the back of my mind as first I wanted to enjoy my last full day to myself. I planned to make the most of it - like a girl untamed.

In Kathmandu, there are a couple of important sites that everyone ticks off. First on the list - Swayambhunath Temple perched on top of a hill reached by 365 steps dotted with the fiercest monkeys on this land. After surviving the monkey gauntlet, I was rewarded with the whitewashed dome representing earth rising to a gold spire, from where four iconic faces of the Buddha stare out across the valley. The 13-tiered, tower-like structure at the top symbolises the 13 stages to nirvana. Talk about drawing you in. I felt like in a trance, under the Buddhist spell. Situated on a hilltop, the instantly recognisable stupa attracts a steady stream of pilgrims and, of course, all the trekkers. The views out over the valley are simply stunning. Most locals and tourists join in the tradition to ring the prayer wheels at the base of the Stupa embossed with the sacred mantra *om mani padme hum*: "hail to the jewel in the lotus." As I heard the ring of the prayer wheels, I knew Nepal was going to be that place that I would credit with becoming more mindful, present and connected. It felt real. Thousands of prayer flags flutter above the Stupa with similar mantras, to be carried to heaven by the wind. This place kept my attention - I strolled about taking it all in.

I managed to avoid a monkey attack, as they roamed freely around the site, and I also managed to pick up a new travel friend. While crouching down to take some photos, I looked up and caught the eye of an American traveller. We were soon deep in travel chat, taking photos of each other while enjoying the chilled life. It seemed we shared similar plans for the rest of the day, so we left the Stupa shrine and walked towards Durbar Square, where the city's kings were once crowned. The square remains the traditional heart of the old town and Kathmandu's most spectacular legacy of traditional architecture. The square was sadly impacted by the 2015 earthquake damage. Temples collapsed, some now stand under restoration, others waiting patiently to be brought back to their former glory. The entire square, designated a world heritage site, felt like a real-life open-air museum where the architecture styles blend, drawing you in to consider the history of this city. We enjoyed a pit stop to recharge over some beers and my new favourite food - moo moos. After a lovely day exploring Kathmandu together, feeling all the spiritual vibes and having the best chats, it was time to say goodbye as the next day he headed off to start the Mount Everest Base Camp trek - I wished him luck. Another person who left his footprints on the world and my life – we still follow each other now, online. I was completely set for a day by myself, but the universe had different plans for me. I was grateful for the company.

As I headed back to the hotel, I knew my trek adventure was about to begin - first I would meet my new roomie. Gulp. I know, I know, I seem outgoing, but secretly I think I am an introvert who has practised enough to become an extrovert. I feel being around people all the time a little exhausting, especially strangers. I value and adore my own personal space. "Please let my new hike buddies be the best," I thought, "and not space invaders."

As I turned the key to open the door, there stood a girl who introduced herself as Beth. I could quickly tell we would be trek besties - thank you universe for bringing me the best new roomie. She immediately admitted that she spotted my name on the check-in sheet and found my profile on social media, where my wee travel face appeared through my profile picture. She concluded she thought I looked fun. "No pressure Jacquelyn," I thought.

Beth, a fellow modern-day explorer, seemed like me, with the exception she was English. Same but different. Having found herself with some free time over Christmas, she wanted to explore the world rather than spend Christmas at home. I felt relief when I heard she was a Nepal veteran, having trekked to Mount Everest base camp a couple of years before. Her face glowed when talking about her previous experiences in Nepal and trek life. This excited me and I felt any unease slowly fade away. She seemed a pro.

That night we met the tour leader, Chandra, and the rest of the group - another two girls. Based on my India tour, I expected a bigger group than four. We were meant to be a group of five, but a girl found herself in the hospital before the trip even began. We never really found out why, it seemed puzzling. I found myself considering the situation - just the four of us, with ten whole days trekking in the wilderness, with no outside distractions or anything really to do. "Would it not get boring?" I thought. How wrong was I.

That night they took us to a cultural dinner and dance show as a welcome to Nepal and a way to get to know each other. It felt a little forced. All I wanted was to be in the local place with a plate of moo moos, but I fully embraced the feast as I glanced awkwardly at the dance show. After this, our leader Chandra provided a detailed overview of the ten-day trek. I intensely over listened to every word, trying to envisage trek life and follow his English. A little bit of unease crept in as I thought of venturing into the unknown. We were soon back in the room to pack and get ready. No time to overthink or worry. Gulp.

We left Kathmandu early the next morning and seven bumpy hours later, after all the girlie chats trying to figure each other out and start to build up a trek girl group friendship, we arrived in Pokhara, where the adventure would start the next day. The town sits on the edge of a gorgeous lake beneath the snow-capped peaks of the Annapurna range, making it an incredible place to relax and contemplate what lies ahead. That afternoon we set off to make sure we were kitted out with all the walking sticks, all the snacks, and importantly a sleeping bag. This the start and end point for every trek in the region that undoubtedly changes everyone that takes the step into the unknown towards the Himalayas. I could feel a mix of nerves and excitement start to bubble away. Eek.

As a group, we shared our last dinner in comfort before trek life would begin bright and early the next morning. As we sat in a lakeside chilled restaurant, enjoying some moo moos, naturally, and a beer, I started to feel a bit sick. With hiking in the Himalayas, there is a risk of altitude sickness. In the previous night's briefing, the symptoms were discussed. Some people take pills to curb the sickness. I didn't bother.

I think, somehow, I convinced myself I had altitude sickness, although we were not at altitude. Of course, I did. Sounds wild now, but the situation felt real. I popped to the toilet, thinking I might bring up my moo moos. Is this the calm before the storm - my mind playing tricks with me? No going back now. We were a small group - alongside Beth, we were joined by a lovely Spanish girl Clara, now based in LA, and the youngster of the group, miss Aussie. And one tiny tour guide, Chandra. I wasn't convinced he was strong enough to protect us from any looming risk as he was so tiny.

Finally came the time for a few goodbye 'I am going offline' text messages as this girl prepared to get lost in nature, hopefully not literally. Next up, ten days with no Wi-Fi, booze or luxury. My music playlist chosen, some books and movies downloaded, extra portable batteries packed, earplugs for any snoring and an eye mask to sleep. I felt trek ready.

On Christmas Eve, the four of us, led by tiny Chandra, his super cool assistant Dev and the two sturdy Sherpas, set off for the start of an adventure that would change me to the core.

We arrived at the start of the adventure to Annapurna base camp, at 8,091m, one of the highest mountains in the world surrounded by its sister mountains, all equally imposing. We soon discovered they would create magnificent panoramas from any viewpoint. Full of the joys of the first day, blue skies, and excitement after a quick group selfie, we were off. We walked, talked, smiled and laughed. Trek life seemed the dream.

The trek covers a wide variety of terrain, from lowland pastures to peaceful villages. We wandered through farmland amazed at the blue skies, complete tee-shirt weather and so different from the smog of Kathmandu - this felt like the nature release I expected and longed for. We stopped for our first lunch of the trek. After enjoying some fresh veggie noodles in full sight of the terraces filled with homegrown food, where the locals plant, grow, cook, and share their produce, the Spanish girl picked up a guitar and started to play a tune.

She explained back in LA, she felt fed up with single life and losing hours of her life on unsuccessful online dates, with all the nonsense chat that accompanies it, so she took up playing the guitar as a hobby and a way to meet like-minded people. I loved her mindset. Why sit about waiting to meet someone when you can be out learning, jamming and socializing. It made me think about how much time you waste chatting online or chasing after guys when you could be learning, growing, and finding out what makes you happy, rather than placing all your hopes on a guy to bring you happiness. She looked so happy, content and deep in concentration. I made a mental note of this moment as a reminder we can make ourselves happy.

As we continued to stroll along the route, our attention turned towards our Sherpas. The word Sherpa derives from the *shar* ("east") and *pa* ("people"), which refer to their geographical origin of eastern Tibet. They are native to the most mountainous regions of Nepal in the Himalayas. Studies identified their genetics make their bodies well-suited for high altitudes. They are the invisible men that make the trek effortless - effectively porters who transport your bigger trek bag with your sleeping bag, extra clothes, snacks and toiletries, so you only trek with a lighter day bag filled with essentials. We were supported by two Sherpas. They always started ahead of us so when we reached our location our bags were there waiting for us. I found it difficult to watch them at times, as it looks, and is, back-breaking work in the terrain we cover. It is their job and lifeline. A job that many carry on in their family line as a Sherpa tradition. Our tour guide, Chandra, started as a Sherpa so understands the life. If we could, I am sure we would all have carried our bags – they would not allow it, though. They were fascinating to observe. Sadly, as they spoke little to no English, we couldn't establish a relationship or find out much about them. But they were a vital part of our small trek group. They would place our bags outside the bedroom where we would sleep. I loved this little touch. I would always try and find them to acknowledge this, mainly through eye contact and a smile. They could have dumped our bags anywhere for us to drag back to our rooms, but not our guys. Maybe they could sense even strong independent females like a little help every now and then. Thank you to the Sherpa community.

The natural landscape of the trek route broke up with colourful teahouses dotted along, with the vibrant colours of flowers blooming as if from nowhere. We wandered across swing bridges, past dramatic waterfalls before continuing onto the final steep ascent, a challenge mentally and physically due to the 3,500 stone steps that stood in the way of our much anticipated first-night accommodation at Ulleri.

A welcome sight after five hours of trekking across farmland. In the distance, we were rewarded with our first glimpse of a snow-capped mountain. The camp teahouse included basic bedrooms with a concrete base for the bed, a small thin mattress and, if you were lucky, some thin curtains to pull across to shut out the morning sun, or the locals so you change with a little privacy. Everyone shares the same toilet facilities, with only a hole in the floor for the loo. No western luxury here. There is a communal tearoom, with simple tables and chairs, where meals are eaten and groups reflect on the day or discuss the next day's plans. 100% basic, but everything you need.

I noticed I slowly introduced a daily routine on the trek. I would change into my colourful yoga style leggings for that comfy stretch factor and pop on some extra layers. As soon as the sun disappeared, it became a race to wearing all your layers before the sharp coldness hit you. As part of this daily routine, I introduced another little luxury where I would slip off my hiking socks and bulky trek boots to slide into a fresh pair of big comfy slouch socks and my super soft trainers. The little things in life. My feet felt like they were walking on fresh air after hours of pounding up and down a variety of trek terrains.

The next daily routine started that first night - let me introduce the daily 'Follow Your Joy' jump. This is where Beth and I would glance around our camp to select the best jump for joy setting. On the first day, we agreed it ought to be the snow-capped mountain backdrop. I would get into position and when she instructed, I would jump, and jump, and jump more, hands in the air squealing with delight until we captured the moment. Looking back at the photo of that first jump, I can see the pure joy on my face. Thanks Beth, you legend!

That night I experienced my first Dal Bhat. A dish made of yummy hearty lentils, rice and a combination of side veggies, the choice of veggies depended on the available produce that day. Considered the national dish of Nepal, I became an instant fan. The big draw for trekkers is the free refills of rice and side veggies - as much as you can fill in your tummy. I would always opt for one refill. It also arrived with a popadom. This felt sacred as you knew there was only one, no refills on the popadom. Noted. The comforting combination of flavours and warmth from the food made it my daily dinner of choice.

The night before would follow the same routine. First, we would order breakfast, then Chandra would explain the next day's plan, including the 'be ready' time. I always remember the excitement of deciding on breakfast – ah the simple life.

We woke on Christmas Day to open the super thin and flimsy curtains to look out to the blue sky of the Himalayas. Again, I caught a peek of the snow-capped mountains. I felt pure joy as I considered the fact I was spending Christmas in this enchanting part of the world, today would be a bit different.

After transforming from a sleepy trekker into a day hiker, I knew breakfast would be waiting. I discreetly changed clothes while still in my sleeping bag - it became an art form - freshening up with a wet wipe and a spray of body mist. Breakfast became my favourite part of the day. You could sense everyone's eagerness to spend more time at one with the mountains, lost in their thoughts and energised by nature. We sat relatively quietly, waking up our bodies and minds to the surroundings, glancing around at trekkers in different stages of departure. Considering the broken night's sleep and contemplating the day's plans. Making sure everything packed for the Sherpas to start the day's hike ahead of us. There was a calmness.

That morning there seemed an extra buzz in the air. This continued for the rest of the day. Everyone on the trek route keen to make eye contact and merrily shout, "Merry Christmas" to every passing hiker. We stopped for a bit to talk to a family with two young children. We cheekily asked for a loan of their Santa hats so we could make a Christmas Day memory - Himalaya's style.

The trek continued with a fun vibe singing, or at least humming, Christmas jingles while meandering the route on another blue sky day. We strolled through various terrains, sometimes with passing donkeys for company. Walking in a group or in twos chatting, listening in to other chats or in solitude with music playing through your earphones. We arrived early at tonight's camp, Ghorepani at 2,750m. As a group, we stood in front of the 'Welcome to Poon Hill' entrance - all these moments created to look back on and sigh as I consider the feelings I felt, the smells, and the sights I could see beyond that one-dimensional photo.

As we set up our sleeping bags ready for another zero degree night of sleep, I glanced out the window and stopped. I stopped and peered out, mouth wide open in awe, turning into a smile as I whispered to myself, "The Himalayas." The panoramic views from the bedroom, that looked out over the basketball pitch, simply breathtaking. From far, what looked like clouds turned out to be the snow drifting off the mountain peaks. All the Sherpas were playing a game of basketball. For some reason, this made me so happy. Normally you would see them performing back-breaking work, so to see them let off some energy and free their bodies seemed more natural.

After exploring our new camp area, we made sure we were back for the sun setting slowly on the panoramic view that made me stop on my tracks earlier in the day. We sat perched with our faces up against the windowpane in silence, each experiencing our own sunset reflection moment.

As Chandra explained the next days plan, Beth and I were too distracted to listen as our Christmas song humming continued. Things soon escalated and we took it upon ourselves to entertain, well, ourselves. We took things into our own hands, headed to the dancefloor and danced along to the Christmas tunes being played out as background noise like no one was watching us.

Technically no one really was. Some guides, including ours, came onto the dancefloor and were all side shuffling around while Beth and I were giggling like mischievous schoolkids. I smiled so much.

The rest of the room filled with big groups of Chinese trekkers, all ignoring us as they were deep in chat while we enjoyed ourselves, having the best time. We continued to encourage others around to join in - some more guides slide onto the dancefloor trying to western dance alongside us. What a sense of freedom. There is nothing more liberating than freestyle dancing - completely going with the flow. As the night continued, we sensed the locals wanted to party - without us. After an hour of playful dancing, our beds called our name! We had used up all our energy. All of it. As we tucked into bed for an early morning rise, I heard this deafening noise. Turns out all the guides and Sherpas were going crazy downstairs having their own Christmas party - Nepalese style. They loved to dance erratically to traditional Nepalese music. We were soon dreaming of more trekking as our playful dancing became a distant memory.

After a few hours of sleep, we woke at 4 am from the slumber of our cocooned sleeping bag sleep to hike up to Poon Hill, in the pitch black, ready to reach the summit for sunrise. With our head torches switched on, we set off in the freezing temperature to hike up to one of the most special spots of the trek. The stars glistening in the sky, a reminder that you need to work for the sunrise highs - they are not delivered to you, so rise and seize the day. We walked in a single file, part of a bigger single file ahead of us. At one point, I looked back and stopped in awe. The red, pink, orange and yellow of the emerging sun splashed across the horizon with the silhouette of the mountains. Talk about stunning. It made my half-asleep body feel energised. After an hour of slow walking, we reached Poon Hill standing at 3,210m. This spot the equivalent of the Eiffel Tower in Paris or Big Ben in London – tourist central, with trekkers swarming around everywhere. With the sun rising, we grabbed some group photos next to the Poon Hill sign. More memories made. Whenever I look at my photo of that moment I see tired but vibrant eyes.

I spotted the striking watchtower in the distance, where I introduced a new mission - to get up there for the sun rising. As I stepped onto the last step, I looked up at the 360-degree views and felt I had to catch my breath. The views ahead simply beautiful. Although the viewpoint was crowded with trekkers, it still felt peaceful, in a busy sense. Everyone taking it in, feeling the energy from the sacred mountains. These are the experiences you play back in your head. In front of me stood some of the highest peaks in the world. Jagging out into the horizon, snow-capped, where the dark shadows turned to light with the sun rising, sweeping colour over their gigantic forms. We decided Poon Hill was today's spot for a 'Follow Your Joy' jump. I loved that jump. Cold, sleepy and a little tired, but my soul full of hope and possibility. Seeing a sunrise in a new country or any location is inspiring. To jump at one of the most scenic points, in a sacred part of the world, felt liberating. Forever chasing those nature highs.

For the rest of the day, I felt on a natural high – if only you could store this feeling up. Today's trek continued to bring that feeling of gratitude into my life. Grateful to be in Nepal, to be awake at 4 am, to see the sunrise, to be curious, and choose to explore the world. We can capture the sights in a photo, but only you feel it, and only you experience it, by being fully present. The power of nature is something else.

We set off along the Deurali Pass, a climb to the same altitude as Poon Hill, with spectacular views of the Annapurna range. The pass runs along the ridgeline of the hillside dotted with mini Buddha shrines and prayer flags fluttering in the wind. I slowly warmed up, and as I took off some layers, I stood glancing back at the mountains.

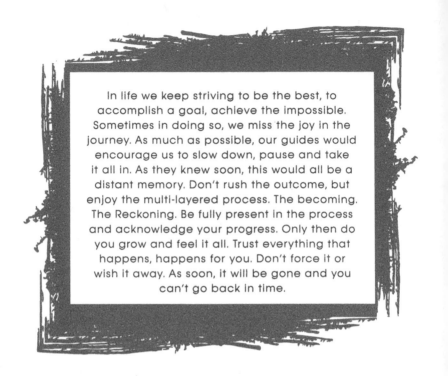

In life we keep striving to be the best, to accomplish a goal, achieve the impossible. Sometimes in doing so, we miss the joy in the journey. As much as possible, our guides would encourage us to slow down, pause and take it all in. As they knew soon, this would all be a distant memory. Don't rush the outcome, but enjoy the multi-layered process. The becoming. The Reckoning. Be fully present in the process and acknowledge your progress. Only then do you grow and feel it all. Trust everything that happens, happens for you. Don't force it or wish it away. As soon, it will be gone and you can't go back in time.

Every day when we hiked up and the altitude increased, we knew very soon there would be a long descent. On this day it was 1,000 slippery steps. The trail sweeping down deep into the valley with waterfalls leading into rivers, the blue skies masked by the luscious green foliage and a cooler air filled with the sounds of nature.

After what felt like the longest day, we reached our camp at Tadapani to find the most basic lodge where the rooms were made from plasterboard walls and rickety old window frames. Everyone sat along the walls of the communal room journaling, reading, playing cards, checking the day's photos, chatting or just waiting for the daily Dal Bhat to power us up – ready for bedtime. After an evening chilling and with a tummy full of all the amazing, tasty food, I knew I needed sleep. The fresh air, early rise, the up and down hiking left me lacking energy. I slept like a baby that night.

A new trek day started with another breakfast waiting for us. The hike would start, and meander through the various landscapes until the first break of the day, morning tea. I always sipped the same drink - hot lemon. Today's pre-lunch hike involved swing bridges with sheer drops into the valley, tiptoeing through farmlands with chickens running loose, terraces of rice and excitable sheep jumping along the path as we stood still against the edge trying not to get in the way of normal mountain life. We also posed for selfies with some very cute girls who looked a little shell-shocked as I suggested a photo – surely this happens a lot - with their snotty noses from the coldness a reminder of the altitude.

We eventually stopped for lunch. Our next task to pick our meal from a simple menu, which had enough variety to choose a new meal each day. Each teahouse had an identical menu. The variety of food, although simple, was so flavoursome. I would usually order one of two lunch meals - vegetarian noodles or fried rice - not wanting to complicate the simple life. Then you guessed it, another couple of hours trekking before we reached the camp for that night. This was usually by 4 pm. Then nothing.

Nothing to do except be. Be with nature, other hikers, your group, or your thoughts. Just be. We would order dinner and have an agreed time when we would eat. In between, you would set up your bed for the night, put on more layers, and simply wait for the meal to be prepared. Maybe play cards, check your photos, read a book, or chat with some others. Then after the excitement of mealtime, always the same, the Nepalese classic - Dal Bhat, it would be bedtime. 9 pm at the latest.

It took a couple of days to understand and appreciate the Nepalese trek life. Then I loved it. I loved the predictability, routine and structure. Everything felt easy. We were so pleased with the smallest of things - extra rice with dinner or a hot drink at the end of the trek. I listened to the same playlist for most of the trip, and I never got bored with it. We sometimes chatted as a group, sometimes with the group leader, or the assistant. Or, my favourite, you would walk solo in amongst the group but quiet, with music usually in one ear, and nature in the other. At times I felt something deep, hard to explain at the time but now I know. An appreciation for life, for the wonder of nature, for your body, and for being wholly present in the moment. For being alive.

We stayed at Chomrong, perched on top of a sweeping valley. That evening, after the 'Follow Your Joy' jump, we sat in the guest house communal area with a new set of characters to join the many we had already met along the way. These new additions would become big characters in our future trek stories. They were a family known as 'The Aussies'.

The Aussies were made up of the eco-warrior mum and her three sons - all in their early 20s and all very different. So very different. As a collective, they were very noisy. At times it felt like a sensory overload. Sometimes I stepped away from the group as the noise was deafening. I mainly sat watching them from afar - like a new breed of traveller. The most fascinating set of people ever who deserved their own documentary - I couldn't take my eyes off them for a second as at any minute they would say something so intriguing but wild. Like casually telling a story and slipping in, 'remember we nearly died that night,' and the mum would nod to confirm the bold statement.

They were so untamed and chaotic, free and loud, yet warm and nurturing. I needed to know their story. Everyone hiking in Nepal has a story. Well, everyone in life has a story. They were adventure junkies. Having recently completed the two-week trek to Everest base camp, they were not done and added on the Three Pass Trek. This strenuous trek, earmarked for experienced trekkers intent on crossing the high altitude passes in the Himalayas, sounded wild. They described it in such a way that it sounded like heaven and hell. Again, not done they added on the Annapurna basecamp trek, and here they sat in front of us. They hadn't been warm in months. I felt colder being around them. The coldness of the Nepal evenings can get to you. I think it started to turn them a bit delirious. Mostly the mum sat in all her clothes – shivering.

They paid the same guide from their initial trek to keep extending their adventure 'holiday', and he joined them as they boldly traversed the various routes. The mum a totally inspiring female with a carefree spirit. She wore leggings and hippy style dresses half-hidden with all her layers on top. Each son the product of her, but a complete and unique individual. The eldest seemed thoughtful, always found perched on some nature-infused boulder pondering life. The middle one seemed eccentric, an artist with a wild imagination. Always scribbling and drawing in a journal. Then the youngest, Jono, so hard to explain. Full of energy, a whirlwind of noise and thoughts. Everyone seemed to walk on eggshells around him or wind him up until he exploded. All very exhausting to be around. We sat for hours that first night with the Aussies, playing games. In the end, exhaustion and coldness kicked in, or maybe the headache the Aussies brought on with the intenseness. Either way, my bed called.

The next morning, we were greeted with a light snow flurry. I stood enjoying it as I watched the breathtaking views of Annapurna and Macchhapucchhre in the distance – our distant goal. By now, I felt so deep inside the Himalayas. Day five, and five days with no connection to the outside world - no Wi-Fi, phone calls, or text messages. I felt cleansed, present and so alive. Your mind stopped looking for external distractions and settled with knowing this was the simple life.

We knew looking down into the valley the route we would follow, the steps dotted way into the horizon. At our morning tea break spot, we encountered a second snowstorm. It brought a bit of excitement. Groups came and went. You would spot them at the tea break or lunch spot, maybe even stay in the same guest house or you would never see them again. Just a fleeting moment in your adventure.

Guess who we bumped into at the lunch spot – yes, the noisy Aussie family. They were a whirlwind of energy, wound up like a jack in the box and released out into the world. Always armed with a back catalogue of intriguing stories. I sat smiling at them.

That afternoon we arrived at our camp spot Dovan. All the teahouse bedrooms looked out onto the main trek path. We all sat on the edge of the steps that led to the bedrooms, enjoying the rest of the day and some stillness. The Aussies were staying at the same teahouse, so there wasn't much silence. After we all watched the sunset, we took refuge from the cold in the communal area. Even with all my layers, I could feel it in my toes. Once you feel the cold, it is hard not to feel it. We sat and played cards, patiently waiting for the Dal Bhat.

Whenever we saw Dal Bhat arrive on the kitchen serving hatch, we would try not to show our excitement in case it was not for us. Then when it came towards us, we would do a mini clap of hands to show our appreciation. We would survey the yummy goodness in front of us then make grateful noises eating it. Each night I would decide not to have seconds, then the minute it got offered, I would gladly accept. Once the food glow wore off and the coldness set in, it would be time for bed.

The next day we set off to reach our first Base Camp, Machhapuchhre, at 3,700m. The overall trip seemed to be speeding up as the days progressed. I always thought I was a day ahead of the actual schedule, before realising my mistake. Not quite ready for the Annapurna base camp experience we all seemed to focus our efforts on, but also wishing away the cold nights thinking ahead to luxury as next up the heat of Oman waited for my arrival. A true reflection of life. Wishing away the weekdays, for the weekend to arrive, to then attempt to pause Sunday before Monday starts again.

Today the terrain and landscapes felt different. We were leaving the farmland and rice terraces for more thrill-seeking views. The lunch spot at Deurali had a ski resort vibe to it. With a backdrop covered in snow and ice, the tea house sat on the mountain pass with the best sun trap, where the daily veggie noodles were served. We decided to lift the vibe a bit more and played some music from my playlist. Tunes on, shuffle dancing, while taking in the sweeping landscape, knowing very soon we will be on the final afternoon trek to the first basecamp of the adventure. I smiled and laughed a lot that day with all the ski resort vibes. Blue skies and warm sun on your face. What more could you want from life?

After we left the pretend ski resort, things got livelier. First up, we walked through an avalanche risk area - thanks for the sign to bring that warning to life. Then walking, or attempting to, across an ice sheet, slipping and sliding. Talk about Bambi on skates trying not to topple over. Followed by a tip toe crossing over an icy bridge of bamboo stepping 'stones' with a sheer drop - we were walking across an iced-over waterfall. Simply terrifying if you considered the danger levels. I tried not to.

Our wonderful guides helped us over. Soon we entered an open valley and the Machhapuchhre Base Camp stood in our sight. "This is it," I thought, we were on the verge of Annapurna. Everything we had been focusing on was, literally, just around the corner. Machhapuchhre became my first base camp experience.

The busiest, most crammed tea house ever waited for our entrance. That night we experienced more ski resort vibes where the 'Russians' were celebrating a birthday and somehow, by some means, shared a massive yummy cake with the teahouse guests. Beth and I sat perched like meerkats watching as no one 'helped themselves'. We changed this up and boldly helped ourselves - it tasted amazing. I know you are thinking, "Who are the Russians?"

They were spotted a few days before as we crossed the same route. I watched them from a distance. The mum didn't seem to speak and always looked miserable. The dad chain-smoked, drank straight whiskey and wore the brightest orange jacket. Then the son, who spoke English and seemed relatively normal, appeared to be chaperoning his parents around the Himalayas. That night I heard the dad speak. Not much, but a little English. I thanked him for the cake, hoping he hadn't spotted me watch him whenever I spotted them at one of our stops.

That night the Aussies were being loud. Jono, the youngest, carrying a cough from the first night we saw them. I generally thought that boy might not make it overnight with the intensity of the coughing. The mum never seemed overly troubled. I sat watching the Aussies out the corner of my eye, still fascinated. Jono, having conquered Everest Base Camp, was now being talked out of trekking to Annapurna to stay in bed to recover from clear overexposure to the cold. It became clear no one stops Jono at anything in life. He made this very clear. Once again, if only there was a documentary on the Aussies and this trek.

That night the four of us in my trek group slept in the same bedroom. It felt a bit like a sleepover, a very cold version where we slept in cocoon sleeping bags, eye masks on, and earbuds in. Trying to block out the cold and outside noise. Next door, the Aussies and Jono's cough kept us awake most of the night. The next day I woke, at first to silence before I heard the cough start again. Arghhh. "Send Jono back down the mountain," I thought. Trek life - a rollercoaster of emotions.

On day seven, we finally approached the Annapurna Base Camp. We took it slow, with all the time in the world, we wanted to saviour it, appreciate this mountain as we slowly ascended into the cavern. The basecamp was the goal of the trek - but I soon realised it wasn't. It was a moment, a milestone but it wasn't the end. I can remember it like yesterday. We strolled higher into the mountain range, sheets of snow our landscape, everyone walking single file. Some other groups we knew ahead of us.

We soon stopped to enjoy the snow, make snow angels, and capture our own moment with lots of photos. I felt nervous and excited. Then I saw it, basecamp sitting perched at 4,130m. We reached it - this felt special. There are lots of signs, prayer flags, and international flags signifying the achievement. A symbol of one of Nepal's highest base camps. It felt a little carnival-like as everyone queued to capture their group and individual photos at the famous signs. I didn't care. I earned this memory.

As you stand in the glacial basin and glance up at the mountains, you gasp a little at their sheer size. People have died scaling the Annapurna summit, and you are reminded of this in the main hall where everyone congregates. One memorial really touched me. It told the story of a European man who lost his life performing the activity he loved, scaling the Annapurna Mountain range to the summit - one of the highest peaks in the world. He lost his life in the cathedral, the mountain his sacred place. Here's an extract from a passage written by him:

"I wanted to achieve something essential in life, something that is not measured by money or position in society. My fate was to be an athlete. In their presence, I attempt to understand my life, to purify myself of earthly vanity, greed and fear. On their alter I strive to perfect myself physically and spiritually. From their vantage point, I view my past, dream of the future and with unusual acuteness I experience the present. My ascents renew my strength and clear my vision. In the mountains I celebrate creation, on each journey I reborn'.

Wow. It makes you stop and realise we need to cherish life.

When you walk outside and away from the main hall, towards the soaring mountains, there is an area covered in peace flags and more memorials. One inscribed 'Forever lost to Annapurna' for a Korean woman who lost her life scaling the mountain in 1999 at the age of 40. As I read it, I felt the presence of the mountains and knew I would be changed forever. With a 360-degree view of some of the highest peaks in the world, it's hard not to feel humbled. A lot of people reach basecamp and quickly start the descend. We savoured it - I felt lucky our group stayed here all day and overnight.

When we first arrived at the basecamp and set up our bed for the night, it seemed early, maybe midday. I thought I would be bored, as once again there was nothing really to do. Having fully adjusted to the simple life, I slowly allowed myself to be. I wandered outside and sat a bit, watching the daily life play out. Helicopters arriving and, just as quickly, departing, taking people on a completely different adventure high up in the air. There seemed to be a collection of basecamp resident dogs, sleeping out on the snow enveloped in the heat of the soaring sun. Weary new arrivals, making their final steps into the basin, where the mountains encase the manmade camp, supported by their trusty walking sticks, my face greeting them as they looked up from that final step.

Nepal taught me to be. Be still, present, and grateful.

That night we all sat in the main communal room, trying to keep warm with our layers, the extra rice of the Dal Bhat and the energy from the other hikers, except the girl suffering from altitude sickness - she lay in a cocoon. I convinced myself she wouldn't make the night. In the end, I grabbed my sleeping bag and sat in my own cocoon – trying to zone out the coldness. As I got ready for bed, I stood brushing my teeth outside, gazing up at the dazzling starry sky, knowing soon this trek would be finished and I would be leaving Nepal. Although we reached the trek destination, I told myself to enjoy the last few days as the journey wasn't over. The journey is never over. The journey of life constantly hurtling you along, where you need to decide when to jump off to start the next chapter.

We woke cold and early on New Year's Eve, ready for sunrise at the spot where the memorials stand, standing in the footsteps of those whose shrines we read from. It gave me shivers. I stood, myself, in solitude, taking it in. Letting it reach my soul. The shadow of the sun appearing on the mountain range as the sun rose. The coldest I have ever felt but the most alive – nothing can prepare you for this. I will always remember this trip for what I call the awakening. When you realise life is for living, taking chances, exploring and pushing the boundaries. The silence and stillness provided real clarity. I knew each day I felt more grounded and wanted to return to the UK a little different. Hard to explain, and maybe I will never understand what changed, but I felt a new appreciation for life. A new urgency.

After watching the sunrise, we enjoyed breakfast knowing today would be one of the longest hike days back down through the mountains, crossing the paths we used to guide us here. It felt like a challenge, but one I needed. The past couple of days were a max. of three hours of trekking a day. I am the kind of person that needs to be active, this girl is not a sloth. I felt so energised after spending a day in the stillness of the mountains. Everyone in high spirits, with a spring in their steps. We shared lunch at the same spot where we meet the Aussies a few days before. It turns out this would be the last time we saw them on the trek. I'm not sure we were prepared for this. Especially the Aussie girl in the trek group, she developed a definite soft spot for the two older brothers. It was the entertainment we needed on the trek.

We reached our destination – Bamboo - after seven hours of trekking. From the high-altitude snowfields, back into the green valley with the enchanting rice terraces and the cattle grazing the fields, through the endless man-made steps, so thankful now for my walking sticks. I remember stretching my body outside with the sun on my face, grateful when I heard the showers were warm again. I needed a pick me up as my body now showed the stress and strain of eight days of trekking across the most varied terrain. My poor knees and lower back – it started to feel like survival now. That night, officially New Year's Eve, we sat and enjoyed some time speaking with the Sherpas and our tour leaders. We were the only tour group in our tea house. The eight of us. All on our own journeys in life. All sharing a moment in each others. I wouldn't have swapped to be anywhere else.

About four hours after we arrived, in the pitch black, a new tour group arrived. They were British of Indian origin, all-male, all in their 30s or 40s, except for a little boy about eight. As they walked through the door, all twenty of them seemed shattered and ready for Dal Bhat. I glanced at their faces and remembered them from the morning where we overtook them at the basecamp as we started the descent.

"Wow," I thought, they have been hiking literally all day.

Chandra told us we were a great hike group, all with good levels of fitness, and we always seemed to surprise him when we took on the challenge of the day with fun and playfulness. We shared some chat with the new group, mainly as we wanted to know if this was a pilgrimage, and who owned the tiny eight-year-old. Can you imagine at that age casually being in Nepal, hiking with your dad, uncles and dad's friends? What an experience. Every single person I met on the trek opened my eyes and urged me to tear up the society blueprint. We slipped off to bed at 9 pm, exhausted. Goodbye 2018.

Hello New Year's Day. Today felt like a good day, something different was going to happen. We had an incentive, a carrot dangling in front of us, involving changing into our bikinis. Yes, bikinis in the Himalayas.

After six hours of hiking, we reached our destination in the early afternoon. Another day where the trek descended endlessly. I could feel it, my mood shifting a little. With the basecamp done, it felt like a race to the end, and you had to motivate yourself as the trek down felt brutal. I felt less engaged in the group and would seek solace in my music. As we arrived at Jhinu Danda, a low 1,780m, we changed and strolled down to a nearby hot spring by the river for a well-deserved rest. I have never felt so grateful for these Nepalese makeshift hot springs filled with different trek groups.

When we woke on our last full day on the trek circuit, I felt I found some new energy, I didn't want to be ungrateful and wish away these last few experiences. Sometimes we need to catch our thoughts and reset. Remind ourselves to be mindful and present. This trek a constant reminder to be grateful. Now trekking through villages, crossing some of the longest bridges of the trip that seemed to float through the air connecting the remote communities. We would pass farmers and their mules transporting supplies across the terrain.

There is no Amazon delivery or Uber Eats in the Himalayas.

After another long day of trekking, we arrived at Pothana. The location of the last group dinner and dance – cue incoming awkwardness. Since day one, I could sense the Nepalese love a dance – literally Bollywood style i.e. over the top and very dramatic. After another meal of Dal Bhat – and before you ask, no, it is impossible to get sick of this meal – I enjoyed my first alcoholic drink in ten days. A whiskey or rum, I can't remember now. We then each expressed our thoughts on the tour and thanked our two guides, tiny Chandra and the very chilled Dev, and our two Sherpas.

It was a little emotional as you feel like a family.

Before I could allow my emotions to take over, the music started. They played some Bollywood inspired Nepalese music videos on this screen showing us the dancing they expected. It was wild. Never one to be rude and turn down a dance, each of us awkwardly and slowly entered the dancefloor and danced with our guides. I think I squealed with laughter as they kept encouraging us to loosen up and lose ourselves in the music. What a slightly cringe-worthy Nepalese kind of night. Always expect the unexpected in the world of travelling and go with it. And 100% scream with laughter.

And just like that, our very last day of the trek arrived. The teahouse, where we danced the night before, set up breakfast outside on their grounds. I could have cried – I nearly did when I found a rat had nibbled away at my last energy bar during the night. Traumatic. It felt so magical and surreal that this was the end. We could still catch glimpses of the snow-capped mountain peaks so far in the distance now. As we left the last teahouse, I paused for a minute and smiled as I reminded myself of what I achieved. I just trekked for ten days in the most amazing place in the world, the Himalayas. Never take for granted the stuff you do that feels normal, when in fact, it is out of this world.

We enjoyed a final downhill trek motivated by the thought of an incoming massage, real coffee and cake fix, and finally being able to connect with the outside world.

The minibus waited for our arrival and took us back to Pohkara, the lakeside destination. That feeling of sitting in the minibus knowing soon you will be out of your smelly trek clothes, in a hotel room with a hot shower, fresh towels and an actual bed - bliss. This is why we trek - to appreciate the things we sadly take for granted. We arrived back in Pohkara early in the morning, allowing us to enjoy a day just as I imagined as we meandered the trek route. Lakeside cocktails, the most amazing massage ever with all the herbal tea treats after a deep tissue massage, then cake and coffee in the backpack trendy spot, where I switched on the WI-FI to tell the world: I hiked the Himalayas.

The next day we drove the seven hours back to Kathmandu. Everything felt the same, but also a little surreal. Returning wiser, more in tune with the world, but still the same in some regards. Knowing that over time, and usually when you need it, you will slowly realise all the life lessons from this trip, which will form your future and inform your life decisions.

The next morning I boarded a flight to Muscat, Oman where the cold of the Himalayas soon became a distant memory. Just as we start one adventure, our minds race onto the next. As I triple-checked I had my passport and scanned my e-visa, I noticed I entered the incorrect passport number into the visa application. I felt that anxious feeling in your tummy when you realise the mistake is all yours, and there is nothing you can really do. I googled the potential outcome - Google said 'no entry' if any details are incorrect. Aww man. I sat with those anxious feelings, then told myself overthinking and lying awake would not solve anything, so breathe it away. I said goodbye to Beth as we both lay in bed - the last time as roomies. I knew I would be seeing her again, someday. And guess what, I sailed into Oman.

Always remember the majority of things we worry about never happen, so stop wasting your energy overthinking something you can't prevent. I know easier said than done, but from everything I have learned on my travels - it does feel accurate.

Nepal is a great place to learn about the simple life. Everything from Buddhism to moo moos. Experiencing first hand the traditional mountain life at a slower pace, the energy from the powerful glaciers you tiptoe across, the stunning mountain views which hurt your head glancing up at. Lost deep in the rugged mountain scenery, encountering the mountain communities and the super friendly Nepali hill people as they go about their daily life.

The trek provides a chance to learn about local cultures, enjoy the tranquillity that comes with no external distractions. Cross icy rivers on those swing bridges flagged with peace flags fluttering in the clear blue skies and rewarded with all the Dal Bhat.

The goal at the beginning of the trek appeared clear - reach Annapurna Base Camp. I learned an unbelievable amount from that trip, about myself and life. In the end, the goal was never base camp but the journey. Every single second spent in nature, walking, sitting, stretching, listening, eating, moving, sleeping, sharing, or lost in my own thoughts. The simplest of life, where you are focused on the next two to three hours. Nepal offers one of the world's great travel moments, the ultimate goal for mountain lovers.

Eventually, I spent ten days with no Wi-Fi, no connection to the outside world or my family. I didn't feel lost, sad, or disconnected. I felt free, connected to a higher purpose, grateful, healthy, and present. I actually felt anxious when I thought about reconnecting. I felt different and know how easy it is to get sucked back into a mindless life where you operate on autopilot. Losing time on social media, or wasting energy on people who don't share your passion for life.

Over the ten days, my footsteps crossed the same path as some amazing souls now lost to the mountains. I encountered trekkers from all walks of life. We all are so deeply interconnected - we have no option but to understand and appreciate that. People from so many different walks of life. Normally we would maybe share a glance, nothing more, and now we shared some of the most amazing sunsets and sunrises in the world. The ripple of human connection. The highest blessing of the Universe. When we stop judging people and really listen, we will hear our own voices - as everyone is a mirror back into our own lives. We are all the same curious, playful beings who are trying to find and follow what brings us joy in the short time we have on this planet.

I found my joy. Nepal started a chapter of my life that brought me to today - where I am the modern-day explorer, now comfortable to share my words. I am on my own journey and path, fully aware one day I will be gone and only hope someone will follow in my footsteps and have all the fun I have. This book and my words are my prayer flags, fluttering in the wind with the wisdom I pass on through my travel stories. Thank you Nepal for teaching me to strip back my life and be authentically unique. Fly like a butterfly and express my true self into the world.

To every single person I connected with on that trip, you shifted or challenged my perspective.

To the Aussies, I am still years later processing why the universe plotted for our paths to cross. Maybe they showed that a family doesn't need to follow the blueprint that society expects from us either. They now have a collection of unbelievable experiences which can only be created when you step into the unknown. I want the world to be filled with more people like that, rising each day and deciding their own joy.

The friendship I shared with Beth, my roomie, will hopefully continue as we both share the same curious and playful outlook on life. In 2020 we caught up on life over brunch in London. She was also my virtual guide through a trip to Sri Lanka, a country that allows us to be surf chicks. Thanks to the universe for connecting our paths.

To the girl, me, who realised once you step out of the shadow of excess, you take control of your life. That night, at Christmas, when I danced in a room full of strangers, completely sober and lost in enjoying myself fully. Realising we create our own fun in life when we get out of our way.

Nepal

"As each day arises,
welcome it as the very best
day of all, and make it your
own possession. We must
seize what flees."

– Seneca

Belize & Guatemala: Slow Down

Belize, if I am honest, was an afterthought. A beautiful afterthought. After exploring South America as part of my big 2016 trip, I flew from Rio, Brazil to Cancun, Mexico to add Central America into the mix. The plan involved travelling to Guatemala then over the border into Mexico to make my way back to Cancun through the Yucatán peninsula. To travel to Guatemala from Mexico, there is a tiny country sandwiched between them which rests nestled onto the Caribbean Ocean. That country is Belize. The only English speaking country in Latin America. The minute it appeared on my radar, and I spotted the dreamy Caye Caulker, I knew I wasn't just passing through. The new plan, to stop over for a couple of nights for a slice of the Caribbean in Central America.

Previously known as British Honduras until 1973, Belize was the last British colony on the American mainland and achieved independence in 1981. Retaining its historical link with the United Kingdom through the Commonwealth, the common language of English and weirdly Queen Elizabeth's face on the currency. Pint-sized Belize is packed with islands, adventure and culture. It is the owner of the second-largest Barrier Reef in the world, after Australia, attracting divers from all over the world to explore underwater caves and the world-renowned Blue Hole. Mind-blowing – check it out!

The journey to Belize involved the standard struggle when travelling into a new country on an overnight bus. As I sat at the pretty shifty bus station in Cancun, I must have asked the same guy ten times, "is the bus coming?" and "is this the correct platform?" Each time he would answer, "soon" and "yes." Finally, the bus arrived, it always does, and as I boarded and sat down, I remembered a blog I read. Night buses can be targeted by locals who pretend they are passengers, then when you sleep, they rob you. Ideal.

The next hurdle involved a fake border checkpoint scam where they demand you pay a made up departure tax. I tried to get some sleep on the overnight bus, while keeping one eye on anyone attempting to rob me. The minute the bus rumbled to a stop, I knew it was scam time.

The backpackers formed a line, all weary and half asleep. An Aussie guy took it upon himself to explain the same scam to everyone in the queue. I nodded as I explained I wasn't paying any tax, preparing in my head for the incoming drama. All the others in the queue seemed shocked. As the first couple of backpackers entered the cabin, the rest of us stood waiting, trying to imagine what was happening inside. Each time the person would return, some paid, some didn't – in one case, some shouting came from the cabin and the door slammed shut. I felt some nerves but also wasn't in the mood for another scam. Next up, my turn.

As I entered, I spotted a male and female dressed in official outfits, the female pointed at a bit of paper explaining the made-up scam. I shook my head and said I wasn't paying. She pointed again, then the man came over. They now had my passport – I think it was a legitimate border, but they were using the opportunity to turn it into a scam goldmine. One thing I gained from travelling South America was an awareness that each country has several scams on the go. Once you are aware of them, you gain the power. Knowledge is power. I showed them a printout of my flight receipt with the tax outlined. They kept repeating the same scam details, while I kept pointing to the receipt. In the end, he shook his head at her and nodded. She handed back my passport and pointed to the door. I walked through the door and felt relief flood from my body. The rollercoaster of being a traveller.

Back on the bus, with my eye mask back on, I drifted off to sleep. When I woke and slid off my eye mask, I glanced out the window. I felt a little shocked at my first view of Belize. It wasn't the Caribbean-esque dream I was expecting. The streets filled with run-down prefab housing. As I looked out the window again, I saw grey skies and eerie looking deserted streets – most travel books don't recommend stepping into Belize city and this bus was driving into it. My slight unease rumbled along inside as my thoughts swirled, "Should I stay on the bus and head directly to Guatemala?", "Would Caye Caulker be worth it or just more potential hassle?". I think I was just tired from the overnight journey and surviving another scam.

The bus stopped at the jetty for San Pedro – the gateway to the tropical paradise I was here for. I hopped out and knew I would be on the next boat towards a slice of paradise. A lack of sleep and a scam-fuelled overnight bus journey wasn't stopping this girl from experiencing a new culture. I could smell adventure in the air.

Just off the coast of Belize lies a sleepy little island called Caye

Caulker. As soon as I read blogs describing the pastel wooden houses on stilts, palm trees swaying slowly in the breeze and Caribbean infused vibe, I knew I would be visiting. A couple of days to wind down, relax and reset before I started the last part of a four-month trip. Sounded like the island dream.

As I boarded the next water taxi, I glanced around to see it crammed full of excited backpackers, all seeking that hammock island getaway. As the choppy journey started, I felt my initial unease float away. I made eye contact with some fellow solo travellers, a Canadian girl and an American guy, and we were soon sharing our travel tales.

When you arrive on the island at San Pedro, you instantly feel the slow vibe float over you. There is a strict no car policy, with everyone using bicycles to get around. As you catch a glimpse of the white sand beach, fishing boats bobbing along in the jetty, pockets of colourful ocean lined beach huts, and the smell of island life, I could feel the excitement of a new setting bubble away. I said bye to the chatty backpackers, knowing I would likely see them again at some point as the island felt small.

Off I strolled to locate my guest house, aptly titled 'Sun n Sea'. Simple and to the point. As I turned down a sandy lane, I spotted the sign flutter in the breeze and felt a sense of calmness. Sometimes the photos on the booking websites are not as they appear. This place was more than I expected. The wonderfully friendly owner appeared to make sure I checked in smoothly and gave me a very honest rundown of the island. Let's just say she was frank.

The owner didn't shy away from the topic and made it very clear the local men could not be trusted, that although they appear friendly, they want sex – full stop. She continued to explain under no circumstances should I wander down a street or lane alone if a local man is there, to keep on the main sandy street, and watch your back. "Oh, Okay," I thought.

Belize is a multicultural community with the largest ethnic group, the Mestizos, who represent a combination of Spanish and Maya heritage. Next are the Creoles, people of mixed African and English/Scottish heritage. On the island, there is a large Rastafari population. I remember standing there half listening and half thinking, "Talk about killing that dreamy island vibe." I respected her honesty, though.

Running on empty, I felt grateful that she provided a room with a side balcony overlooking the ocean. I lay swinging from the balcony hammock feeling super chilled. Talk about the dream. After too many restless nights in hostels, I needed this guest house to recharge a little. Everything felt as it should – serene. With the guest house owners words rattling about in my mind, I took my first cautious steps to explore the island. Once I hit the main street, I consciously avoided eye contact with the locals, although they were soon shouting me down. Eek. As I walked assertively along, they were shouting, "Go slow," and even pointed to a canopy scribed with the same words. How funny. Not sure how to explain, "My guest house lady told me to go fast past you." After a few over-friendly interactions, I felt at ease. It isn't only on this island you get attention, so once you gauge the danger level it becomes like anywhere else in the world – you keep your wits about you. With enough locals and backpackers strolling around I never felt unsafe. Plus, I didn't want it to hang over my island experience. You set boundaries and go about your travel life.

In Caye Caulker, life moves at a snail's pace. No one is in a rush. No roads. And the bluest of skies and water. You feel like you are floating through the air. The island is small enough that you can get by on foot if you want to. There is one main place where everyone hangs out. That place is the Split, a channel that divides the two halves of the island. Caye Caulker was one solid piece of land until a hurricane struck. The hurricane effectively split the island in two. On one side are the mangroves of the Caye Caulker Marine Reserve and, on the other, well, the inhabited part of the island. The Split is the place to be seen on the island and is where everyone meets to lounge around, swim, snorkel, and of course, drink. Enjoying that Caribbean vibe.

It's where I bumped into the Canadian and American from the boat trip.

We were soon a threesome, not literally, and hung out that first
g wanderlust. We strolled about enjoying our paradise
ding ourselves distracted by island life. Stumbling on
ngling from palm trees on the beachfront – the perfect
ckdrop, and as they attempted paddle boarding, I sat
de laughing at their attempts.

he excitement and playfulness, we needed a refreshment.
d a local food shack where we sampled the tastiest tacos
joying some beers and cocktails. There was soon a twist

to the threesome when the American announced a friend was due to arrive on the next water taxi onto the island. A friend from back home in America, they were looking to see if they could be more than friends. This created a high level of excitement. We prepared for an exciting reunion, in Belize of all places. His friend arrived, and we were smitten. She seemed the best, and they seemed the best couple. It may have been the cocktail fuelled playful tipsiness, but we were convinced they would get married. The world can feel very small at times.

Where we sat overlooked the back of the island, home to the mangroves. As we all laughed and shared stories, the sun set on the island. I felt such happiness and forgot those frank words from my guest house owner. Strength in numbers and all that. My overnight journey and, maybe, the booze brought on a big dose of sleepiness that a power nap could only fix. Back at my guest house, I shut my eyes for a nap and woke up hours later in the middle of the night. Day one done, I felt okay with that. Sunset drinks are the best.

The next day I woke up feeling fresh, energised and ready to be an ocean explorer. Except for one slight issue, the boat company cancelled my snorkelling trip that morning. With one last day in this part of the world, I was not taking no for an answer. Storm or no storm, I wanted to experience the Belize coral reef. As I optimistically paraded myself along the beachfront strip, looking for a potential boat trip, everyone shook their heads and pointed out to sea. Dark clouds were swirling around dark and gloomy, a bit like my mood. That is until I found one boat going out. Alongside an American family, with a teenage son and two young girls, we were a full boat of explorers. Yes, to that. As I enquired about the storm, they shrugged and explained it shouldn't be a concern. I remember feeling a sense of achievement, my plans back on track. The storm put to the back of my mind, ready to be an ocean explorer again.

Things progressed quickly as I sat eagerly wearing a life jacket in a pretty flimsy boat, sailing through overcast skies following a splattering of other boats towards the Barrier Reef. I swam in the Australian Great Barrier Reef and although it was truly amazing, I struggle a little with snorkelling. I'm ok until I hear my breathing, or think about how you can't just stand up when you feel tired. At the first spot I popped on my snorkel, I felt genuine excitement as we followed the boat skipper into the ocean. Although the skies were stormy, the feeling of calmness as you swam through the ocean brought a feeling of peace, with beautiful coral gardens and the fishy residents appearing in view through my mask. Soon back on the boat, we headed to the incredible Shark Ray Alley. The boat skipper kept saying something about swimming with sharks, to which I would smile. I didn't understand the shark comment and thought it was a joke.

As I glanced out of the boat, I couldn't see any sharks.

The skipper soon saw to that by throwing in some fish, and then carnage unfolded. From nowhere, Nurse sharks surrounded the boat, much to my bewilderment. Tons of them. No idea how many, but let's just say loads. Everywhere I looked. The boat started to rock with the activity in the ocean. Gulp. Although they are slow-moving and harmless to humans, they are huge - up to 14 feet - with very strong jaws filled with thousands of tiny, serrated teeth. I sat perched on the side of the boat, taking some photos with them, not planning to get any closer. After they enjoyed the fish, they disappeared. The next thing I know the skipper convinced me to jump in with the sharks still around somewhere in the distance. Aww man, that feeling in your tummy as you slide into the water. Terrifying and invigorating at the same time. Soon we are all back in the ocean, snorkelling following the skipper again. Things went from wild to cute, when I spotted some sea turtles. I've swum with turtles in the Philippines, they are fascinating, majestic even. You can't help but follow them along, a little mesmerized.

Suddenly woken from my sea turtle daze with the skipper shouting, I'm mega confused. As we all come up for air, the American dad explained we saw a stingray. "What?" I thought, "a Steve Irwin stingray". All around the storm developed, and the sea changed from peaceful to crazy choppy, making swimming tricky and tiring. I am a strong swimmer but started to feel tired and uncomfortable in the conditions. I got back in the boat and asked if we should turn back. The skipper's mate shook his head. We sat and tried to enjoy some lunch on the boat in the choppy waters. The weather continued to deteriorate - I felt this uneasy feeling. I am the girl that is all up for an adventure, those spontaneous trips, enjoying life to the max, but I also don't want to die and not in Belize in the Barrier Reef. Life is more precious than that. Plus, my mum wouldn't be impressed.

Slowly the Americans wised up and after a few words with the American mum, she got onto her husband to speak with the skipper. Thankfully, we agreed to skip the last spot and head back - I couldn't believe they wanted to keep us out on the boat any longer. As we headed back, still a good hour away from the island, the storm came in and the waves splashed wildly into the flimsy boat. With no covering or shelter, I sat crouched in my bikini, a soaking wet towel clung to my body trying to keep warm, my teeth chattering non-stop, shivering away. I couldn't even look up as the waves slapped straight off my face. Up until now, we shared fun energy on the boat. The American mum and dad were on the 10 am cocktails for that full island life experience, the teenage kids were lots of fun - the mum even roped the teenage boy into being my personal photographer. Now it felt like a race against the impending storm, and the demise of our flimsy boat. None of us looked up, we all clung onto the side of the boat as the skies continued to darken. When you travel solo, these are the moments you want someone alongside you for reassurance, to give you that knowing look to signal, "we won't die out at sea in Belize." Instead, I was trying to convince myself of the same.

After what felt an actual lifetime, where I went through all the worst-case thoughts of being lost at sea, found washed up, or maybe saved but traumatised, I felt relief when I saw the island come into sight. The heaviness in my body eased away and I knew I would not be lost at sea in a storm - all so I could tick off the Barrier Reef. "Take note Jacquelyn," I mumbled.

I thought we were done with any more surprises until we seemed to head through the split towards the back of the island. "What now," I thought. Mentally and physically exhausted, looking like a drowned rat, I just wanted to be on land – preferably swinging from my hammock. We entered the Marine Reserve, home to mangroves and a plethora of sea, plant, and birdlife. We were in for one last surprise! I didn't know what to expect and nearly fell out of the boat. As one of the kids held a fish in their hands to tempt the final act out of the water, from nowhere, the most frantic Giant Tarpon jumped out of the water and grabbed the fish. Terrifying to witness with no warning. I couldn't take any more drama and needed to be back at the sanctuary of my guest house hammock. "Please," I whispered.

As we landed at the jetty, I looked like a drowned rat. As I handed back the soaked towel to the skipper, I had that moment of realisation that I would need to walk through the island wearing only a bikini and equally soaked skimpy sarong. Eek. This led to lots of catcalls from the locals. I didn't even acknowledge them, too exhausted for any 'friendly' sexual harassment. I kept my head down as I scurried to the sanctuary of the guest house.

As I stepped through the gate to the guest house, I bumped into the owner. She looked at me like I was a survivor of shipwrecked. After a shower and a chance to relax, I made some dinner in the shared kitchen. This led to a friendly exchange with an American lady travelling Central America solo. I shared some travel stories with her, small talk really. From the little I shared, she suddenly opened her purse to show photos of her son back in the US. Next up, I knew his height, job and relationship status – divorced. Things escalated even further, next she asked for my email so her son could correspond with me. I know, I know. The mum setting me up with her son miles away. I don't even know what correspond meant – like a pen pal via email. Is that even a thing? I didn't have the energy to explain this plan was too wild and that I would not be emailing her son. So instead, I shared my email and smiled like this was perfectly normal. She treated me like her future daughter-in-law, showering me with all the attention. I needed to escape this matchmaking situation. "Why are people you meet travelling so untamed?" I thought.

After making up an excuse to leave this awkward exchange with my potential future mother-in-law, I ventured out to experience the island nightlife. I found myself at the local sports bar on the beach drinking beers with a Canadian couple, and mainly avoiding eye contact with any locals. The couple were very tipsy from day-drinking and the female kept whispering she needed to travel solo. "Eh, don't let your husband hear this," I thought. The bar suddenly livened up and the locals were clearly trying to enter dance-offs with the drunk travellers. I felt a little uneasy and once the couple left to grab some food, I quickly shuffled back along the well lit main sandy street to my guest house, again completely ignoring any suggestive calls from the locals. A little relieved to see the 'Sun n Sea' sign.

The next day, I said my goodbyes to the loveliest guest house owner. Throughout my two day stay, I would pop into her little office to give her updates on my day and let her know I was safe. She wished me well on my trip to Guatemala. There was no sign of my future mother-in-law. This had been exactly what I needed.

I felt so chilled, even after the crazy boat trip, and started to feel excitement as I headed into the next stage of my trip.

As I walked to the jetty, I once again got shouted at by the locals. The constant sexual comments and attention did become exhausting. Belizean men catcall every foreign woman walking down the street, even if they are with their male partners, so you don't feel a victim. Weirdly it doesn't feel threatening, as it's usually said in a light and friendly tone. I wouldn't let it keep anyone from travelling to Caye Caulker, even if you're alone. Apart from this, it is the most chilled island with an opportunity to witness the famous barrier reef and unique culture. Like nearly every island I visit, Caye Caulker felt like a slice of 'Go Slow' paradise.

After a five-hour bus journey, I arrived in Flores - my first taste of Guatemala. Well apart from when an over-friendly local man jumped into the minibus that transports you over the causeway to the island and, of course, tried to scam us.

"Welcome to Guatemala," I thought.

Most backpackers seemed unaware they were walking into a scam as he instructed the minibus to the nearest ATM then tried to sell us some cut-price tours. Luckily the hostel I was heading to emailed me earlier to warn about Eddie. How ridiculous is this, everyone knows who the scam artists are by name. Up until he mentioned his name, I sat half asleep near the back. In a split second, I turned into assertive Jacquelyn again. Travelling can be a little exhausting but, of course, highly rewarding.

With its pastel houses cascading down from a central plaza to the emerald waters of the lagoon, the island town of Flores feels a little like Venice. Surely this would be the end of the dodgy characters. It felt like a slice of Europe in South America. A causeway connects the cute island to its humbler sister town on the mainland. After a quick trip back across the causeway to assertively collect the pesos my little sister had wired over to me, I was ready for the Guatemala adventure to properly begin.

The next day I spent hours exploring the inviting streets and cobbled lanes of Flores, enjoying some lunch in a cool arty café while listening to some brash travellers discuss their trip in great detail. As a solo traveller, you can't help but listen in. The creative vibe of the island, highlighted by the colourful buildings, continued by the lake where local musicians sat and jammed. A truly chilled atmosphere encircled me and I decided to explore a little – nothing too wild. I was enjoying the new chilled vibe of this part of the trip.

I jumped on a small taxi boat for the five-minute journey across the lake to enjoy the views back to Flores and experience a mini hike to a forest viewpoint. As I gazed at the views of the colourful cobbled-together buildings back on the dreamy island, I found myself sitting in amongst some locals. The coolest locals ever, made up of a girl about my age, her male friend, a teenager and a baby, oh and a couple of dogs. They took me in after they heard I intended to hike the same route as they explained it can be dangerous on this side of the water. I didn't want any more drama, so felt grateful for their offer. You know when you get a vibe from people, these people were free-spirited, warm and welcoming. I felt my shoulders drop, thinking I would be in good hands.

We walked to the lookout while we chatted, shared stories and giggled. Along the way, the terrain became a bit jungle-like, and every time a moped whizzed by, they would signal to watch out. Arghh. The constant unease of not knowing whether a robbery would happen in broad daylight seemed to follow me around.

After a slow walk, we reached the lookout which appeared like a treehouse. Another group were playing some chilled music with various instruments, so we rested at the top looking back towards the island over the glistening lake. Everything felt so peaceful, the girl singing a traditional song to the baby while dancing soulfully. I wanted to be her, she carried this nurturing essence - naturally stunning and vibing high - you know, one of these magnetic types.

We weren't done with the hike and decided to extend the day by walking further into the jungle. The route would take us to a stunning beach, where we sat and watched the sunset while throwing stones in the water, with the dogs running around. Talk about tranquil. What a perfect day. That was until we got a bit stranded. There should have been water taxis to take us back, but after much discussion, it became apparent that wasn't the case and we would have to walk back to the spot we got dropped off - about an hour walk away, in the pitch black, through a jungle. "Aww man," I thought.

ou know when a lovely, chilled day escalates into a pitch-black anger fuelled return trip, and to make it worse, I felt hungry. As e walked, the mood changed as I think we all wanted to be ack in the safety of Flores, not walking in the pitch black. The ietness of the jungle blackness only interrupted with the whizz a moped in front or behind. I would hold my breath each time king, "Please don't rob us." The next vehicle that drove past was a full tuk-tuk. The guy in our group shouted to the driver if he would come back. He shouted something back – everything unclear.

After what felt like a lifetime, where all I could think about was my rumbling belly, we saw the bright lights of the tuk-tuk return. I don't think we thought he would come back for us. I heard a little cheer inside my head. With no way to fit us all in, I jumped in the tuk-tuk with the girl, the baby - yes we still had a baby - the teenager while the guy ran behind us with the two dogs. This must have looked the funniest thing ever. A grown man and his dogs chasing the tuk-tuk in the pitch-black jungle.

As we reached the shore, I felt relief as a boat sat bobbing ready to depart. We flung ourselves out of the tuk-tuk onto the boat, but the guy and dogs were nowhere to be seen.

The girl cradling the baby seemed pretty frantic looking out for her wayward friend. Meanwhile, I sat on the boat with one eye on the safety net of Flores where some Guatemalan veggie food waited my return. Just as the boat skipper - listen to me, I survive a boat nightmare in Belize, and now everyone is a skipper - threatened to leave, we saw the blue tee-shirt of the friend and the panting dogs running into sight. Hurray. We were all reunited and bundled together on the boat. Everyone else on the boat looked at us like a bundle of inconvenience.

As we reached the shores, I thanked them so much for sharing an amazing day with such beautiful energy and for making sure I returned safely. I was done. Even when you plan a chilled day, the universe decides to bring in a little bit of chaos. That nicely sums up most of my travel experiences – you always think you are one step away from some danger, but in the end nothing bad ever really happens. A lesson for us all – stop worrying so much, you always make it back safely.

The minute I turned away, I knew I needed food, then an early night as in the morning I would witness one of the most amazing Mayan sites in the world, and I felt truly exhausted. This is travelling. You spend a whole day with some people, share some really fun moments, then they are gone. Never to be seen or heard of again. No idea where they are now. Life – a constant wave.

The major reason for most backpackers making their way to Flores is to visit Tikal, one of the most impressive sets of Mayan ruins in all of Central America. Tikal is thought to have existed since the 4th century BC and reached its peak as the capital of one of the most powerful Mayan kingdoms by 200 AD. It was eventually conquered and gradually declined as everyone left. The city was rediscovered by the Guatemalan government in 1848, when a team began archaeological digs to restore the ancient structures. Nowadays, only 10% has been uncovered. Hidden beneath those jungle canopies are countless more structures waiting to be discovered. It adds to the sense of adventure to know that there could be hidden ruins at every turn. When the tour guide explained this on the day, I kept repeating in my head, "Only 10% discovered." Goosebumps.

What they have discovered is incredible. The site scattered with vast temples, houses, altars and plazas. A national park, the same size as the entire country of Israel. The guide, like most guides around the world, loved showing off all the knowledge of this stunning sight. What interested me the most was not the stories from the Mayan times, but the stories from my new day trip friends. They were the best. They all shared a great dynamic and the best energy. We were all in awe of Tikal. It is always better to share these experiences with cool people.

Having witnessed Chichen Itza a week before in Mexico, I felt torn. Chichen Itza is one of the new wonders of the world. A complex of Mayan ruins where a massive step pyramid dominates the ancient city. When I visited, I expected to be blown away. It is impressive, but after seeing Tikal, I couldn't help but think this should be a new wonder. Sorry Chichen Itza, Tikal is a true hidden gem where you can freely explore most of the temples and sites. It is ten times quieter, providing an intimate setting and experience – with lemures scurrying about. This felt more raw and real. Maybe this was left deep in the heart of Guatemala as a present to those who choose the less travelled road. I liked that idea.

As we headed back to Flores, I knew I would remember the feeling from earlier that day as we sat on the edge of the massive main temple looking out over acres of forest treetops to where the top of neighbouring temples popped out. Making you truly appreciate the scale and epicness of this site. My mind wandered to what they would unearth when they explored the remaining 90% of this city. Think of the possibility. This is travelling - it stirs something inside you. A thirst for more.

After a post day trip drink, I said my goodbyes as that night I was leaving on an overnight bus. Now ready to arrive at the second destination of my Guatemala trip, where this country would show off its nature and cultural charm.

I arrived in Antigua early the next morning, like an eager feral girl with my big humid hair. This, the destination that excited me the most when I planned Guatemala. Its colonial beauty and charm seducing you the moment you arrive. Local life unfolds to the backdrop of cobbled streets, beautifully restored colonial buildings with facades, picturesque ruins sitting in nature surroundings, all beneath the watch of three incredible volcanoes. Every time I glimpsed up at the volcano backdrop, I would gasp. Sometimes completely covered by low-lying clouds, and as the clouds drifted away, you would see the awesomeness. Volcanoes have this imposing power. Knowing the destruction they could cause, makes you respect their presence.

After a few hours exploring the streets, soaking it all in, I became part of a new travel gang at the hostel. They took me under their wing. We enjoyed a gastro tour of the town. First up, my chance to sample the famous Guatemala coffee from the neighbouring plantations, followed by tasty tacos with some beers while enjoying everyone's travel stories and the random stuff we would spot in the town, like the chicken buses. The name originates from when locals used the buses for the transport of livestock. What looks like an old school bus from the United States, brightly painted in powerful colours and patterns. The definition of fun. From that day on, if I saw a chicken bus, I would pause and smile, like I had never seen one before. Live your life through the eyes of a child - it is way more fun. Trust me.

That night we all sat about drinking and playing cards. As more newbies arrived at the hostel, we welcomed them into the card game which got louder and sillier. We drank shots as the forfeit. Travel life, wholly centred around drinking card games – I still have flashbacks from a messy night in Poland. We ended the night across the road in a trendy hipster bar with live music, a nice mix of locals and travellers. Completely unexpected from this laid back town. We were all in a boozy silly mood and I felt pleased to have added Guatemala to the mix. I felt part of the worldwide travel community. All a little lost but more connected than people realise.

The next day most of my new friends were moving on or leaving for one of the hike excursions to the nearby volcano. Antigua is the perfect spot to be a backpacker and lose yourself in the day-to-day life. A few of us went off to explore the churches, plazas and markets. They were vibrating with activity. We wandered the stalls at the markets, checking out the trinkets. This is where I first stumbled upon the Mexican artist Frida Kahlo. Her paintings were all over the town. Remembered for her self-portraits, displaying pain and passion, and bold, vibrant colours. Celebrated around the world for her unique style and by feminists for her depiction of the female experience and form. And we can't forget that unibrow. I now have one of her self portraits in my lounge, a nod to the females in this world who have stood up against society's blueprint. Yes, Frida.

After a day in amongst the hustle and bustle of the markets, I found myself back alone walking up to this mega chilled viewpoint looking back over the town, with glimpses of the volcanoes to bring goosebumps. The town, enveloped by the volcano's energy, shines with the vibrant colour of the colonial architecture as horse carriages, chicken buses, and locals, dressed in traditional clothing, stroll through the streets. Throughout its history, this city has suffered earthquakes, floods, and volcanic eruptions. But in recent decades, it has re-emerged as the colonial jewel of Guatemala. I was under its spell. A place where you could settle for longer.

I wanted to stay longer, so many people do to learn Spanish at language school. Most travellers in my hostel were effectively living there as they attended the local language school. But I had plans. The next day I headed towards my last destination – Lake Atitlan. Arghh I didn't want this part of the trip to end. Guatemala felt like a big warm hug.

In the minibus to the lake, I bumped into my next two travel friends. A couple of English girls cradling a hangover. We were heading to the lake known as Hippie Central, dotted with small villages, all magnets for backpackers looking for an alternative chilled life. Depending on what you are into you, you pick the village to visit: yoga, meditation, language school, lakeside bars and bustling nightlife. Each village with its own vibe, attracting a different crowd. San Pedro is for the nightlife, my chosen village. A girl can only be chilled for so long before she goes off the rails.

When we arrived, I felt that energy from the lake, the volcano that overlooks it and the Guatemala culture. The village is a mix of indigenous Tz'utujil Mayans and Christians. I checked into my party hostel; the dorms reminded me of a prison cell. My room filled with guys who seemed on a comedown. I left them to it, as I wanted to explore. This felt as rural as it could be, with farms perched on the lakeside surrounded by Christian themed murals. Locals walking carrying their produce on their heads. Very impressive. Tuk-tuks scooted about the village, transporting backpackers from the taxi boat port to their party accommodation. Around every corner, buildings splashed with vibrant colour, hectic markets with day to day life in full flow and some stunning Christian churches – sitting pristine. As I headed back to the hostel, I watched a parade. A religious parade. I stood clapping and smiling along as the procession strolled past in full costume. I do love a random parade where you have no idea the occasion but find yourself fully emersed in it. Catching the locals eyes, them looking back welcoming you into the parade party, as if to say 'Welcome to the parade' over a shared nod.

With only one night here, I planned to sample the lakeside nightlife. I left the parade and the day drinking started at the hostel bar where I chatted to the barman. Soon joined by the English girls who had thankfully napped off their hangover. We sat around the lake, sharing our travel tales and vibing off each other, fuelled by the ever-changing happy hour. Each hour the spirit on offer changed. At one point, the rums were 50p. I can still taste them now.

As we got tipsier, we moved onto the bar along from the hostel. A bigger space, housing massive shared tables with a random mix of backpackers and more happy hours. A flow of new backpacker friends would come and go from our table, and some guys the girls knew joined us. It felt like a community in free flow. The girls were pretty wild, and the drink ridiculously cheap. This was everything I expected and so much more. With one night to sample the nightlife, I went all in. Why can't I be the girl that knows when to stop.

The end of the night is a little fuzzy, but thankfully I made it back to my prison cell, where I woke up the next day with the hangover from hell. I lay in my dorm bed, scared to move. My head ached and all I tasted - rum, the 50p rum. I regretted meeting those wild girls! I slowly crawled out of the dorm bed and delicately made my way outside for fresh air. I found myself swinging on a hammock, mesmerised by the lake views hoping the energy from the volcano would transfer to me. I knew there was only one thing to fix me. On the way to my hangover fix, I bumped into one of the

English girls, she stayed out somewhere – you know, no questions asked! After trying to piece together the night, I left her to get sleep and I went for breakfast. I must have stank of booze. I could barely hold my head up, it hurt so much.

Sadly a Pad Thai breakfast couldn't save this hangover. Yes, Thai for breakfast in Guatemala. I am a child of the world after all. I felt better for about five minutes as the greasy noodles soaked a little of the cheap booze and provided some veggie energy. Honestly, this hangover felt next level. Soon back at the hostel lying, dying a little, on a sun lounger overlooking the lake - sweat dripping off my body from the sun and rum fuelled session the night before. This should have been the most idyllic spot ever with the most stunning volcano highland backdrop. Instead, I wanted to curl up until the hangover disappeared - just now I was surviving minute-to-minute. Like a restless feral child, not quite sure what to do.

The sun shone down baking my sleepy body. I knew I should leave this lakeside retreat to make it to the town of Panajachel. You know when you get the hangover fear, that low-level anxiety that bubbles away deep inside as your body tries to relegate the hormone levels after the alcohol binge highs from the night before. I felt it bubble. As I grabbed my backpack, I told myself I would be better in a bigger town, the town where I would depart for the next leg of the trip into Mexico. I would feel less trapped. I started to turn against the party village. It gave me an almighty party high but now the lows were casting a shadow over it. My mind was buzzing with all the thoughts. Even the thought of travelling into Mexico made me feel anxious.

Hangover fear and travelling over a new border anxiety bundled together with the sweaty heat, not a good mix. I thought I might spew up that Pad Thai at the thought, and the only slight glimmer of hope came in the form of knowing that a hotel room waited on the other side of the lake. I needed to be by myself and ride this out.

As I arrived at the village jetty, I jumped into the next water taxi and suddenly felt claustrophobic. I don't get claustrophobic unless I have a hangover. The thought of being stuck in a water taxi made me feel worse. I took a seat up the front, and as we took off, I hadn't thought about travelling with my hangover on a bumpy boat ride. This day couldn't get any worse. I sat in a trance. My mind now in overdrive, my current train of thought involved the boat sinking as the waves splashed in. I felt torn as I quite liked the cold waves as they splashed onto my sweaty skin, providing a soothing coolness to take the edge off the hangover. After what felt like the longest time on the lake - I think it took thirty minutes - I half crawled off the boat, like a true survivor. Just thankful no one I knew could witness this.

As I made my way along the main road carrying my hangover and backpack, which felt like the heaviest thing in the world, I kept shaking my head at the constant stream of market stall owners and tourist shop keepers trying to grab my attention. "I have a hangover people, get out my way," I mumbled to myself in my head. I honestly felt like this was survival. Meanwhile, these people are trying to sell me a fridge magnet. When I reached my hotel, I expected to be filled with joy. My sanctuary from this hangover hell. Instead, I felt a new form of anxiety rise.

As I entered the hotel, which sat on the busy and danger-filled main street, I couldn't find a reception area, just a note on a hatch to contact someone. As I contacted someone, they appeared from nowhere and let me into my room. The room with no windows to the outside world. With hindsight, the hotel room seemed perfectly fine, but the fact there were no windows, no security on reception, or even really a reception, I decided I booked a prison room. When you have hangover-induced and crossing a new border anxiety, you do not want to be in a prison cell. I thought I would sleep it off, enjoy the peace of my own space and slowly turn back into normal Jacquelyn. Nope, I carried my hangover onto the streets like a restless wild animal.

There were no real attractions in the lakeside town. As the gateway into Mexico or out to the lakeside villages, most people use it as a one day base to get to the next place. I booked my minibus to Mexico from a travel agency in the party village – before the day drinking took over. I glanced at the flimsy slip of paper with tomorrows departure date scribbled on it. This led to my next anxiety episode as I convinced myself I didn't have a booking, and I couldn't even double-check the validity of what I held in my hand unless I wanted to travel back to the other side of the lake to check. Argh. Why is hangover anxiety so wild? Now, living on the last of my Guatemala money with no access to an ATM, I couldn't even try to relax in a luxury spa. Instead, I tried to enjoy my last day by exploring the lakeside markets, while avoiding eye contact with everyone as I convinced myself anyone I make eye contact with would try to kidnap me. Obviously.

That evening, still cradling my hangover as I hadn't napped it off, I knew Guatemala held one last experience, and I wanted to soak it in as I may never set foot in this country again. I walked to the edge of the lake and sat on the steps to gaze out at my last sunset. The volcano, which looks like it floats over the lake, sat in front of my eyes with the powdery pink colours of the sunset sky floating over it. I felt a calmness – finally. I will forever treasure Guatemala for its picture-postcard panoramic views.

Thankfully, I survived the hangover anxiety and felt grateful to have experienced Guatemala - it is hard to explain. Serene and energetic. Rural and old fashioned. It isn't showy or in your face. It is the calm ripple that trickles through the water when you throw a stone into a lake. It is a knowing smile from the locals. Like everything is going to be alright.

That sunset reminded me I am alive and present, and on the trip of a lifetime. We can get so lost in our thoughts that we forget to be alive. Always fighting the constant chatter distracting us from living.

As I sat reflecting, I could sense someone trying to catch my attention. At first, casually, then more obviously, moving towards me to sit on the same step. As I glanced up, I caught eyes with a young local guy, who seemed pretty keen to chat. He seemed interested in my nationality, my travelling and decided he wanted to ask me to go for dinner. Dinner, I thought, with a local man. No chance. I explained I had a boyfriend back at my hotel. All made up of course. After waving goodbye, I scurried down the main street, looking back to make sure he wasn't following me, again my wild hangover anxiety filling my mind with danger fuelled thoughts – what a joy. Finally, after packing and checking my passport, I drifted off to sleep, knowing in the morning I may or may not be crossing the border to Mexico. Eek. Just glad to have survived this day. It had been long and way too wild – this girl was mentally exhausted.

The next morning, feeling back to normal, I turned up at the vague pickup point where I handed over my last Guatemala pesos for a roadside coffee and a fresh pastry. At the end of the street, I glimpsed the sunrise over the lake showering the volcano with those early morning glows. Again, I felt torn. Travelling is a constant struggle of being present in the moment but allowing your mind to wander into the future as you move onto the next adventure. A mix of goodbye sadness, new horizon excitement and what could possibly happen next anxiousness. Ahh all the emotions.

Slowly a few more backpackers came to the makeshift bus stop on the edge of a back road on the outskirts of town. This made me feel at ease a little. After chatting to an English couple, I felt the anxious thoughts rise again as they waited for a different minibus operator. From speaking to a few more people around the bus stop, no one seemed to have a ticket for my minibus. Eek.

Everyone seemed a bit on edge.

My heart jumped as the first minibus arrived. A local appeared shouting names. People were grabbing their bags and excitedly stepping foot onto the minibus, ready to head towards Mexico's border. My name, as we would expect, not shouted. I approached the man to gain a little comfort that I would not be abandoned here. When I showed him the slip of paper, I looked him in the eye for some sign that this wasn't a scam and my bus would arrive. From the distance another bus approached – my heart jumped a beat again. Surely this is my bus.

He looked at my slip, then at the new minibus arriving and said, "not this one, but next." Yes, to that! Would the next minibus arrive? Of course, it did. My face turned into a big smile when the man dangling out the next minibus grabbed my slip of paper and ushered me in as if to signal, "Welcome to the next chapter of your four-month dream trip."

I jumped onto the bus smiling at everyone already on it, tempted to high five someone but decided not to jinx it, and grabbed a seat, feeling my anxiety, for now, float away. This girl survived the craziest hangover ever, forever blamed on those two English girls and cheap rum. Now I felt a little smug. I still don't know how the slip of paper booking system works, but doubt it at your peril as it is the gateway to the next adventure. The minibus took us to the border. The border as wild and crazy as you would expect. I wouldn't have expected anything else.

And that is Belize and Guatemala.

Two countries on paper that could easily be skipped. It is only until you learn a little more about them, that you discover they are home to some of the most incredible hidden wonders of the world. They filled my life with so much natural joy and deep perspective. I will always remember swimming in the second largest Barrier Reef in the world, surviving the stormy waters to swim with docile sharks, stingrays and turtles. Swinging on the beach swing with my travel friends from the boat ride to Caye Caulker. Meeting my future mother-in-law, remember the lady at my guest house. I never heard from her son – how rude. And then Guatemala.

Central America's most diverse country captivates you with its extraordinary volcano infused landscapes and the Mayan villages in the highlands. The mind-blowing Tikal, with the most intriguing temples rising from the dense jungle and the colonial gem of Antigua, where the Spanish left behind plenty of footprints from their colonial conquest of Guatemala. And we can't forget the natural beauty of the volcano-ringed Lago de Atitlán, home to my heavy hangover.

In 2019, I stopped drinking. Years of wasting weekends with tiredness and the dreaded hangover, travel trips made more difficult by the wild thoughts that come when your body and mind are out of sync. Life doesn't need to be overly difficult, and I am a big believer in the mantra 'Get out your own way'. My drinking, and the hangover, never became a problem or stopped me from living what to outsiders looked like my best life, but I knew it felt more difficult than it needed to be. I felt tired.

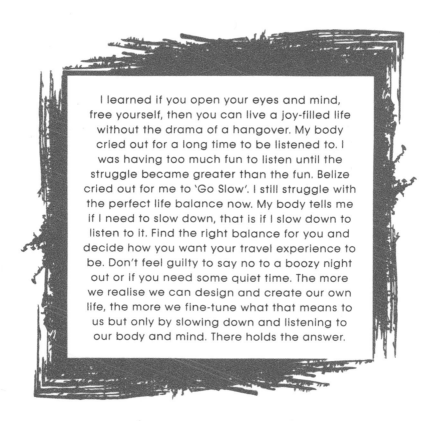

I learned if you open your eyes and mind, free yourself, then you can live a joy-filled life without the drama of a hangover. My body cried out for a long time to be listened to. I was having too much fun to listen until the struggle became greater than the fun. Belize cried out for me to 'Go Slow'. I still struggle with the perfect life balance now. My body tells me if I need to slow down, that is if I slow down to listen to it. Find the right balance for you and decide how you want your travel experience to be. Don't feel guilty to say no to a boozy night out or if you need some quiet time. The more we realise we can design and create our own life, the more we fine-tune what that means to us but only by slowing down and listening to our body and mind. There holds the answer.

These two were the perfect combination. Perhaps teaching me to live a well-balanced life and stop doing everything in excess. Balance is a feeling derived from being whole and complete, it's a sense of harmony. It isn't something you achieve 'someday'. The only way we figure this out is by playing in life and adjusting.

Thanks to Guatemala for planting a seed that one day would lead me to take back control of my life. The day I said goodbye to my hangover and hello to freshness! Find the balance in your life. I know my life got easier when I worked out what was getting in my way. This is our only shot at life, and I know I don't want to waste a second. What is holding you back in life?

Belize & Guatemala

"Live with no excuses, travel with no regrets and never be so busy making a living that you forget to make a life."

– Unknown

Italy: Live a life full of purpose and passion

Italy, the one country that fills my soul and leaves me wanting more at the same time. Each region with its own culture, art masterpieces and passion-filled locals. With more UNESCO World Heritage cultural sites than any other country on Earth, Italy inspires you to want more from life, and to leave your own legacy. Now we are talking the same language.

The epicentre of the Roman Empire and the birthplace of the Renaissance, this is Europe as we all know. With style, beauty and flair, you can't help but fall in love with the Italians and their daily life. Those standing immaculately dressed sipping espressos, like a scene from a movie. The root of Italian psychology is a dedication to living life well. After watching Eat, Pray, Love countless times, I always felt like a star in my own movie when I visited. Italy and I have enjoyed a long love affair.

I first visited Rome at the start of my ten-year relationship. Young and in love, with him and life. Still developing my personality, my likes and dislikes. I fell in love with Rome, the everyday life, wandering the streets where you encounter a stunning plaza to discover it isn't in the guide books. Their day to day, your treasures to be found. To experience the classics - everyone will always remember when they first set eyes on the Colosseum, Roman Forum, and the Pantheon. I know, I do. That trip felt special, to witness the passion of a Rome football derby - Roma versus Lazio – talk about chaos. Then the next day, wandering into the Pope's speech at Saint Peter's Square. A truly intriguing moment, surrounded by crowds of worshippers all here to catch a glimpse of a man they love and idolise, delivering the morning prayer to cheers below. Very surreal. Finally, the Sistine Chapel in the Vatican City. Vatican City, a country within a country. Italy, you had me hooked.

Soon back to witness Venice on a blue sky picture-perfect Christmas trip. The way of life captivating. Three days travelling the canal circuit and exploring the laneways. The locals using the same route to transport their produce and supplies. Climbing the bell tower to glance down at Saint Mark's Square, then further out to the islands that surround Venice – hypnotising you. The Italian passion slowly rubs off on you.

After a very long break, where life got in the way and I found myself living on the other side of the world, I finally returned to Italy. My first trip back, this time solo. I meandered through the streets of chic and cosmopolitan Milan, sunglasses firmly on – mainly so I could check out the handsome locals. Everyone remembers their first sight of the cathedral, the Duomo di Milano. I do. Absolutely captivating.

I strolled through the nearby neoclassical shopping arcade, known as the meeting place of the city, captivated by the architecturally stunning gallery - an attraction featuring intricate mosaic floors, art masterpieces and glass domes. A magnificent archway leads you out to face the cathedral. To where I would gasp.

Over the trip, I caught more glimpses of the cathedral. My favourite, from the rooftop where you can join a tour to explore some of the most amazing hidden gems. A must. Milan grows on you. I left for the day and travelled three hours south towards the coast to come eye-to-eye with Cinque Terre. A collection of five seaside villages on the Italian Riviera coastline each filled with colourful houses and quaint harbours lined with fishing boats. The cliffside trail filled with tourists hiking to each village, enjoying the sweeping sea vistas. Another must. When there is so much to see and experience, it is hard to pause for a breath. I didn't stop all day, invigorated by the sea air and a love for life. Travelling is a natural energy boost.

When I returned to Milan, tired but inspired, I spoke to some female travellers. They gasped at the fact I day tripped to an incredible part of Italy. Somewhere they wanted to visit. Instead, they had been clothes shopping. I shrugged.

If this is your one life, do what fills you with joy. Clothes shopping isn't up there.

That night I did stop to breathe, enjoying some beers in the hostel bar with a lively lot of backpackers. When they ventured out to soak up the nightlife by the hip canal region, I sneaked off to bed. I drank back then but had also learned to make better choices on my travels. The next day I jumped on a train to enjoy the city of Verona. Awaiting my arrival, a stunning hotel with a rooftop hot tub and views overlooking the amphitheatre. What a location and what a city. Morning runs to Juliet's balcony - what a time to be lost in Italy. I boat tripped around Lake Garda, sipping wine and grazing on pizza. Nothing can beat this feeling of freedom and travel grandeur. As I said, I, Jacquelyn, the star of my own movie – filmed in Italy.

I returned in 2019, this time to explore Sicily for an incredible trip where day-by-day, I fell in love with an island so mystical and epic. Beautiful Sicily lures you in with the diversity of its landscape and cuisine. Pasta Alla Norma is the signature dish, sharing the imagery that links it to Mt Etna: the tomatoes are lava; the eggplant, cinders; the basil, leafy greenery; the ricotta, snow. This dish followed closely by the simplest cannolo, tube-shaped shells of fried pastry dough, filled with a sweet, creamy filling, my new favourite travel foods. I ate both at every opportunity. Anything goes when you travel.

Sicily is a real-life dream, taking you on a journey any Hollywood director would be proud of.

From gritty Catania, where I flew into, to Taormina – home to Mt Etna and the most stunning Greek amphitheatre. Beach days and sunset runs in the magical old town of Ortigia where I stayed in the most awesome BnB with breakfast served on the rooftop. Day tripping to Noto, with its baroque architectural masterpieces, to enjoy a Banksy street art exhibition. That evening enjoying an outdoor Opera performance at the Roman amphitheatre in Syracuse - all in Italian. I would travel back in a heartbeat. No two days the same - each site or attraction leaving you inspired. A trip completely created by me. My very own Italian masterpiece. Living life on my terms.

You can't attempt to ignore the north of Sicily when you travel to experience it all. A train ride later, I walked out into the capital Palermo filled with artistic and architectural gems - street art infused districts home to Arabic domes and arches, Byzantine mosaics and Norman palace walls. That trip ended in the enchanting Valley of Temples. The most important ancient classical site in Sicily. Simply out of this world. As I plotted this part of the trip, I would constantly consider if this day trip was one too many. If I didn't see it, I would know no difference. But now that I have, I am incredibly grateful and more enriched. Sometimes finding the balance in life needs to be left back home as you chase down everything you are passionate about. Travelling the world, for me, is about experiencing as much as possible.

Remember we all have the same 24 hours in the day. Don't waste it.

Sicily, you opened my heart to some incredible experiences. I have a photo where I am sitting perched on the edge of the valley, looking out to the main temple. I can take myself back there in a heartbeat. Alone, but not lonely. The more we go within, and find the strength to be ourselves, the more we experience from the world. Our hearts and eyes open to the wonder of life. Sicily felt pure and unfiltered. What the Romans left to the world in the Valley of Temples deserves to be seen by the world, but sadly very few will even know it exists. With that in mind, my curious mind knows for every Valley of Temples, there are a thousand more sites equally spellbinding. The game of travelling is endless.

That same year I returned, this time to the mainland to explore the Puglia region, hooked on this passion-infused country. I think this may well have been one of my favourite Italian travel trips – don't tell the others - sneakily added it into an already jam-packed year. I flew into a very hot and sweaty Bari after a three-hour delay, where I ended up making money on the trip when the airline compensation came in. Result – silver lining and all that.

When the taxi dropped me off at the main square in Bari, it already felt like home. Bari, the gateway to some of the most incredible jewels in the Puglia region. As I followed my Google map route, I couldn't quite remember where I choose to stay. Located deep in the old town, I struggled to find it. The locals live in the old town, and I couldn't see any sign of a BnB. A friendly local man helped and I finally found the door. The door opened, and I felt confused.

An elderly lady stood in front of me, wearing a floaty dress and a massive grin. She introduced herself as Paola and waved over to her husband, Claudio, in the lounge.

"Where am I am?" I thought.

I followed her through the most amazing house, to the upper floor where she presented the choice of two rooms jam-packed full with history. Wood beam ceilings, original frescos on the wall reliving the fascinating Renaissance era and gorgeous furnishings fit for a sweaty delayed princess. In her element, Paola continued to explain the history of the region, the day trips possible and of course, all the backstory to the BnB – not your standard BnB but an actual palace built in 1598. I began to wither. After a 4 am alarm clock, the thirty-degree heat enveloped me and I wanted her out of the room so I could change and explore. She wouldn't stop talking, though. What a woman, I could sense we would become close friends. But first, I needed to be outside into the fresh air.

After changing into an attire ready for a day exploring in Italy, I found Paola in the room where breakfast would be served. This room simply stunning. Covered in original artefacts, treasures, and bookshelves. All providing a glimpse into the history of this region. A set of doors lead out onto a balcony the full length of the room. We were standing outside enjoying the cool breeze. I felt excited to explore this amazing quaint authentic old town, the nearby fishing harbour and promenade leading to the white sand beach. We bonded as she took my photo on that balcony. When I look back now, I see tired eyes filled with excitement and a mischievous smile. Paola's energy radiating out of me. I could tell she had a few stories to share and had lived a full life.

That day I made all my plans for day-tripping around the region. After five minutes in the tourist office, some local youngsters working the summer sorted me with maps and train times. When you have three full days and three incredible destinations to experience, you get yourself sorted immediately. I knew it would be full-on and didn't want the unknowns to worry away in my mind. I love this life and don't care if I need to wake early, change trains, ask locals for directions – I design and make this life my own. I found the beach and lay chilling, simply reading my book for the rest of the afternoon, and also enjoying some people watching - trying to work out what everyone was saying and what their lives were like.

Do you ever sometimes dream of having other peoples lives?

That night, after an outfit change and a catch up with Paola, I watched the sunset from the fortress walls. I wandered into the old town where I stood alongside the locals waiting for my order number to be shouted, soon presented with a Sicilian inspired arancini ball in a slip of paper ready to be eaten then and there. So, I did. I sat on the high wall outside, legs crossed, eating away as the locals mingled around. Feeling the most at peace and present. Part of a wider community. Here I am experiencing a way of life and culture I dream about. Out of office on and one plane ride later, you get to experience it, fill up your soul ready for the daily grind when you return.

I remember my first morning. Awake bright and early, feeling fresh. Ready to rinse every second out of this trip. I run on my trips, I love it, probably more so than running at home. You can properly explore. I love running first thing in the morning when the streets are empty, you and nature colliding. That morning, wearing my tiny shorts, I waved into her as she stood in the kitchen prepping what would become my breakfast. The excitement of breakfast in a new location! Hands up for the simple things in life.

After a sweaty run, showered and dressed into an appropriate day trip outfit, I walked into the amazing breakfast room feeling grateful I somehow choose this 'bed and breakfast'. You could feel the history seeping out the walls. Paola became my hero. She presented a ravenous me with a bowl of fresh fruit covered in natural yoghurt and freshly squeezed orange juice. This followed by home-baked pastries. A mixture, all from her family recipe book. Then, just when I thought Paola couldn't possibly excel, she appeared with a plate where a warm chocolate cake sat with melting ice cream. Yes, to that! That taste washed down with fresh Italian coffee is what we travel for. I thanked her from the bottom of my heart. No guilt here.

Day trip number one: destination Matera. Matera is a city on a rocky outcrop home to a complex of cave dwellings carved into the mountainside. Abandoned in the 1950s due to poor living conditions - known as the shame of Italy with widespread poverty and disease - the residents were relocated. The crumbling city, thought to be the third-oldest in the world after Aleppo and Jericho, lay empty for the first time in 10,000 years. This part of Matera now houses museums, cafes, small independent artisan businesses, and even boutique hotels – marketing 'come sleep in a cave'. Talk about rejuvenation. A playground of culture with rock churches and underground caves hosting spectacular frescoes. I set off to seek out all the views. This city, the definition of enchanting. As I wandered down to the valley, crossing the brick bridge, I glanced back in awe at the cave city made from limestone, where each building appears to be layered on top of the other. The 13th-century cathedral sits at the top of the layered old town, known as Sassi, reached via a steep tangle of alleyways. Absolutely enthralling.

As one of the European capitals of culture, Matera is now a destination to rival any other in Italy. Declared a world heritage site and set as Jerusalem in Mel Gibson's movie, it is the dream. It keeps you on your toes. With giant bronze Salvador Dalí reproductions dotted around town, it definitely plays up to its year of culture status. I sat watching a live music performance, eating my second double ice cream of the day, in the 40-degree heat. Happy I choose this mind-blowing day trip.

Seven hours later, I returned to Paola after exploring every inch of the cave town. Exhausted but full of culture.

The next morning started as it would each day. Wake up early feeling fresh, 'Morning' shouted into Paola, another sweaty run, a quick shower, dressed and excited about breakfast. This time when I walked into the breakfast room, some fellow guests sat at the shared table.

Two sisters from Peru, who now lived in the United States, on tour around Europe. They were surprised when I shared with them where I visited in Peru. They looked at me like Scottish people don't travel outside Spain. We also shared our love for the cake and ice cream breakfast combination. They were moving on that day. Meanwhile, I turned into the star guest. Wearing one of my favourite summer dresses, I persuaded Paola to pose for a candid post-breakfast photo in the antique-filled breakfast room. She wasn't convinced at first, she didn't feel photo-ready. I told her she looked the part, she eased into it and I now have the most adorable photo of us. Another memory I hold close.

Day trip number two: destination Alberobello. A strange and picturesque destination. This town quickly added to the itinerary. The minute I saw it, I fell in love big time. The small town, a world heritage site for its unusual white-washed conical-roofed houses that pop up everywhere. A trullo is a small dwelling built from the local limestone, with dry-stone walls and a characteristic conical roof, all to fiddle taxes and fool the authorities. It has a toy town vibe to it.

The centre of Alberobello looks normal enough until you spot a few trulli buildings dotted about, a signal that this is actually not a normal town. As you wander up towards the most touristy part built on a slope, you see them all, thousands of them. The white cone-shaped houses. Rows of them. Everywhere. Some along narrow lanes with others sweeping along the hillside. Many buildings are now tiny 'bars', where you can sample local wines, or little boutique shops. It feels like a hobbit town. My imagination couldn't keep up. At one point, I crept up on top of a normal building to experience the most stunning panoramic view of them all. Talk about the definition of picturesque. Another 40 degrees day, I tried to cool down with lots of gelatos. Any excuse really for a gelato fix!

What a place to explore. Around every corner I turned, I would experience surprise and pure joy as I spotted a trullo building in front of me. The world is filled with peculiar gems that no matter how often you see them, your mind still doesn't accept them as normal. Sometimes I need to tell myself to stop muttering "wow" under my breath. I looked back on my photos recently and could hear the familiar word come out my mouth - "wow." What a day trip.

Anything you see online or in a book that makes you stop and say "wow", definitely needs to be seen with your own eyes. No question. That day in Alberobello confirmed this.

That night, my last in Bari, I ate like a local. I ordered takeaway pizza and sat on the castle wall where they like to sit perched, enjoying the simplest of food. Making happy noises. This girl doesn't need a travel boyfriend or flashy eatery to feel full. All I need is to be surrounded by real people, eating the most soulful food in the perfect natural setting. I went to bed feeling overfull that night – both in mind and body.

Day three. Not only did I enjoy another Paola infused breakfast delight, but I also encountered a handsome Australian at breakfast. May I emphasise the levels of handsome - very handsome. A little confused about where he came from as no other guests were on my upper floor. He and his fiancée - yip my heart broke when he made that announcement - were travelling Europe, mainly Croatia and Italy. Surfing, island hopping and enjoying all the gastro delights. The three of us raving about the hidden gem that is Paola's. I quizzed them on where they were staying, a little confused until the fiancée led me into this hidden compartment behind the main wall of the breakfast room to reveal their ginormous sleeping quarters. They couldn't believe it, neither could I. I stood stunned and we all agreed this would be a BnB we will recommend forever. Today's breakfast – a slice of chunky apple pie with a berry sauce. We salute you, Paola.

Now for the final day trip. Beach-ready, I arrived in Polignano a Mare, a shiny gem on the coast perched atop a 20m high limestone cliff above the crystal clear waters of the Adriatic. I first caught a glimpse of the beach through the arches of the viaduct. Simply stunning.

Polignano offers you an enchanting experience. The tiny old town, reached through the ancient Roman gate, combines white-washed streets with beautiful old churches, tiny colourful doors, quaint balconies, colourful shutters, and quirky restaurants built into the limestone cliffs. I found myself lost in the winding streets. This location, again, felt like a movie set. Panoramic terraces offering breathtaking views, a million miles away from my daily life.

After watching people cliff jump and snorkel, I made my way to the super crowded beach to enjoy a little sunbathing. Cliffs flank the beach with crystal clear waters on both sides for the most dramatic sunbathing setting. I sat and took it all in, as soon I would be on a flight back to Scotland. Back in the office and switching off my 'out of office'. Once again grateful that I 'sneaked' in a four-day trip when society wants us to work ourselves until we earn our annual two-week holiday. No thanks.

As I returned to Bari to collect my bags and jump into a taxi to the airport, I felt a little sadness. This felt like home, as shown by the warmth and enthusiasm from Paola and Claudio. A special couple. Each morning I would explain my plans, and she would nod knowingly. She knew I had little time and big ideas. And no one would get in my way. Each evening I would fill her in on my experiences, then she would ask, "breakfast time?" By now, she knew I ran. Each morning we would mouth morning as I tiptoed out the thick wooden door, out into Bari ready to explore and free my mind. The morning run a joy and struggle in equal measures. The intense heat making it a struggle until the last kilometre when I knew a yummy breakfast surprise awaited my return. They opened their home so I could discover the architecture, history, local traditions and gastronomy of the Bari they experienced.

Paola shared one last gem.

She opened a biscuit tin storing many brooches, homemade from a variety of buttons that she lovingly glued together. Talk about being moved by a brooch made from buttons. I could feel myself getting a little emotional. I glanced at her, smiled and grabbed one with an orange button. What a memory - I still cherish the brooch today. This is why I travel, to be allowed a glimpse of people's life so full and vibrant. Knowing I will bring this energy back into my life. You never know, I might even have my own BnB one day.

We hugged as I dashed into the taxi to head to the airport, clutching the most precious gift from a special lady. What a whirlwind trip. Just when you think you are done with a country – you realise you are only just warming up.

In 2020, I flew back to Italy for a second time that summer. This time I flew into passion-filled and gritty Naples. Italy forever pulling me back by its charm.

The Covid-19 pandemic still hung over much of Europe. On paper, the Italian Covid rules seemed a lot stricter than Greece, where I was flying in from after island hopping. This signalled a heightened awareness in my travel-fuelled mind. I may look spontaneous and untamed, but I am very aware of the rules of life and how they can dampen the positive vibes of an adventure, while in 'winging it' mode. The Covid rules were now an extra dimension to contemplate.

We always rush from A to B to C, never acknowledging how we got to C – operating in autopilot mode. I try to pause, as much as possible, and replay back the journey. A reminder that for every anxious thought that pops into my mind, nothing outrageously difficult ever happens. Life always works itself out. Right or wrong.

The Naples part of the European trip involved a trip within a trip. After two nights exploring the wonder that is Italy's third-largest city, including a day trip to the epic Pompeii, I jumped off the train at Sorrento. The gateway to the Amalfi Coast.

Too early to check-in, I left my bags at the hotel and went off to explore. As I wandered back to the main street, a poster for a photography exhibition caught my eye. I tiptoed in and spotted a very Italian looking man hover around - hair in a ponytail kind of look. As I paid the entrance fee, he mentioned a swing on the balcony and that if I wanted, he would take a photo of me on it. I agreed to this playful photo opportunity while thinking, "what is going on here," of course, while playing it cool.

My eyes immediately stumbled onto this intriguing photo in the far corner. A photo of a group of nuns being ridiculously playful around the swing. The same photo referenced in the poster which first enticed me in. It seemed to be an iconic shot in the collection. If I am truthful, it felt staged. I looked around for Mr Italian. When I found him, I asked what I had been thinking - was the photo staged? He immediately declared, "No," as if he knew, which confused me a little. I asked how he knew, then I realised. Not only is he the Italian guy that works the counter, who I reference as Mr Italian for ease, but he is also the exhibition owner and the photographer of all this amazing work. He took the photo of the nuns.

He reached for his phone and showed a photo of eight nuns who appeared on his balcony the day before. I found this surprisingly funny. A group of people I am fascinated with, now the centre of my universe. Whenever I see nuns on any trip, I usually feel they can sense your soul and all your life adventures, good and bad. I always wonder what they do each day.

It turns out in Sorrento they love that balcony and swing. As he showed me the photo on his phone, I realised the nuns know the secret we are all chasing. How to be happy by slowing down and doing the things that fill us with joy as kids, when life seemed uncomplicated and pure. No filters, expectations, or agendas. This is a moment in my life I will treasure. A reminder to challenge my perspective. Nuns are not some weird, odd collection of females hiding from the world and temptation. They have found their calling and purpose. And enjoy time to embrace the playfulness of life, in the community they serve.

I soon embodied their spirit and found myself dangling off that swing, squealing with delight as Mr Italian instructed me how to pose. The pose seemed elaborate, involving several steps: how to hang off the swing, one leg extended, one leg perched, and my overly long hair dangling in the Sorrento sea breeze. What a moment. Those nuns certainly knew the secret. I felt as free as a bird. "Follow your joy," I mumbled.

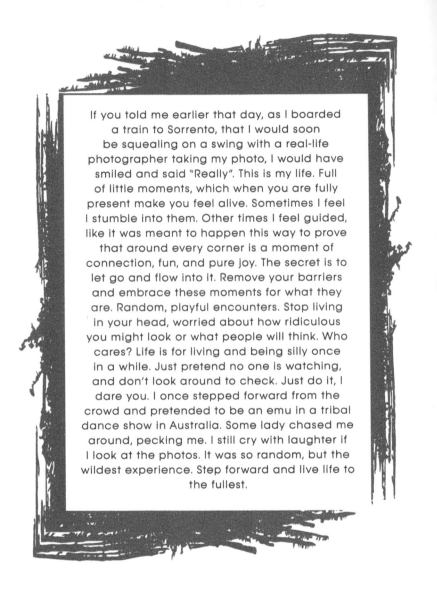

If you told me earlier that day, as I boarded a train to Sorrento, that I would soon be squealing on a swing with a real-life photographer taking my photo, I would have smiled and said "Really". This is my life. Full of little moments, which when you are fully present make you feel alive. Sometimes I feel I stumble into them. Other times I feel guided, like it was meant to happen this way to prove that around every corner is a moment of connection, fun, and pure joy. The secret is to let go and flow into it. Remove your barriers and embrace these moments for what they are. Random, playful encounters. Stop living in your head, worried about how ridiculous you might look or what people will think. Who cares? Life is for living and being silly once in a while. Just pretend no one is watching, and don't look around to check. Just do it, I dare you. I once stepped forward from the crowd and pretended to be an emu in a tribal dance show in Australia. Some lady chased me around, pecking me. I still cry with laughter if I look at the photos. It was so random, but the wildest experience. Step forward and live life to the fullest.

Mr Italian handed back the camera, I really wasn't sure what was next. Of course, what was next would again leave me feeling a bit speechless. Are we ready to meet Mr and Mrs Sheffield? I didn't know they were incoming, but they made an entrance.

The second part of the exhibition focused on the Nepalese way of life which, from my experience over the previous two days, seemed 100% accurate. It demonstrated how the Nepalese hang their clothes over their balconies to dry. You could tell a person's underwear preference from a glance at the balcony. As someone brought up by a mother who would never have her knickers on show in the garden, this fascinated me.

As I wandered through the hanging knickers in the outdoor exhibition area, I bumped into a couple from Sheffield. From their body language, I could sense they were up for a bit of a chat. Interestingly, the wife visited the Amalfi Coast 23 years earlier as a solo traveller, when 23, on a package holiday with a bus full of older couples - you know the type. My mind quickly whizzed back and thought, "Wow - can you imagine a bus tour back in the day?" Driving from England to the South of Italy - it must have taken days.

Mr Sheffield seemed eager to share the next part of the story. The bus tour stayed at a family-run hotel in Sorrento, where they explored the surrounding region on day trips. The hotel owner's son became interested in the 23-year-old Mrs Sheffield (who obviously wasn't a Mrs then). Eager for some fun, he would call her hotel room to offer personal massages - What!? She smiled off the advances until, with the encouragement of the tour bus crew, decided on the last day to give in to his advances.

They met that night at the hotel reception. As the conversation turned to what 'fun' they could have with the little time left, they both spotted the grand piano in the corner of the hotel reception. The owner's son signalled for the reception desk worker to finish for the night. He then led the bold Mrs Sheffield towards the piano, where they enjoyed wild, untamed holiday 'fun' in the reception of the hotel. As casual as that.

At breakfast the next morning, Mrs Sheffield gave the couples on the tour the nod and smile, as if to say, "Yes, mission accomplished." At this point, as they were being bundled onto the bus to leave the Amalfi Coast, an Italian lady arrived to say goodbye with a couple of kids. The lady turned out to be the owner's son's wife, with his children. The son who the night before enjoyed Mrs Sheffield on the piano.

What a story, all told under the exhibition knickers floating in the breeze. No idea how this story even made its way out of their mouths.

Not 100% sure how to follow up, I shared I recently stayed at a hotel in Heraklion, the capital of Crete, where a handsome local man worked the reception desk. At the same hotel, a grand piano stood in the reception. I chuckled, thinking maybe I missed a chance for some wildness. Can you imagine? They both smiled and explained they watched my interaction with Mr Italian from afar as we were being playful on the swing. I bet they did - these two notice everything.

Mrs Sheffield thought I flirted with Mr Italian, whereas Mr Sheffield thought it was the other way around. Either way, they suggested we shared some chemistry, and I should explore this. Right, Mr and Mrs Holiday Blind Date, this isn't a game show!

We shared two final exchanges. I asked if they planned to visit the hotel with the grand piano to see the owner's son. The answer a strong NO. And secondly, I told them I would now be looking for a fellow grand piano opportunity of my own since, well, you need to live a little. They told me to start right now, with Mr Italian.

As I turned the corner into the next exhibition, a Sophie Loren photo display, I paused a little to process the pretty wild exchange with Mr and Mrs Sheffield. I have no idea why people share so much of their lives. Can they sense I am an open book? Or did they see the exchange on the swing with Mr Italian and think, "We need to overshare with that traveller." Or is it when you are travelling solo, you are presenting a more vulnerable side of yourself that rubs off on others. No idea really, but I am aware of it, and it is something I never take for granted. I learn so much from these exchanges.

It turns out passion waited just around the corner. Instead of a wild chandelier swinging exchange, it involved an interesting and thought-provoking conversation with Mr Italian. I spotted him perched on the balcony near the swing. I strolled over where we chatted about photography, my passion at the time, and something I am keen to continue to learn about. He explained on a recent photoshoot there had been a stormy day where he took a young female to the coast. He prefers working with real people instead of models. He feels there is something wonderful and free about them – not staged. He used a female, a bit like a mermaid, naked and wet from the waves rolling about on the rocks as the waves crashed over her. He seemed to have a quality about him. A way to make people open up and become free. He explained, when you are truly being you, people also become themselves.

"Real people, attract real people," I muttered to him. He nodded.

As I finally left the exhibition space, I remembered some of his last words, "Real people are freer, more expressive, not trained in the experience. Their expression is the truth."

I stepped back onto the main high street of Sorrento, where I paused again to consider what just happened. If you keep rushing and moving on, then you miss the true essence of these moments. That exhibition experience was intense but so much fun. Life can be fun if we go with the flow and not shut down interactions. To think I arrived with no plans for this town. It turns out this town had plans for me.

As I turned and walked away, I knew I had come to Italy to experience all this. The life of a girl 'lost' in the world, but not in the traditional sense. Lost in its beauty, wonder, calmness, and spontaneity. This day a complete rollercoaster and I loved it. I giggled, as I appreciated everything I learned. This is what slowing down has given me. Time, patience and reflection. A curiosity of myself, and others.

What is the saying, "When life imitates art."

I am forever learning from other experiences. That is what Italy gave me, and what the nuns showed us all in that one photo. Let go of all expectations and be playful. When we get out our heads, nice experiences happen when we let them in and go with the flow! Live a life full of purpose and passion. Let go of what others think of you, stop following the herd and live in the present.

Why did I finish this book with Italy?

I feel I have grown up and matured through my Italian adventures. First as a young girl in love in her early 20s, to an untamed and playful woman in my 30s. Completely walking into some wild experiences and just going with it. I am passionate. I am open to learning about myself and adapting to life. That is Italy. It takes you on a journey of a lifetime. Italy has inspired thinkers, artists, and writers for centuries. It has inspired me. Am I done with this country? No way, we are only warming up. I have the mighty Dolomites on my horizon.

Keep chasing what brings you joy and fills your cup.

Italy

Epilogue: Follow your joy

"Like a butterfly stuck in a chrysalis, waiting for the perfect moment, I waited for the day I could burst forth and fly away home."

Some search their whole life to feel alive. I found that feeling the moment I followed my joy.

When I jumped on a plane for my first solo trip in 2015, I didn't know how Japan would be or where I would end up in life. I stood at a crossroads. My long term relationship over - I knew I had a choice, the choice to discover who I am and what makes me happy. I choose to become my own cheerleader and pilot my life. I became the maker of my dreams. A pretty cool side hustle.

Since then, I've explored what's important to me and what I'm passionate about. Uncovering who I really am, and what fills me with joy. I am sure from this book you can tell I have my own personal collection of joyful moments. All stored away deep inside ready to take me back to that moment in time, whenever I need it.

I also have a daily practice of joy, filled with the simple things in life. The energy from a run, the goosebumps when you hear your favourite song, the calmness of sipping a coffee in silence, the joy of reading the first pages of a new book, the feeling of adventure on a bike ride, being silly with my niece and nephew, giggling with family and friends, capturing city life through a lens, or surrounding myself with colourful art - bright, modern, colourful art. We can all be the makers of our own joy. I pass that superpower onto you.

Every trip, you learn a little more. In every country, your eyes are opened wider than before. Every trip I think will this be the last - I know it won't be. It can't be. There is so much out there waiting to be found. I continue to grow and expand, and so does the world.

Since Japan, I've been very lucky to travel to over 60 new countries leading to that significant moment when I tiptoed into country number 90! Teeny tiny San Marino. The third-smallest country in Europe. In the end, a 14-hour day trip, all completely planned and designed by me.

My advice to you, start living today. Wake up and be grateful. Try something new. Surround yourself with like-minded people. Live life in the moment and remove the seriousness. Be present, be connected, be motivated, be curious, and be you.

Life is a gift. We all have the same 24 hours in the day, and we all have choices. Sometimes our greatest achievements or experiences are one choice away. But we never make the choice that could change our lives, as we admit defeat too quickly. Listening to self-doubt and settling.

I only hope by sharing a little of my travel experiences, I have shown how the world, and life, is one big playground, with various hidden gems and experiences waiting on the other side of courage. The courage to speak your truth and say out loud, "I am willing to walk into the unknown and be guided to discover what the world has to offer." The courage to live a life against society's blueprint and demand more.

Is anything by chance? Or are our lives a sequence of curated events? Either way, you need to be playing the game of life to find out. Not stuck on the sofa, a spectator to the outside world. Only then will you discover the possibility of what could be. Don't be afraid of what you don't know, but excited about what you may learn and become along the way.

There is only one of each of us, and every experience in life is unique to you. Every single sunrise and sunset one of a kind. Each new day an opportunity to let go and discover the path to your future.

You are the author of your own life - be bold, be brave and be courageous.

Act today and create your own dream life by doing the stuff that brings you joy.

About the Author

Jacquelyn doesn't like labels, as they box you in. No one likes to be boxed in.

She constantly designs her life to follow that feeling of joy and freedom. Seeking out her next life adventure to learn a little more about life and herself.

Writing this book has been some adventure.

Currently living in Glasgow, Scotland. She is training for another marathon, recently hiked the highest peaks in Scotland and England solo, and can be found exploring the UK while she waits for the world to open back up again.

She has a list of stuff to tick off and doesn't plan to stop anytime soon.

Follow Jacquelyn here and keep across her adventures:

Instagram.com/followyourjoy_ja

www.followyourjoy.uk